# INFORMATION SYSTEMS PLANNING FOR COMPETITIVE ADVANTAGE

# Books and Training Products From QED

## DATABASE

Data Analysis: The Key to Data Base Design
Diagnostic Techniques for IMS Data Bases
The Data Dictionary: Concepts and Uses
DB2: The Complete Guide to Implementation and Use
Logical Data Base Design
DB2 Design Review Guidelines
DB2: Maximizing Performance of Online Production Systems
Entity-Relationship Approach to Logical Data Base Design

## SYSTEMS DEVELOPMENT

Effective Methods of EDP Quality Assurance
Handbook of Screen Format Design
The Complete Guide to Software Testing
A User's Guide for Defining Software Requirements
A Structured Approach to Systems Testing
Practical Applications of Expert Systems
Expert Systems Development: Building PC-Based Applications
Storyboard Prototyping: A New Approach to User Requirements Analysis
The Software Factory: Mananging Software Development and Maintenance
Data Architecture: The Information Paradigm
Advanced Topics in Information Engineering

## MANAGEMENT

Planning Techniques for Systems Management
Strategic and Operational Planning for Information Services
The State of the Art in Decision Support Systems
The Management Handbook for Information Center and End-User Computing
Disaster Recovery: Contingency Planning and Program Analysis
Techniques of Program and System Maintenance

## MANAGEMENT (cont'd)

The Data Processing Training Manager's Trail Guide
Winning the Change Game
Information Systems Planning for Competitive Advantage
Critical Issues in Information Processing Management and Technology
Developing World Class Information Systems Organization

## TECHNOLOGY

Handbook of COBOL Techniques and Programming Standards
1001 Questions and Answers to Help You Prepare for the CDP Exam
1001 Questions and Answers to Help You Prepare for the CSP Exam
VSAM Techniques: Systems Concepts and Programming Procedures
The Library of Structured COBOL Programs: Concepts, Definitions, Structure Charts, Logic, Code
How to Use CICS to Create On-Line Applications: Methods and Solutions
CICS/VS Command Level Reference Guide for COBOL Programmers
Data Communications: Concepts and Systems
Designing and Implementing Ethernet Networks
C Language for Programmers
Data Network Concepts and Architectures
SQL Spoken Here for DB2: A Tutorial
SQL for dBASE IV
Systems Programmer's Problem Solver
CASE: The Potentials and the Pitfalls

## THE QED INDEPENDENT STUDY SERIES

Managing Software Development (Video)
SQL as a Second Language
DB2: Building Online Production Systems for Maximum Performance (Video)

**For Additional Information or a Free Catalog contact**

QED INFORMATION SCIENCES, INC. • P. O. Box 82-181 • Wellesley, MA 02181
Telephone: 800-343-4848 or 617-237-5656

# INFORMATION SYSTEMS PLANNING FOR COMPETITIVE ADVANTAGE

**QED Information Sciences, Inc.**
**Wellesley, Massachusetts**

© 1989 by QED Information Sciences, Inc.
P.O. Box 82-181
Wellesley, MA 02181

Library of Congress Catalog Number: 88-35464
International Standard Book Number: 0-89435-284-9
Printed in the United States of America
89 90 91 10 9 8 7 6 5 4 3 2

**Library of Congress Cataloging-in-Publication Data**
Information systems planning for competitive advantage.
     ISBN 0-89435-284-9
     1. Strategic planning. 2. Business--Data processing.
     I. QED Information Sciences.
     HD30.28.I52 1989
     658.4'012--dc 19

This material was developed by the Chantico Publishing Company, Carrollton, Texas, in association with the Profit Oriented Systems Planning program.

## TABLE OF CONTENTS

# TABLE OF CONTENTS

# TABLE OF CONTENTS

# TABLE OF CONTENTS

## TABLE OF FIGURES

## TABLE OF FIGURES (Continued)

## TABLE OF FIGURES (Continued)

## PREFACE

New ways of thinking about the corporate possibilities of the use of computer technology are forcing Information Services personnel to re-evaluate their position, direction, and management style. There has been a change in emphasis over the years from the Computer Room, to Data Processing (DP, EDP, and ADP), to Management Information Systems (MIS), to Information Resource Management (IRM), to Strategic Information Systems (SIS). The Information Services Planning group must move with this change, and provide the direction and methodologies for developing the business-related plans that are required by the organization. The new center of interest is strategic planning, simply because it is at the heart of the organization. This puts a new and higher value on the systems and computer work, and introduces the idea of information systems as competitive weapons. The possibilities are limitless, the stakes are high, and there are many opportunities for Information Services to move in this new area. The goal is to integrate Information Services into corporate plans to win the competitive battle.

This new way of thinking does not put an end to the efforts required in operational planning and budgeting, both long-range and short-range. These methods have been proven over time. The supplying of computer and information services is complex, and must be dealt with systematically and analytically. Budgets must still be prepared for all parts of Information Services. Computer hardware and software must still be ordered and installed under management control. Systems must still be delivered on time and within budget. In addition, all of this analysis work must be integrated with the work being done on the more "interesting" competitive strategic systems.

One of the opportunities for Information Services today is to apply all that has been learned from the classic planning methodologies to the new requirements of strategic planning. Obviously, there are many differences to be considered, but there are also many similarities, and the wheels do have to be reinvented. By using their understanding of the planning process, and by automating the process with spreadsheet analysis programs and the use of microcomputers, strategic systems can be more effectively planned. This will also enable planners to communicate with senior management more effectively.

One of the purposes of this book is to point out the similarities and differences of the proposed strategic methods and to clarify the relationship involved. In the past, opportunities for IS planners to improve company profitability were minimal. With most strategic systems work, however, planning discussions must be held with users, corporate planners, and management as well as the systems staff. The possibilities of information technology reducing costs or gaining competitive advantage through new, computer-related products or services can only be discovered through broad discussions, brainstorming, and systematic, cooperative analysis, resulting from the interaction of both business and systems planners together.

These opportunities for Information Services planning do not come automatically or easily, of course. The great majority of IS planners operate in a departmental staff role, and have only rare access to managers who may be interested in strategic systems. The theory is fascinating, but the chances for its practical use are hard to find. What is needed to increase the probability of realizing strategic opportunities for information systems is a planned effort to:

1. Understand the concepts of strategic information systems and competitive advantage.

2. Assess your industry and company characteristics and the impact of your company's competition.

3. Assess your products/services value chain and look for value-added possibilities.

4. Understand the possible strategic planning methodologies and their variations, as described in this manual.

5. Identify and select an appropriate methodology for your organization.

6. Attempt to get a hearing and to discuss your plan.

These points will be discussed at length in the book. Obviously, they are not all easily handled. Few planners will be able to go through these steps without considerable help from a number of managers who are interested in the subject. However, all planners should be prepared for the opportunity for strategic planning should it occur by studying and being aware of all aspects of the subject and their ramifications in the Information Services area.

# SECTION 1

## THE STRATEGIC POSITIONING OF INFORMATION SERVICES

### SECTION OVERVIEW

There are new opportunities for Information Services in the rapidly developing ways of thinking about strategic information systems. This does not end the effort in operational planning and budgeting, but is in addition to it. IS planners must take a new view of the business process and their role in it. Some ways of realizing these opportunities are listed. There must be a planned effort to understand these new concepts, assess the company's position, and identify and select appropriate methodologies.

Strategic planning is the development of a plan to employ the resources of an organization to provide the maximum support to adopted policies. While much traditional strategic planning has been in response to business initiative, some current thinking is to plan information services to create business initiatives. Different information systems may be technically similar, and have similar functions, but may be designed for quite different organizational uses. Most strategic planning is for the **identification** of strategic information systems.

Strategic information systems planning is planning for the **development** of strategic information systems. This usually starts with an assessment of environmental characteristics, and examination of the product value chain to look for opportunities. **Issues** and **objectives** are the keystones of IS strategic planning. Strategies are practical methods to resolve unsettled issues into the final, desired objectives.

Strategic planning should not be confused with long-range planning, but the difference is largely a matter of perspective.

Strategic planning is complex, and the technology is little understood by management. William Gruber popularized the idea that this "planning amid change" must be started by "creating a vision" that can be understood by management. Vehicles are described for communicating this vision to others.

1

Cornelius Sullivan has pointed out that there is no single strategy for
IS planners, but that the strategy must fit the characteristics of the
occasion. His ideas of **contingent planning** are briefly reviewed.

**Reactive planning** is being prepared to respond to initiatives from
management. **Proactive planning** is taking the initiative in advocating the use of information systems for competitive advantage.

John Rockart's ideas for engaging top management in strategic
planning are outlined. They are based on a three concepts, critical
success factors, decision scenarios, and prototyping.

## 1.1     OPPORTUNITIES FOR INFORMATION SERVICES

New ways of thinking about the corporate possibilities of the use of computer technology are forcing Information Services personnel to re-evaluate their position, direction, and management style. There has been a change in emphasis over the years from the Computer Room, to Data Processing (DP, EDP, and ADP), to Management Information Systems (MIS), to Information Resource Management (IRM), to Strategic Information Systems (SIS). The Information Services Planning group must move with this change, and provide the direction and methodologies for developing the business-related plans that are required by the organization. The new center of interest is strategic planning, simply because it is at the heart of the organization. This puts a new and higher value on the systems and computer work, and introduces the idea of information systems as competitive weapons. The possibilities are limitless, the stakes are high, and there are many opportunities for Information Services to move in this new area.

This new way of thinking does not put an end to the efforts required in operational planning and budgeting, both long-range and short-range. All of the functions and the planning steps that are described in the first two volumes of this manual are still valid and necessary. These methods have been proven over time. The supplying of computer and information services is complex, and must be dealt with systematically and analytically. The first two volumes of this manual* provide the techniques for dealing withh complexity and inter-department cooperation over one year and multi-year spans. This third volume, on strategic planning, should therefore be considered as an extension of the work of Information Services planning, rather than a replacement of method, as some authors would have us believe. Budgets must still be prepared for all parts of Information Services. Computer hardware and software must still be ordered and installed under management control. Systems must still be delivered on time and within budget. In addition, all of this analysis work must be integrated with the work being done on the more "interesting" competitive strategic systems.

Speakers at meetings and external consultants will, of course, have little to say any more about the basic aspects of planning. They are considered to have been learned by most organizations, yet the reality is that there is much refinement that can be made in the planning approaches of any company, and the points made in the first two volumes are well worth review at any time. Basic planning methods are generally of little interest at meetings, however, and agendas now include talks illuminating aspects of strategic planning. There are so many presentations given, and so many differences of opinion about the subject, that one of the purposes of this manual is to point out the similarities and differences of the proposed strategic methods, and to clarify the relationships involved.

One of the opportunities for Information Services today, therefore, is to apply all that has been learned from the classic planning methodologies to the new requirements of strategic planning. Obviously, there are many differences to be considered, but there are also many similarities, and the wheels do have to be reinvented. By using their understanding of the planning process, and by automating the process with spreadsheet analysis programs and the use of microcomputers, strategic systems can be more effectively planned. This will also enable planners to communicate with senior management more effectively.

The greatest opportunities for Information Services lie, of course, in the management exposure of work with strategic systems. In the past, IS planners have

---

* Published as "Strategic and Operational Planning for Information Services," Second Edition, QED Information Sciences, Inc., 1989.

frequently worked in the restricted area of computer systems planning, while systems development people were the only contacts with corporate management. This led the planners to work almost exclusively with the project and system information that other staff in Information Services gave to them. Opportunities for helping to improve company profit were minimal. With most strategic systems work, however, planning discussions must be held with users, corporate planners, and management as well as the systems staff. The possibilities of information technology reducing costs or gaining competitive advantage through new, computer-related products or services can only be discovered through broad discussions, brainstorming, and systematic, cooperative analysis, resulting from the interaction of both business and systems planners together.

Information Services planners must, therefore, take a new view of the business process and their role in it. They must be constantly looking for new possibilities for the use of information technology. Instead of viewing business as a set of individual computer systems, they must view business as a related chain of activities, and examine the value added of the information content of possible products or services. Business systems are no longer free-standing computer applications, but are part of the business cycle, from business planning and organization through production, distribution, marketing, and service. At any point in this chain, there may be real opportunities for Information Services to provide information technology for competitive advantage.

These opportunities for Information Services planning do not come automatically or easily, of course. The great majority of IS planners operate in a departmental staff role, and have only rare access to managers who may be interested in strategic systems. The theory is fascinating, but the chances for its practical use are hard to find. There are a number of avenues of approach to this problem of realizing the opportunities. Some of them are:

- Planners should sell the idea of strategic systems to Information Services management, and provide strong enough staff support so that their usefulness will be appreciated.

- Help to arrange for a prominent consultant or authoritative speaker to work at a high enough level in the organization so that the concept will be understood, and there is likelihood of you participating in it.

- Arrange for a brainstorming session on strategic planning with both operational and IS participants so that mutually acceptable ideas result, and you can participate in their development.

- Work with Systems Development on a Business Systems Planning (BSP) type of approach where possible ideas can be generated bottom-up, then presented to higher management for their consideration.

- Work on producing key indicators, such as Critical Success Factors (CSF), that will be interesting enough to lead to further discussions with management, and introduce the idea of strategic systems and planning.

- Engage top management in the ideas of strategic planning through the methods developed by John Rockart (discussed in **Section 1.4, Engaging Top Management in Strategic Planning**).

- Distribute papers written by any of the authorities reviewed in this manual, if their approach seems to fit your particular company's requirements, and try to have discussions about their possible application.

- Use descriptions of the successes of other organizations in strategic system development to arouse interest in the possible opportunities.

None of these methods are guaranteed to work, but any of them may give just the right fit for your particular set of circumstances. Each group must assess their own particular situation and open as many doors as possible. One thing is clear, there is no use waiting for a classical strategic opportunity such as those that have been described in technical literature. On rare occasions, a senior manager may hear about the use of strategic information systems, decide on one, and call on the staff to implement it. Such occasions are not worth dreaming about. What is needed to increase the probability of realizing strategic opportunities for information systems is a planned effort to:

1. Understand the concepts of strategic information systems and competitive advantage.

2. Assess your industry and company characteristics and the impact of your company's competition.

3. Assess your products/services value chain and look for value-added possibilities.

4. Understand the possible strategic planning methodologies and their variations, as described in this manual.

5. Identify and select an appropriate methodology for your organization.

6. Attempt to get a hearing and to discuss your plan.

These points will be discussed at greater length in the following sections. Obviously, they are not all easily handled. Few planners will be able to go through these steps without considerable help from a number of managers who are interested in the subject. However, all planners should be prepared for the opportunity for strategic planning should it occur by studying and being aware of all aspects of the subject and their ramifications in the Information Services area.

It should be clear that the whole process of strategic planning is considerably more complex than operational or budget planning. First, it moves out of the technical realm into an area where projections require business experience. Second, it is a convergence of business and systems planning with many more players, some of whom will have little appreciation for the technical problems involving computer systems. The opportunity for Information Services to develop strategic systems is available, however, because the methodology has been tested and proven, and the payoffs can be great. The Information Services planners are the ones who have heard the most about the successes of others. They must attempt to position themselves so that strategic opportunities may be discovered, management may be convinced, and useful plans may be developed.

## 1.2     THE MEANING OF STRATEGIC PLANNING

The concept of "strategic planning" has been used for thirty years in data processing literature, and very much longer elsewhere. There have been some modern shifts in thinking about the strategic planning process, however, that call for a delineation of some of the meanings that are used for terms that are modified by the word "strategic". The same terms can have greatly different meanings for different authors.

### 1.2.1     STRATEGIC PLANNING

Strategic planning is the careful development of a plan to employ the resources of an organization to afford the maximum support to adopted policies. It is planning for competitive advantage. It anticipates future business changes and trends.

The term "strategic planning" has been in general use in the Information Services plans of major corporations for at least thirty years. It has the usual connotation of operational planning that is related to general or specific strategies of the corporation as a whole. There are still many articles written that refer to strategic planning in this sense, and some examples will later be given. A new concept has become well-known in the last ten years, however, that emphasizes the possible use of information systems as competitive weapons for the business. It concentrates on the search for those unique information systems that can provide special advantages to the business, to the point of improving market share or profit. No amount of careful definition can completely separate these two points of view, as they are really on a continuum of approaches. In reality, the difference is in perspective, or in attitude. The traditional approach to strategic planning is **planning in response to business initiative,** while much of the current thinking is **planning information systems to create business initiatives.** As will be discussed, the first approach is **reactive,** while the second approach is **proactive.** Both are acceptable approaches for an Information Services group to adopt, but the second can have the greatest payoff to them, and is the approach that is most often discussed by speakers today. The fact is, however, that most Information Services planners must work with the first approach.

In all cases, the purpose of strategic planning for information services is **to link business and computer strategies.** It is the process of identifying and achieving important business change through the use of information technology. It is the explicit connection of the organization's business plan and its systems plan to provide better support of the organization's goals and objectives. It gives closer management control of critical information systems to help achieve desired ends.

Although strategic planning is described in the literature in many ways, it should never be confused with long-range operational planning, since strategic planning may refer to a time span of several years, a single year, or an immediate, rush project. It will all depend upon the rapidity with which the organization wishes to move on a critical project. In the past, strategic planning has sometimes been used synonymously with long-range planning. It should never be used that way now, as it has come to mean planning that is concerned with issues and objectives, while long-range operational planning means lining up a broad range of projects and organizational actions.

Strategic planning for IS attempts to match Information Services resources and actions in response to strategic business opportunities where the computer systems will have an impact on the products and on the business success. Strategic planning is not defined by calendar cycles or budget periods. It is defined by the effort required to impact the competitive environment and the strategy of a firm.

## 1.2.2 STRATEGIC INFORMATION SYSTEMS

Strategic Information Systems (SIS) are computer-related systems that are used for strategic purposes in the corporation. They are systems that are designed to support or to shape the competitive strategy of the business.

Charles Wiseman, in his book **Strategy and Computers,** argues convincingly that a completely new **perspective** is required to identify strategic information systems. He claims that the conventional perspective over the years has led to the search for two information system opportunities, either **management information systems** (MIS) or **management support systems** (MSS), which may be called either decision support systems or executive information systems. He says that these latter systems are intended to serve organizational purposes that are associated with the conventional perspective. That is, the perspective of MIS has been to automate basic existing processes and to produce routine reports. Also, the perspective of MSS has been to satisfy the information needs of managers and professionals, usually in planning and control decisions. On the other hand, the perspective of strategic information systems is that they are designed to support or shape the **competitive strategy** of the business. All the different types of information systems may have similar physical structures, and they may be used for either transaction processing or query and analysis, or both. The key to SIS is that they are designed and operated with a perspective that is entrepreneurial and competitive.

Different information systems may thus be **technically** similar, and have similar **functions.** That is, they may deal with transaction processing, or with highly structured analyses, or they may provide query and ad hoc analysis capability. On the other hand, they may be designed for quite different **organizational uses.** The purpose for which a system is designed will depend on the perspective, or the business point of view, that is applied to its design. To get at strategic information systems, you have to start thinking about a different kind of organizational use, a use of the system that is quite different from the traditional planning and control focus of information technology.

This does not mean, incidentally, that all the much-publicized successful strategic information systems started out to be strategic systems. It seems likely that Robert Crandall of American Airlines invested $300 million in the 1970's simply to get an excellent reservations system. In retrospect, the Sabre system was a conventionally analyzed information system. They wanted efficiency, capability, and rapid response time for their reservation clerks, and it was not until much later that they were able to introduce some bias into the system and, along with United Airlines and its Apollo system, preempt the principal distribution channels for airline reservations. Similarly, in the early stages of the American Hospital Supply system, they did not realize that it would have the impact that it finally did.

Thus strategic information systems (SIS) have no technical or functional difference from MIS or MSS. They also process predefined transactions and produce fixed-format reports on schedule, together with ad hoc query and analysis capabilities. They may already exist in a corporation and may be run regularly as an MIS. They can be called SIS, however, only after they have been identified as useful to support or shape the competitive strategy of the business. As soon as management realizes that a particular information system can be used to give them a competitive advantage, or to directly support their competitive strategy, that information system becomes an SIS.

Strategic information systems can be planned within an Information Services group if they have good communications with the operational management of the organization. They should be planned systematically, with all participants aware of their roles. Many corporations regularly look for strategic opportunities in their planning. They may not produce major breakthrough systems that will be discussed in the literature, but they maintain a goal of steadily increasing their firm's profitability.

Summaries of most of the views about SIS that are given in **Section 2, Strategic Information Systems,** are primarily concerned with the **identification** and analysis of SIS. They are not particularly concerned with the details of planning, systems analysis, and program development. Those subjects are discussed more fully in **Sections 3 and 4.** The authorities and consultants on SIS are principally concerned with showing how to introduce management to the possibilities of using the computer as a competitive tool, and the strategies to prove that point. SIS may be found by adaptation and extension of conventional systems. They may also be found by direct analysis of the competitive situation, and considerable cooperation between operational and IS management.

In summary, strategic planning usually refers to planning for competitive advantage, or planning **for the identification** of strategic information systems. Strategic information systems planning is then the planning **of the development** of strategic information systems.

## 1.2.3    STRATEGIC INFORMATION SYSTEMS PLANNING

Strategic information systems planning is an umbrella term for a great deal of staff work that must be accomplished to convert strategic systems concepts and ideas into reality. Possibly senior management has heard a presentation by an effective consulting group. Possibly Information Services has sponsored a lengthy brainstorming session with operational managers after a convincing description of SIS has been heard. Possibly alert managers have presented certain ideas and issues to IS and asked if an approach can be automated to reach their goals. The idea of using a computer system for competitive advantage has been accepted, and IS is asked to separate the wheat from the chaff, and develop a working system that will have the desired functions. The stages that follow are not fixed. In fact, there are a number of different approaches that have been put forward, but there is always a logical progression that may be followed to produce computer results efficiently and effectively.

SIS planning starts with the identification of the target SIS that is to be developed. This should include an assessment of the industry and company **character-istics,** in terms of customers, suppliers, competitors, geography, market segments, and so on, to set the framework for the system development. There should also be an analysis of the **value chain** to formulate sound competitive strategy by concentrating on the key driving forces. The planning methodology should then be discussed and agreed upon. Some managers may want a conservative, step-wise approach taken, with many control steps. Others may favor moving swiftly to a prototype model, which may be effectively used even while a fuller system is being developed.

Whatever planning methodology is used, the first step is always the "plan for the plan." The SIS planning approach must be documented, with its requirements, priorities, and checkpoints, and presented for approval at the highest level of management involved with the proposed strategic system. It must make sense to operational management and concentrate on their strategic interests before extensive work is started. An SIS can never follow the path of some traditional system approaches, and disappear inside the Information Services Department for months as it is being developed. It must be continually visible, and retain management interest.

Strategic plans are usually complex, and simply cannot be developed in a vacuum. They must draw on past company experiences, the current competitive status, and technological possibilities. Strategic plans are not a listing of IS projects that are started over time, but are working documents grounded in the business purpose of the enterprise. They may well be prototyped, since they must always be modified as the circumstances of the business dictate. The objective of SIS planning is to arrive at near-term decisions that coincide with the longer-term direction of the company. In essence, they are communication vehicles that highlight key business and IS issues. They do not necessarily afford definitive solutions, although such solutions will later be incorporated in the IS operational plans.

Strategic planning may involve lengthy analyses, preparations, and discussions, with many iterations, or it may be a rapid, all-out effort leading to a prototype model. In whatever way they are produced, they are always built on a solid base of studies, records, and reports that have been systematically developed and produced by IS personnel. The broader the base on which strategic plans are built, the quicker they will come to fruition.

**Issues** and **objectives** are the keystones of IS strategic planning. Their statement helps to resolve the organization's critical business issues, and the organization's business objectives are attained by setting the IS objectives, measuring their attainment, and accomplishing them. All the other familiar elements in the planning process, such as feasibility studies, proposals, analyses, projections, action programs, resource estimates, and so forth, are simply the tools for attaining the business objectives and resolving the business issues.

The events or elements of most strategic IS planning processes are:

- The **mission statement,** or the setting of new business boundaries.

- **Business objectives,** which are the management aims or goals to be attained.

- **Opportunity areas or problem areas** including the anticipated conditions that could favorably affect future profitability, and those that could have an adverse effect.

- **Pressure points or impact points** that touch on the factors influencing the business both externally and internally, and which may be changed through efforts by management.

- **Business issues** are aspects of the business which management has selected to be addressed, which are under their potential control, and can have a significant effect on the bottom line if control is exercised.

- **Strategies** are methods used to resolve unsettled issues and lead to the desired objectives.

- **Targets** are the measure of the benefits to be received from a strategy, and of the time when the benefit will be substantially received.

- **IS objectives** are the specific IS systems to be produced to follow the strategies and to reach the management targets or aims.

- **Implementation programs** are the outlines for carrying out a strategy, or achieving an objective, giving estimates of the expected duration, costs, resources, performance measures, and benefits.

- **Performance measurement** is following the criteria for the acceptable level of achievement of the program over a period of time in a specific way that is representative of the objectives desired.

Strategic information systems planning is concerned with special situations that have differing time demands and a wide range of management interest and urgency. The process must be adapted to the requirements of the unique business situations, and be timed according to the business necessity that is dictated by higher management. There is an optimum process for conducting strategic systems planning for a large project, however. Variations of, and approaches to, the strategic planning process will be discussed more fully in **Section 4, Strategic Information Systems Planning.**

## 1.2.4   STRATEGIES

There are two complementary definitions of strategy which are used in SIS planning:

- A general statement of the way in which the resolution of an issue will be controlled by management to attain the desired effect on profits.

- The practical method used to resolve unsettled issues into the settled, or final, objectives.

The first definition of a strategy is from the management viewpoint. An issue is turned around in a positive manner to become a strategy. A problem is recognized, and a working objective is stated. This is not the final objective, but a process to be followed. For example, if the issue is that too few customers are using a particular service, the strategy may be to offer services that are tailored to particular customers. Note that this is a strategy stated by management, and it is then up to IS to provide a strategy for its solution.

The second definition of strategy is the approach to be used by IS to settle the issues, resolve the unanswered questions, and refine the results of the strategic analysis into a statement of specific objectives. Where the management strategy simply gives a direction and a target, the IS strategy may involve many steps. These steps in the strategy could be business plans analysis, environmental analysis, forecasts of trends, assumptions, analysis of internal strengths and weaknesses, risk analysis, contingency analysis, economic analysis, and so on. The **management strategy** states the **direction.** The **IS strategy** states the **tools and approaches** that will be used to move in that direction.

Only after strategies are considered is it realistic to set objectives and the key measurement factors that will be used. After these decisions are made, a strategic plan, or report, can be prepared for top management, who may be expected to make a decision about whether or not to proceed with the plan as presented. Management can then review whether the IS objectives match the business objectives, and appear to be able to produce the desired strategic results. The statement of IS strategies developed in response to business strategies facilitates decision-oriented planning by management. They can look at the alternatives offered to them by Information Services, and decide on the IS strategy to follow.

If the IS planning process determines that an issue can be controlled in more than one way simultaneously, the various approaches may all be listed in the IS plan, possibly for management selection. They are then called **sub-strategies.** Again, if the issue is that too few customers are using a particular service, and the management strategy is to offer services tailored to a particular customer, the IS response may be a number of sub-strategies, such as expanding product offerings, adding services, and offering products tailored to particular needs. The sub-strategies become a selection menu for management to use.

All that is important in presenting an IS strategy is that it deals with an aspect of the business issue that senior management has decided needs attention and that, if it is addressed, it can improve future profitability. When a strategy is translated to an implementation program, there will be far more detail developed. Statements of strategies, therefore, are bridges between IS and the business units of the company to show what is intended to be done, and how the various courses of action relate to each other and will affect the company's future profitability.

## 1.2.5    STRATEGIC PLANNING AND LONG-RANGE PLANNING

In the past, many corporations have called their long-range planning "strategic planning," and their annual operational planning "tactical planning." These have been perfectly acceptable uses of the terms "strategic" and "tactical," which were originally borrowed from the military usage. In the military, strategic means the whole theater of war, while tactical refers to a specific battlefield at a specific time. When these terms are still used today, however, it should be clearly understood that they have many differences of meaning from the popular current use of the term "strategic planning." (Incidentally, "tactical planning" is a term that is rarely used in the current literature, and the former idea of "tactics" is sometimes interchanged with "strategies.")

Planning is now considered as a process in which appropriate information is systematically assembled and analyzed in order to forecast areas of opportunity and risk. It includes the development of alternatives for management selection, and of strategies to optimize the attainment of the desired goals with minimum risk. Such a definition covers all the types of planning, and therefore the differences between the types may be more conceptual than actual. If a large organization has a good, working system of routinely passing specific top management goals down through the organization as far as the systems planners, the resultant planning may validly be called "strategic." The systems developed will realistically be for competitive advantage, because that was the intent of top management when they set the goals. Such an approach has been publicly described by the DuPont organization, for example, since the 1920's, and it is in general use in a number of large, technically-managed oil and chemical companies.

The fact is, however, that management in some companies may not have an appreciation of technical, computer, and systems potentials, and may not even think in terms of Objectives and Goals. Yet they may have large, well-run, Information Services organizations that carefully plan both long-range and short-range. There is a linkage missing, however, between the IS planning and the corporate strategic goals. Their long-range planning is predominantly concerned with technology changes and very large operational computer systems.

It is to these latter companies, the majority, that the current message of strategic planning as a unique endeavor is addressed. The message is to let the technical long-range planning continue on its cyclical course. It is vitally needed. But also, start linking IS planning with corporate planning for either long horizons or short horizons. There is competitive advantage to be gained, and bottom-line impacts to be made, by purposely adopting a new perspective on the planning process. Link it to business change, and turn the computers into competitive weapons, at the same time as the other operational work is pursued efficiently.

The difference between strategic planning and long-range planning is thus principally a difference of perspective. Long-range planning has the data processing perspective while strategic planning has the business perspective, yet they both interact. **Figure 1-1, Comparison of Strategic Planning and Long-Range Operational Planning,** lists some of the differences of approach between the two types of planning. The columns are labeled "emphasis in", because neither method of planning has a patent on any of the approaches or ways of thinking. It is simply that the attributes listed are more typical of the types of planning listed at the heads of the columns. A detailed analysis of this figure would be redundant. The entries in the columns carry the message.

Figure 1-1

## COMPARISON OF STRATEGIC PLANNING AND
## LONG-RANGE OPERATIONAL PLANNING

| PLANNING AREA | EMPHASIS IN STRATEGIC PLANNING | EMPHASIS IN LONG-RANGE OPERATIONAL PLANNING |
|---|---|---|
| Planning Horizon | Period of Business Change - short or long | Intermediate and Long Term |
| Systems Orientation | Immediate Business Needs | Structured Development |
| Business Assumptions | Possibilities of Change | Projections from Experience |
| Planning Cycle | Foreshortened, Immediate | Routine, Annual |
| Objective | Competitive Advantage | Operational Control |
| Analytical Methods | Critical Thinking, Creative | Technical, Rational |
| Tools | Meetings, Discussions, Brainstorming | Systems Analysis, Statics Operations Research |
| Measurements | Bottom Line | Time, Costs |
| Mind Set | Offensive Optimistic | Defensive, Realistic |
| Output Orientation | Economics | Business Needs |
| Value Added | Effectiveness | Efficiency |

## 1.3     INFORMATION SERVICES STRATEGIES

It was pointed out that, from the viewpoint of Information Services, strategies are the approaches used by IS to settle management issues, resolve the unanswered questions, and refine the results of the strategic analysis into a statement of specific objectives. The steps in the IS strategies include a variety of analytical methods that are used. These are the tools and approaches that are most often described in the literature for showing IS how to move in the direction desired by management. Some of the facets of Information Services strategies that will be outlined are planning amid change, contingent planning, and proactive vs. reactive planning.

### 1.3.1     CREATING A VISION

A concept that has been popularized by William H. Gruber, Research & Planning, Inc., is that the planning task of the Information Services planner is not a routine matter that can be readily structured, but is a problem of "planning amid change," where much of the change may indeed have been generated by the strategic possibilities of information systems themselves. The mission of the systems group has long been the application of information technology to the management of the business. This has been understood, and IS has done substantial, worthwhile work in the transaction processing and other operational areas of the business, always looking at them as situations that could be completely analyzed and established as defined operational entities. IS has proven itself to be completely capable at collecting, organizing, and controlling data, and running systems operationally. IS analysts received instructions about systems, coded them, and ran them. But, Gruber pointed out, the role of IS began to change dramatically. IS has to "create a vision" of the organization's direction, and change their way of thinking. Instead of objectively following directions from individual managers, they have to start building large, integrated databases on the mainframe, interface them with the microcomputers, use a variety of developed and packaged software, and supply new methods of analyzing and using data.

No longer can systems be planned unilaterally, then the equipment obtained to run those systems. Planners who are working on large systems must now also consider that the users will want the data from a variety of sources, whenever they have need of it. They will want to scan a variety of data files, and analyze the data for their own purposes without having to go through others to get what they want. They need to be able to directly access data themselves, and to define their own output at their own convenient terminals. One driving force behind this major change is that data processing technology has changed markedly, and is now making available cheaper hardware and more functional software. The IS planners, therefore, have to take a new view of planning that includes:

- New, interlocking systems architectures

- Data organization for better access with control

The traditional planning by projections while thinking of certain, specific applications has reached a point of limitation. There is no help in doing capacity planning for one application on one computer, when an undetermined number of other groups within the organization will probably want to soon be accessing that application, and using its data in other applications, all on-line. The classical planning methodologies fall down when the requirements for the information involved are a moving target. Planning formulas that concentrate on a single application by itself, as a one-time exercise, are no longer valid. Change must be anticipated and expected. Management issues must be understood, future user needs must be taken into account, and a new vision of computer use must be mutually developed. A new vision must be created of the strategic uses of the computer rather than defined application uses.

For the initial creation of a new vision about Information Services, Gruber recommends a planning session, fully devoted to communication and debate, held away from the normal working office. A consultant may be helpful at such a session as an objective catalyst. The first purpose is to look at the management issues, and determine the Information Services issues. From such a session, many issues should arise, and they need to be first listed, and then put into some sort of priority order. The types of management issues that are drawn out may include:

- The changing role of systems analysts when users develop their own applications

- The coordination of data usage among users

- The networking of the central computer and the PCs

- The physical cabling and control of the local network

- The corporate and division roles in information management

- The ownership and control of the data

The many management issues of this type should then be aggregated according to perceived IS solutions. There may be hardware solutions, telecommunications solutions, software solutions, and so on. The purpose is to make the vision readily understood, so the issues are aggregated in a way that allows ready translation to specific actions.

Another way of looking at the creation of a vision is that it is first, setting the present and projected framework in which IS will be working, then developing solutions to issues that fit into this framework. All the different activities that are proposed will then be perceived as leading to a common resolution. When any group in IS makes decisions on hardware, software, database, personal computing, office technology, systems staff, etc., there is a good chance that those decisions will fit into the common vision that has been created. Each domain will interact and fit. The reporting of specific solutions to issues should then be consistent. The resolutions of issues should all be perceived as falling into the same framework. Every report on an issue resolution should generally follow the form:

- Scope of the problem

- Objective of the problem resolution

- Background issues, opportunities, and problems

- Strategy that is recommended to be followed

The purpose of this type of group discussion to create a vision is to develop an overall backdrop against which daily decisions can be made. It is a vehicle for communicating the vision to others, and securing their commitment to go through the necessary steps. The reports that are produced on the resolution of issues can be used as the starting point to draw out the opinions of others. The planning document will essentially list the strategies for Information Services to meet the corporate objectives. It is important that they be just that, strategies, rather than the traditional lists of projects and equipment, because the users and management can relate directly to the strategic thrusts. Support is then worked on group by group, among the users, management, and corporate staff groups.

This is not an annual occurrence, although the planning meeting may be held annually, but it is a continuing process. It should be reviewed regularly, and new strategies for IS identified. The older strategies can be reworked from experience with them. The great advantage of the process of creating a vision for cooperative planning is that it helps to shift the focus from "data processing" approaches to business approaches. The vision that is created is a business vision, of data processing work directly in support of business priorities.

In most of the strategic information systems approaches that are outlined later in this manual, access to upper management is necessary to gather the issues that will drive the planning process. The difficulty that most Information Services planners have is getting clear instructions from management, or in obtaining a hearing with them. Gruber's suggested method of creating a vision through cooperative discussion has proven to be a useful way of getting original inputs into the planning process that have "strategic" content, and using the resulting reports to get management to discuss the IS directions. In one sense, it is the development of IS strategies that will likely further corporate strategies, then the determination of the fit.

## 1.3.2    CONTINGENT PLANNING

A particular strategy of IS planning that fits a rapidly changing business and technology environment is the contingent approach to strategic systems planning that has been advanced by Cornelius H. Sullivan, Jr.[1] This important strategy of using the best planning process for each specific opportunity will be developed more fully in **Section 3, Strategic Systems Planning - A Contingent Approach.**

Companies are seeking a planning process which can adapt to meet needs which not only vary from one year to the next, but also vary considerably from one business unit to another. This requires a change in the roles and responsibilities of systems planners, and it is occurring at the same time as decentralization of information functions. Systems are now scattered throughout the corporation, and they are often not under the direct control of a central authority. Responsibility has been decentralized at the same time that the strategic impact of systems is being considered.

Sullivan points out that there is no single strategy for Information Services planners, but that the approach will vary characteristically depending on the levels of strategic impact and decentralization. There is thus, no single kind of information systems planning that large firms should use. Each kind of systems environment has a characteristic planning technique which seems to work best. He has correlated the

---

[1]    Cornelius H. Sullivan Jr., **Systems Planning in the Information Age,** Sloan Management Review, 26:2, Winter 1985.

methodologies that will best suit specific organizations by plotting two industry or systems characteristics, which he calls **infusion** and **diffusion.** Infusion is the impact of information technology. Diffusion is the degree to which information technology has been disseminated through the business. Where a corporation falls on the infusion-diffusion matrix will point out the most used planning technique for that type of corporation. This analysis allows Information Services to pick a planning strategy that has been found by others to be most favorable. It will be more fully described in **Section 3.**

Contingent planning, or planning in a contingent framework, is an excellent approach to consider before becoming overpowered by all the variations of strategic information systems planning that have been proposed, and will be discussed. It is a way to cut through the varied claims and convincing arguments and find the best approach for specific circumstances. Even as there are variations from one firm to another, and changes over time, many companies are diversified enough in their use and management of technology that they will face significantly different needs **within** the firm, from one business unit to another.

Any relevant framework for Information Services planning strategies must be based on this planning imperative. Consideration must be given to the importance of various system planning technological issues, to the divergent planning styles in the organization, and to the intensity, or level of effort, with which the planning endeavor is expected to be carried out. These alternative issues, styles, and levels of effort constitute a three-dimensional conceptual framework for Information Services planning strategies. Each planning endeavor is likely to be a unique selection from this set of planning issues styles, and degrees of effort. This is not for just each company, but for each instance of planning within a firm.

The whole purpose of a contingent approach is to allow the process to vary from one instance to the next. It is far less routine and standardized than establishing an accepted approach to planning in an organization. All the strategic planning processes described in this manual are valid in certain circumstances and should be considered. Traditional planning methods are still relevant. Contingent planning in practice is some combination of data collection, value-added analysis, and change management. It simply states that the best approach for specific circumstances should be taken, as long as the following distinguishing traits are present:

- **Responsive:**

    Seek the planning process appropriate to the needs of those for whom the planning is undertaken.

- **Forward Linkage:**

    Systems plans should not just flow from business plans, but there should be a two-way linkage, or information exchange, with technological plans.

- **Backward Linkage:**

    There must be a connection between the strategic planning and the tactical layers of planning, such as long-range systems planning and operational planning.

● **A Corporate View:**

To make the planning process a rational exercise, there must be
a mechanism in place to ensure that the corporation as a whole
will be able to acquire and disseminate the information.

The contingent planning framework is useful not only in understanding the
wide variety of planning processes that are put forward, but also as a way to structure a
planning process for a particular organization.

## 1.3.3   REACTIVE AND PROACTIVE PLANNING

It is popular to call for Information Services planners to discard their older,
**reactive** approach to planning, and adopt a **proactive** stance. Most practitioners find
that this is excellent in concept, but difficult to attain. The problem is that most
planners do not have a ready ear at the senior management levels for their proactive
ideas. They read about the new planning thrusts that must be made, but find it hard to
adopt a recognized, proactive position. One of the purposes of this manual is to present
a wide variety of approaches to methods of creating interest in, and developing,
strategic information systems. If any of the methods offer a possible opening, then the
planner should adopt it proactively.

**Reactive planning** is being prepared to be readily responsive to initiatives from
management. This does not mean taking a wait-and-see attitude. It means developing
computer systems and planning files so that planning information, such as applications
descriptions, equipment and communications inventories, organization charts, and
project reports are all rapidly and systematically available. It means having a broad
understanding of corporate activities, and the routine development of business and
Information Services projections. It means being aware of some of the strategic
possibilities of Information Systems, and watching for opportunities that may be
presented to propose their development.

**Proactive planning** is taking the initiative in advocating the use of information
systems for competitive advantage. It also must flow from a base of carefully-
developed computer systems and planning files. Instead of a waiting preparedness,
however, it is a direct advocacy of possibilities for information systems developments
that will impact the firm's business position. In addition to being aware of some of the
strategic possibilities, and of watching for opportunities to develop systems, it includes
selling the ideas of the systems to senior management.

Much of planning has to be reactive, as the planning work cycles through the
annual operational and budget process, plus the occasional long-range operational
planning work. This work is the basic responsibility of Information Systems planners,
and must be regularly carried out. On occasion, however, new ideas and opportunities
arise that can show promise of great strategic advantage. It is at this point that
planners are urged to be proactive, and to present the ideas of the new possibilities with
vigor. The planner must first do the homework, with the basic analyses and discussions
with knowledgeable operational management. If the indications are favorable, the
opportunity is there for a proactive thrust.

All strategic planning is planning in response to corporate business initiative.
The purpose of strategic planning is to link business and computer strategies, and to

develop a plan to afford the maximum support to adopted policies. Strategic planning facilitates and enhances the efforts of the business that are considered most critical. In **reactive planning**, the Information Services planner simply searches for information about new policies, and new business strategies, and tries to propose information systems solutions for them. In **proactive planning**, the Information Services planner reacts beyond the normally understood approaches and proposes new computer ideas that will have a significant effect on the business. Many speakers and consultants urge planners to be proactive, but the difficulty is usually political and positional. It takes a really powerful idea for a planner to break out of a traditional position. It is interesting to note that many of the famous strategic systems that are repeatedly discussed in the literature started as reactive planning approaches to business problems, then dramatically new possibilities were discerned and proposed proactively by Information Services.

## 1.4     ENGAGING TOP MANAGEMENT IN STRATEGIC PLANNING

The dilemma facing all Information Services planners is that strategic planning, by definition, concerns top management and the basic directions of the organization, yet few planners have ready access to those involved in setting the overall strategies. John F. Rockart, discerned this problem in his study of corporations over the years, and, with Adam D. Crescenzi, documented it.[2]

Rockart describes a successful use of an integrated, three-phase process for management involvement. It is true that outside consultants were managing the process, and were involved in it throughout, but it appears to be a realistic and orderly approach for any group to work with top management. He emphasizes that the process can be replicated in other companies of various sizes and organizations as long as there is good management to supply a clear focus. He says that the process will **not** work at all times in all companies. Timing is key. Management must be ready to be involved. Competitive pressures, a felt need to rethink computer priorities, or sheer awareness of the increasing strategic importance of information systems are all among a list of enabling factors that make possible a successful exercise.

Rockart points out that, with the advent of the personal computer, computer-based assistance for **all** functions of the business is becoming widespread in a number of companies. Top managers have been spectators to system development in the past. Now they are confronting new forces that are leading them into unfamiliar territories, and are creating a thirst for the right information to help **manage change.** Today's information technology has the potential to improve effectiveness and productivity in managing businesses, and it is having a substantial impact on business strategy itself. A number of companies have demonstrated that significant competitive advantage can be gained through judicious use of the new technology.

Rockart's group believes that developing an active engagement of top management with information systems is highly desirable in organizations of every size. They propose a three-phase process that is based on three major concepts:

- **Critical Success Factors** - to engage management's attention and ensure that the systems meet the most critical **business** needs.

- **Decision Scenarios** - to demonstrate to management that the systems to be developed will aid materially in their decision-making process.

- **Prototyping** - to quickly reap system results and to minimize initial cost.

Tying these three concepts together in a single development process not only gets top management engaged in the information systems planning process in a meaningful way, but also keeps management's attention and involvement throughout a rapid development process, since the priority systems are targeted to support their decision-making processes.

---

2    John F. Rockart, Jr., Director CISR, Sloan School of Management, at M.I.T., and Adam D. Crescenzi. **Engaging Top Management in Information Systems Planning and Development: A Case Study,** CISR WP #115, July, 1984.

The CISR study described was with Southwestern Ohio Steel, a major steel service center company. In 1982 they embarked on a major review of their information systems capability to support expected significant growth and to develop a delivery-oriented inventory system. They turned down a conventional systems design and implementation process as too costly and time-consuming. They accepted Rockart's three-phase approach for managerial involvement. This three-phase process consists of:

1.  **Linking** information systems to the management needs of the business, using **Critical Success Factors.** Management develops a clear definition of the business and agrees on its most critical business functions. It begins stating its information needs in these areas.

2.  **Gaining confidence** in the recommended systems, and developing managerial understanding that the **systems priorities** defined would deliver the necessary information to support key decisions. The technique used in this stage is **decision scenarios.**

3.  **Rapid development** of low-risk, managerially-useful systems using a **prototype development** approach. This means implementing initial, partial systems very quickly at low cost. Management can work with these systems to understand their usefulness and to authorize continued system development.

This process is outlined in **Figure 1-2, A Three-Phase Process for Managerial Involvement.**

### PHASE ONE:  Linking To The Business

The emphasis in Phase One is on focusing on the few factors that drive the business, and in engaging management actively in the process. The three steps in this phase include an introductory workshop to develop a management perspective and to outline the objectives of the process, the Critical Success Factor interviews, and the focusing workshop to explore the implications of the CSF's.

The **Introductory Workshop** is the first step in Phase One. This requires a few key members of the management team in order to be successful. Company objectives are discussed and clearly agreed upon, and the process is described. It is emphasized that no one is asking "what information is needed." They are asking, rather, what the critical business functions are, and the information imperatives of those functions. The intent of the workshop is to give management a perspective for systems development, and to start linking information systems needs and priorities to the most important business activities.

The **Critical Success Factors (CSF)** to achieve these objectives are then obtained through an interview process. The CSF's are described as the **means** to the objectives. They are the key areas on which the company must focus. In the interview process, each manager is asked to explicitly state those things that are critical, and their priority. The measurement of the CSF's is also discussed. The interview process helps to clarify the roles of each individual and the culture of the organization.

**Figure 1-2**

**A THREE-PHASE PROCESS FOR MANAGERIAL INVOLVEMENT**

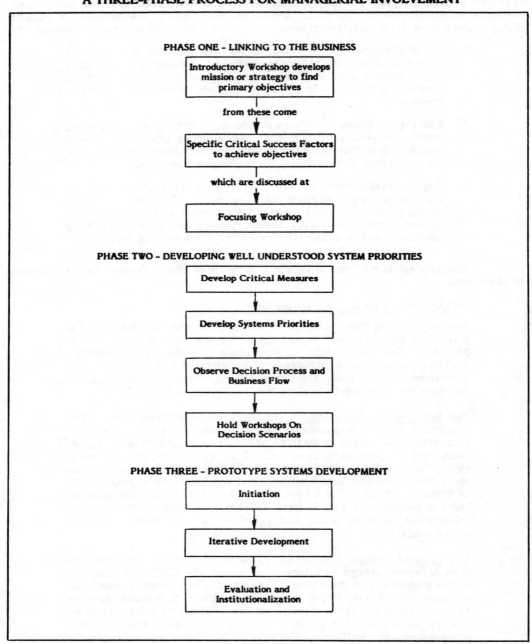

The **Focusing Workshop** is held after the team has studied the CSF's and has developed an initial statement of corporate mission, objectives, and CSF priorities. The top management people constructively criticize what has been found, consider the ramifications, and agree on focused CSF's, organizational relationships, and the preliminary system design. In this step, both business knowledge of the leaders and their interpersonal skills are critical.

### PHASE TWO: Developing Well-Understood Systems Priorities

In this phase, another workshop is held to define a set of measures for the CSF's. An example taken from Rockart's paper is given in **Figure 1-3, Measures of One CSF.** These measures may be either hard or soft data, such as managers are familiar with. The study team then examines the business in more depth, and tries to prioritize the suggested systems. The system needs must flow from the managerial discussion of goals, CSF's, and measures.

**Figure 1-3**

## MEASURES OF ONE CSF

| CSF | MEASURES | DATA TYPE | CURRENT MEASURE |
|---|---|---|---|
| CUSTOMER RELATIONS | - Volume | H | M |
| | - Inquiries | H | M |
| | - Order/bid ratio | H | M |
| | - Complaints and/or rejections of materials | H | M |
| | - Customer turnover or lost accounts | H | M |
| | - Decline in volume with customer | H | M |
| | - Program account actual volume vs. customer and SOS forecasts | H | A |
| | - New Accounts | H | M |
| | - Conversions to program accounts | H | U |
| | - On-time delivery: to first promise date to final need date | H | A |
| | - Trends in credit rejections | H | U |
| | - Tone of voice (esp. during late delivery calls) | S | A |
| | - Finance and credit "handling" feedback | S | A |

DATA TYPE:    H = Hard
                       S = Soft

CURRENT MEASURE:    M = Measured
                                 A = Data Available
                                 U = Data Unavailable

From John F. Rockart and Adam D. Crescenzi,
CISR WP #115, July 1984

The final step of Phase Two is a workshop on **decision scenarios** to develop the technical environment necessary to support the systems, the necessary data in the systems, and the source and frequency of data collection. The object is to make management say that the approach fills their requirements. In these workshops on decision scenarios, typical situations are reviewed, and the questions that may be asked of management are listed. Enough situations are covered, and enough questions are listed and agreed upon, so that management can finally agree that the proposed systems are appropriate. The computer database is always kept in mind, so that it is known whether a particular answer is available or not. This is an excellent time to mock-up screen formats, so that the managers can say whether the particular information is readily available that they want. This is essentially a presentation of "paper models" to determine if they are, or could be, realistic. When everyone agrees that this step has been completed, the detailed design of the system can begin.

### PHASE THREE:  Prototype System Development

The first step in prototype system development is selecting the type of prototype that will be used. Rockart lists three types of prototypes:

- An **information database** for management support. These are preliminary collections of data made available for management use. The manager uses the database to answer typical questions, and gains further insight into what types of data are really needed. This is essentially what is called a **decision support system.** It is frequently what is required in marketing support.

- A **pilot system** is the classical miniature replication of the final production system. Like a pilot plant, it is a scale model of the full system. A pilot system can usually be expanded step-wise into a real production system.

- A **classical prototype** is an initial system that contains the essential features of the full system, but a limited set of functions. As the prototype appears to behave satisfactorily with the initial functions, increased functionality is added in a stepwise fashion. At each step, the model is tested to see if it is behaving as expected.

There are several advantages to the prototyping of systems. First, they have the ability to provide some useful data at all levels of management almost immediately, and can be constantly enriched. Secondly, they produce results while management is still interested in the project, and sustained interest may be generated. Third, they give a smooth education to management of the newer technologies and remove fear of computer systems. Fourth, they can be introduced piecemeal into the management process, and show specific linking to business needs.

The advantages of prototyping are listed as:

- Prototypes reduce monetary risk.

- Prototypes reduce business risk.

- Prototypes allow a manager to inspect, work with, and shape the product as it is being developed, and to become comfortable with it.

As prototyping proceeds, an actual system can be developed. This will normally be with a Fourth Generation Language, such as a report program generator, to allow frequent modification and an evolutionary design. Full systems, with significant modifications and extensions, can be developed in this way in less than a year. Such systems are usually menu-based, interactive processing.

Rockart and Crescenzi do not slide over the considerable "backroom" effort that must be put in by the consultants, staff, and system developers. Considerable detail of the operational activities of the corporation must be obtained. Databases and control procedures must be developed to assure appropriate updating of the data by operational personnel. Such a managerially-oriented process requires a great deal of staff work. In all cases where they have followed through on this three-phase process, however, significant benefits have been perceived at all levels of management. They believe that the process can be replicated in any company where there is management interest and support. They, or course, favor the use of outside consultants to ease the engagement of top management in strategic planning.

The advantages of the process appear to arise from the following factors:

a.  The process makes an easy and quick link to top management and the way it thinks.

b.  The process focuses managerial attention on those areas of the business that are important, and makes them feel comfortable that the work is in those areas.

c.  The process supplies real management involvement.

d.  The consultants (whether internal or external) gain significant insight into the business, and are therefore more effective.

e.  Managers recognize that the risk is lower.

# SECTION 2

## STRATEGIC INFORMATION SYSTEMS

### SECTION OVERVIEW

Strategic information systems are systems that are developed in response to corporate business initiative, which may come from Information Services or from business management. They are intended to give competitive advantage to the organization. They may deliver a product or service that is at a lower cost, that is differentiated, that focuses on a particular market segment, or that is innovative.

There has been a **change in paradigm** in the last decade relative to strategic systems. Where previously "strategic" principally referred to the key business planning of the corporation, now it frequently refers to the use of computers as a competitive weapon. These are currently two co-existent paradigms that overlap in practice.

Some of the key ideas of forefront writers about strategic information systems are summarized. Michael Porter's work on competitive advantage and the value chain has been the foundation for a great deal of subsequent writing, although his theories on competitive advantage are not tied to information systems.

Charles Wiseman's ideas on the use of information systems as competitive weapons is outlined. He is strongly on the side of the new paradigm, but points out that some of the best examples grew from the older thinking process.

Warren McFarlan's work on information technology and competitive strategy has bridged the two paradigms, and has given a basic understanding of how information technology has changed the way organizations do business. He reviews the generic strategies and discusses resource allocation.

Gregory Parsons' concentrates on strategic information technology management. His matrix on the impact of information technology against the impact of competitive forces on strategy is frequently used to show how information technology can affect the firm's ability to execute strategy.

Gerald Loev has had many years of consulting on strategic approaches for information technology. He uses the Boston Consulting Group's familiar characterization of business types as stars, question marks, cash cows, and dogs to show what automation should be doing in specific firms. He describes how Information Services should position itself in firms for strategic opportunity analysis and strategic planning.

Paul Strassman's work on the value-added approach as the best way of looking at productivity is outlined. He advocates a new measure, Return on Management (ROM) as a means of benchmarking management productivity and information technology. He points out that the external marketplace is the competitive equalizer, and must be included in all evaluations. He introduces a comparison and measurement tool to strategic planning.

Jacques Passino points out that businesses are increasingly challenged with intense competition and rapid change. He advocates the consideration of the forces of global competition, and discusses how the information planning process must consider the organizational issue, the scope issue, and the change management issue.

## 2.1    CHARACTERIZATION OF STRATEGIC INFORMATION SYSTEMS

Strategic information systems are those computer systems that implement business strategies. They are those systems where Information Services resources are applied to strategic business opportunities in such a way that the computer systems have an impact on the organization's products and business operations. Strategic information systems are **systems that are developed in response to corporate business initiative.** The ideas in several well-known cases came from Information Services personnel, but they were directed at specific corporate business thrusts. In other cases, the ideas came from business management, and Information Services supplied the technological capabilities to realize profitable results.

Most information systems are looked on as support activities to the business. They mechanize operations for better efficiency, control, and effectiveness, but they do not, in themselves, increase corporate profitability. They are simply used to provide management with sufficient dependable information to keep the business running smoothly, and they are used for analysis to plan new directions. Strategic information systems, on the other hand, become an integral and necessary part of the business, and directly influence market share, earnings, and all other aspects of marketplace profitability. They may even bring in new products, new markets, and new ways of doing business. They directly affect the competitive stance of the organization, giving it an advantage against the competitors.

Most literature on strategic information systems emphasizes the dramatic breakthroughs in computer systems, such as American Airlines' Sabre System and American Hospital Supply's terminals in customer offices. These, and many other highly successful approaches are most attractive to think about, and it is always possible that an equivalent success may be attained in your organization. There are many possibilities for strategic information systems, however, which may not be dramatic breakthroughs, but which will certainly become a part of corporate decision-making and will increase corporate profitability. The development of any strategic information system always enhances the image of Information Services in the organization, and leads to information management having a more participatory role in the operation of the organization.

Three general types of information systems that are developed and in general use may be classified as financial systems, operational systems, and strategic systems. These categories are not mutually exclusive and, in fact, they always overlap to some extent. Well-directed financial systems and operational systems may well become the strategic systems for a particular organization.

**Financial systems** are the basic computerization of the accounting, budgeting, and finance operations of an organization. These are similar and ubiquitous in all organizations because the computer has proven to be ideal for the mechanization and control of financial systems. These include the personnel systems because the headcount control and payroll of a company is of prime financial concern. Financial systems are usually one of the bases of all other systems because they give a common, controlled measurement of all operations and projects, and can supply trusted numbers for indicating departmental or project success. Organizational planning must be tied to financial analysis. There is always a greater opportunity to develop strategic systems when the financial systems are in place, and the required figures can be readily retrieved from them.

**Operational systems,** or services systems, help control the details of the business. Such systems will vary with each type of enterprise. They are the computer systems that operational managers need to help run the business on a routine basis. They may be useful but mundane systems that keep track of inventory, for example, and print out reorder points and cost allocations. On the other hand, they may have a strategic perspective built into them, and may handle inventory in a way that dramatically impacts profitability. A prime example of this is the American Hospital Supply inventory control system installed on customer premises. Where the great majority of inventory control systems simply smooth the operations and give adequate cost control, this well-known hospital system broke through with a new vision of the use of an operational system for competitive advantage. The great majority of operational systems for which many large and small computer systems have been purchased, however, simply help to manage and automate the business. They are important and necessary, but can only be put into the "strategic" category if they have a pronounced impact on the profitability of the business.

All businesses should have both long-range and short-range planning of operational systems to ensure that the possibilities of computer usefulness will be seized in a reasonable time. Such planning will include project analysis and costing, system development life cycle considerations, and specific technology planning, such as for computers, databases, and communications. There must be computer capacity planning, technology forecasting, and personnel performance planning. It is more likely that those in the organization with entrepreneurial vision will conceive of strategic plans when such basic operational capabilities are in place and are well managed.

Operational systems, then, are those that keep the organization operating under control and cost effectively. Any of them may be changed to strategic systems if they are viewed with strategic vision. They are fertile grounds for new business opportunities.

**Strategic systems** are those that link business and computer strategies. They may be systems where a new business thrust has been envisioned and its advantages can be best realized through the use of information technology. They may be systems where new computer technology has been made available on the market, and planners with an entrepreneurial spirit perceive how the new capabilities can quickly gain competitive advantage. They may be systems where operational management people and Information Services people have brainstormed together over business problems, and have realized that a new competitive thrust is possible when computer methods are applied in a new way.

There is a tendency to think that strategic systems are only those that have been conceived at the point where you say, "that's it!" or "I have found it!" It is most pleasant and profitable if someone is brilliant enough, or lucky enough, to have such an experience. The great majority of people must be content, however, to work step-by-step at the process of trying to get strategic vision, trying to integrate information services thinking with corporate operational thinking, and trying to conceive of new directions to take in systems development. This is not an impossible task, but it is a slow task that requires a great deal of communication and cooperation. If the possibilities of strategic systems are clearly understood by all managers in an enterprise, and they approach the development of ideas and the planning systematically, the chances are good that strategic systems will be the result. These may not be as dramatic as American Airline's Sabre, but they can certainly be highly profitable.

There is general agreement that strategic systems are those information systems that **may be used for gaining competitive advantage.** How is competitive advantage gained? At this point, different writers list different possibilities, but none of them claim that there may not be other openings to move through. Some of the more common ways of thinking about gaining competitive advantage are:

1.  **Deliver a product or a service at a lower cost:**

    This does not necessarily mean the lowest cost, but simply a cost related to the quality of the product or service that will be both attractive in the marketplace and will yield sufficient return on investment. The cost considered is not simply the data processing cost, but is the overall cost of all corporate activities for the delivery of that product or service. There are many operational computer systems that have given internal cost savings and other internal advantages, but they cannot be thought of as strategic until those savings can be translated to a better competitive position in the market.

2.  **Deliver a product or service that is differentiated:**

    Differentiation means the addition of unique features to a product or service that are competitively attractive in the market. Generally such features will cost something to produce, and so they will be the selling point, rather than the cost itself. Seldom does a lowest cost product also have the best differentiation. A strategic system helps customers to perceive that they are getting some extras for which they will willingly pay.

3.  **Focus on a specific market segment:**

    The idea is to identify and create market niches that have not been adequately filled. Information technology is frequently able to provide the capabilities of defining, expanding, and filling a particular niche or segment. The application would be quite specific to the industry.

4.  **Innovation:**

    Develop products or services through the use of computers that are new and are appreciably different from other available offerings. Examples of this are automatic credit card handling at service stations, and automatic teller machines at banks. Such innovative approaches not only give new opportunities to attract customers, but also open up entirely new fields of business so that their use has very elastic demand.

Almost any data processing system may be called "strategic" if it aligns the computer strategies with the business strategies of the organization, and there is close cooperation in its development between the Information Services personnel and operational business managers. There should be an explicit connection between the organization's business plan and its systems plan to provide better support of the organization's goals and objectives, and closer management control of the critical information systems.

Many organizations that have done substantial work with computers since the 1950's have long used the term "strategic planning" for any computer developments that are going to directly affect the conduct of their business. Not included are budget, or annual planning and the planning of developing Information Services facilities and the many "housekeeping" tasks that are required in any corporation. Definitely included in strategic planning are any information systems that will be used by operational management to conduct the business more profitably. A simple test would be to ask whether the president of the corporation, or some senior vice president, would be interested in the immediate outcome of the systems development because they felt it would affect their profitability. If the answer is affirmative, then the system is strategic.

Strategic systems, thus, attempt to match Information Services resources to strategic business opportunities where the computer systems will have an impact on the products and the business operations. Planning for strategic systems is not defined by calendar cycles or routine reporting. It is defined by the effort required to impact the competitive environment and the strategy of a firm at the point in time that management wants to move on the idea.

Effective strategic systems can only be accomplished, of course, if the capabilities are in place for the routine basic work of gathering data, evaluating possible equipment and software, and managing the routine reporting of project status. The calendarized planning and operational work is absolutely necessary as a base from which a strategic system can be planned and developed when a priority situation arises. When a new strategic need becomes apparent, Information Services should have laid the groundwork to be able to accept the task of meeting that need.

Strategic systems that are dramatic innovations will always be the ones that are written about in literature on the subject. Consultants in strategic systems must have clearly innovative and successful examples to attract the attention of senior management. It should be clear, however, that most Information Services personnel will have to leverage the advertised successes to gain funding for their own systems. These systems may not have an olympic effect on an organization, but they will have a good chance of being clearly profitable. That will be sufficient for most operational management, and will draw out the necessary funding and support. It helps to talk about the possibilities of great breakthroughs, if it is always kept in mind that there are many strategic systems developed and installed that are successful enough to be highly praised within the organization and offer a competitive advantage, but will not be written up in the **Harvard Business Review.**

## 2.2    A CHANGE IN PARADIGM

Another way of characterizing strategic information systems is to point out some of the key ideas of the foremost apostles of such systems. No attempt will be made to assign priorities for the invention of the ideas, as there was a veritable cascade of publications on the subject from 1980 to 1985, each claiming the true doctrine. The older paradigm, or framework for thinking, was usefully expressed when, in 1965, Robert N. Anthony wrote **Planning and Control Systems: A Framework for Analysis.** [3] This book proposed a conceptual framework that became a classic for the next twenty years and was used by many authors to define and differentiate various information systems. Anthony classified planning and control systems as:

- **Strategic planning:** The process of deciding on objectives of the organization, of changes in those objectives, on the resources used to attain those objectives, and on the policies that are used to govern the acquisition, use, and disposition of those resources.

- **Management control:** The process by which managers assure that resources are obtained and used effectively and efficiently in the accomplishment of the organization's objectives.

- **Operational control:** The process of assuring that specific tasks are carried out effectively and efficiently.

Anthony pictured the processes hierarchically, and discussed strategic planning as the process of determining policies for major decisions having long-term consequences, such as diversification, acquisition, and so on. This coincided with the understanding of strategic planning of many large corporations. It emphasizes moving in the most profitable corporate direction, rather than the modern idea of seizing competitive advantage. Through the 1970's, Anthony's classification was drawn on by many writers, including Scott Morton, Rockart, and others, who moved to the ideas of Decision Support Systems and Executive Information Systems. They were intended to supply operational management with information that could be used directly to provide business advantages that were, presumably, of competitive value. Many systems planning methods were also developed in this period that are still just as useful for the detailed planning of strategic information systems as they are for operational systems planning.

Anthony's model provided a good structure for a lot of subsequent thinking. Actually, some of the now-famous examples of strategic systems were first developed in the 1970's working strictly under Anthony's thinking. It had a different emphasis than the presently-accepted ideas about strategic planning for competitive advantage, however. In its time it was a **paradigm,** or model, containing the rules and regulations of information services planning. It set boundaries, or parameters, around planning approaches. There has since been a **paradigm change,** or shift, which has been a dramatic innovation for Information Services planners. No longer do strategic information systems come merely from step-wise development. They may come from SIS opportunities that may originate with top management, end users, or information systems specialists. There has been a trend change to emphasize corporate competitive advantage, and it has been all to the advantage of Information Services groups that are seeking new possibilities for systems.

---

[3] Robert N. Anthony, **Planning and Control Systems: A Framework for Analysis,** Cambridge, Mass., Harvard University Press, 1965.

The idea of paradigms and paradigm changes started with Thomas Kuhn's book, **The Structure of Scientific Revolutions.** A paradigm change can stop trends in their tracks, or create a radically new trend, and is a dramatic type of innovation. Charles Wiseman, in **Strategy and Computers,** states that those following Anthony's classification did not have SIS as objects to be identified. SIS formed no part of their horizon of expectation when they searched for opportunities to apply computer technology. He says that a completely new perspective on information systems is called for -- the strategic. This may well be true, but the fact is that most of the dramatic and frequently-described Strategic Information Systems were first developed under Anthony's paradigm, then sprang up to a new, competitive life when alert managers and technicians perceived new possibilities for the systems. It would seem, then, that the principal identifier of SIS is the **perception** of their usefulness as competitive weapons rather than any specific structure or mode of planning. Many of the writers point out that the principal use of SIS thinking, in the new paradigm, is in the **identification** of SIS systems, and the gathering of **management support** for them. The great paradigm shift is thus in the perception of value and the identification of possibilities, rather than in the meaning of the terms, or in the stepwise planning methodology.

These approaches offer Information Services managers and planners the goal they have long sought, that of having a bottom-line effect on the organization and having senior management appreciate their remarkable usefulness. In individual cases, however, there is no cook-book approach to follow to gain this pinnacle. There are merely a number of theoretical ideas that have been advanced, and a number of proven successes that have been described. In any specific case, techniques to be used must be selected from a fairly large menu, which has been summarized in this manual.

It should be clear from reading the literature that there has not been a dramatic paradigm shift that **all** will eventually follow in the area of strategic planning, but there are two co-existent paradigms. The boundaries are blurred, and there are many shades of application. These ideas have developed slowly over the years since 1972, and have not suddenly dropped among us. There has been a natural progression of thinking, simply because Information Services professionals have long sought to develop systems that would have an effect on their organization's profitability, although they were usually kept to working on operational efficiency as a goal.

No matter how often American Airlines and American Hospital Supply , and others, are shown to us as exemplary strategic information systems, it should be remembered that these forefront strategic systems originally grew out of senior management requests for considerable operational system development work by Information Services. In the process of the development and use of such systems, striking new strategic advantages were found. The use of such examples is remarkably helpful, however, if Information Services is able to gather responsible corporate managers and show them the possible vision. Such inspiration is usually not possible through the IS planners normal chain of management, but is done by means of a consultant's presentation or a brainstorming session at a corporate planning meeting. The fact is that most strategic information systems will surface in response to corporate initiative. Strong corporate entrepreneurial leaders will develop a vision that can be turned into reality by information systems. Of course, some capable and lucky Information Services people will be able to break through with their own new ideas.

Most inspiration comes from perspiration and preparation. Do the job that you do best. Gather the information. Establish the database. Develop methods of data extraction, tabulation, and analysis. Work for systems that are at the core of the company's operation.   There will be a steady pay-off from baseline strategic systems . . . and occasionally lightning may strike.

In this section there are brief summaries of papers from some of the principal writers in the area of the new paradigm of Strategic Information Systems.   These include:

- Michael Porter's "Competitive Advantage and Value Chain"
- Charles Wiseman's "Strategic Perspective View"
- Warren McFarlan's "Information Technology and Competitive Strategy"
- Gregory Parson's "Strategic Information Technology Management"
- Gerald Loev's "Aligning IS with Corporate Strategies"
- Paul Strassman's "Value-Added"
- Jacques Passino's "Process and Issues"

These people have written and spoken about their ideas at length, and with great clarity.   The only way that justice can really be done to their concepts is to read their original papers.   Some of these, therefore, are referenced.

## 2.3     PORTER'S "COMPETITIVE ADVANTAGE"

Dr. Michael E. Porter, Professor of Business Administration, Harvard Business School, has addressed his ideas in two keystone books. **Competitive Strategy: Techniques for Analyzing Industries and Competitors,** and his newer book, **Competitive Advantage,** present a framework for helping firms actually create and sustain a competitive advantage in their industry in either cost or differentiation. Dr. Porter's theories on competitive advantage are not tied to information systems, but are used by others to involve information services technologies.

In his books, Dr. Porter says that there are two central questions in competitive strategy:

1.   How structurally attractive is the industry?

2.   What is the firm's relative position in the industry?

Both of these questions are dynamic, and neither is sufficient alone to guide strategic choices. Both can be influenced by competitor behavior, and both can be shaped by a firm's actions. It is imperative that these questions be answered by analysis, which will be the starting point for good strategic thinking, and will open up possibilities for the role of information systems.

Industry profitability is a function of five basic competitive forces: the threat of new entrants, the threat of substitute products or services, the bargaining power of suppliers, the bargaining power of buyers, and the intensity of the rivalry among existing competitors. Porter's books give techniques for getting a handle on the possible average profitability of an industry over time. The analysis of these forces is the base for estimating a firm's relative position and competitive advantage. In any industry, the sustained average profitability of competitors varies widely. The problem is to determine how a business can outperform the industry average and attain a sustainable competitive advantage. It is possible that the answer lies in information technology together with good management.

Porter claims that the principal types of competitive advantage are low cost producer, differentiation, and focus. A firm has a competitive advantage if it is able to deliver its product or service at a lower cost than its competitors. If the quality of its product is satisfactory, this will translate into higher margins and higher returns. Another advantage is gained if the firm is able to differentiate itself in some way. Differentiation leads to offering something that is both unique and is desired, and translates into a premium price. Again, this will lead to higher margins and superior performance.

It seems that two types of competitive advantage, lower cost and differentiation, are mutually exclusive. To get lower cost, you sacrifice uniqueness. To get a premium price, there must be extra cost involved in the process. To be a superior performer, however, you must go for competitive advantage in either cost or differentiation.

Another point of Porter's is that competitive advantage is gained through a strategy based on scope. It is necessary to look at the breadth of a firm's activities, and narrow the competitive scope to gain focus in either an industry segment, a geographic area, a customer type, and so on. Competitive advantage is most readily gained by defining the competitive scope in which the firm is operating, and concentrating on it.

Based on these ideas of type and scope, Porter gives a useful tool for analysis which he calls **The Value Chain (Figure 2-1).** This value chain gives a framework on which a useful analysis can be hung. The basic notion is that to understand competitive advantage in any company, one cannot look at the company as a whole. It is necessary to identify the specific activities which the firm performs to do business. Each company is a collection of the things that it does that all add up to the product being delivered to the customer. These activities are numerous and are unique to every industry, but it is only in these activities where cost advantage or differentiation can be gained.

**Figure 2-1**

## THE VALUE CHAIN

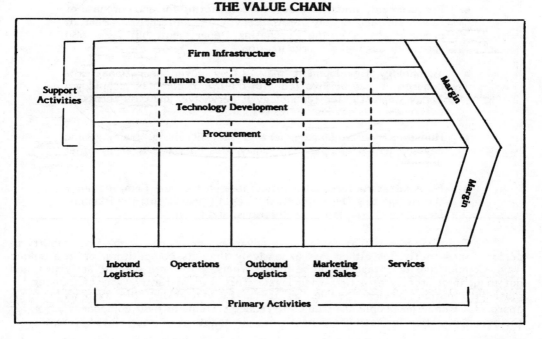

The basic idea is that the firm's activities can be divided into nine generic types. Five are the primary activities, which are the activities that create the product, market it and deliver it; four are the support activities that cross between the primary activities. The primary activities are:

- **Inbound Logistics,** which includes the receipt and storage of material, and the general management of supplies.

- **Operations,** which are the manufacturing steps or the service steps.

- **Outbound Logistics,** which are associated with collecting, storing, and physically distributing the product to buyers. In some companies this is a significant cost, and buyers value speed and consistency.

- **Marketing and Sales** includes customer relations, order entry, and price management.

- **After-sales Services** covers the support of the product in the field, installation, customer training, and so on.

The support activities are shown across the top of **Figure 2-1** because they are a part of all of the firm's operations. They are not directed to the customer, but they allow the firm to perform its primary activities. The four generic types of support activities are:

- **Procurement,** which includes the contracting for and purchase of raw materials, or any items used by the enterprise. Part of procurement is in the Purchasing Department, but it is also spread throughout the organization.

- **Technology Development** may simply cover operational procedures, or may be involved with the use of complex technology. Today, sophisticated technology is pervasive, and cuts across all activities; it is not just an R&D function.

- **Human Resource Management** is the recruiting, training, and development of people. Obviously, this cuts across every other activity.

- **Firm Infrastructure** is a considerable part of the firm, including the Accounting Department, the Legal Department, the Planning Department, Government Relations, and so on.

The basic idea is that competitive advantage grows out of the firm's ability to perform these activities either less expensively than its competitors, or in a unique way. Competitive advantage should be linked precisely to these specific activities, and not thought of broadly at a firm-wide level. This is an attractive way of thinking for most Information Services people, as it is, fundamentally, the systems analysis approach. Computer people are trained to reduce systems to their components, look for the best application for each component, then put together an interrelated system.

Information technology is also pervasive throughout all parts of the value chain. Every activity that the firm performs has the potential to imbed information technology because it involves information processing. As information technology moves away from repetitive transaction processing and permeates all activities in the value chain, it will be in a better position to be useful in gaining competitive advantage.

**Figure 2-2, Value Chain: Key Activities,** gives a brief example of a typical analysis of a value chain for a manufacturing company. It is obvious that information processing plays an important role in all these key activities.

Figure 2-2

# VALUE CHAIN: KEY ACTIVITIES

| | Inbound Logistics | Operations | Outbound Logistics | Marketing and Sales | Services |
|---|---|---|---|---|---|
| Firm Infrastructure | | | | | |
| Human Resource Management | | Monitor labor productivity, Training, Union relations | | | |
| Technology Development | | Design Documentation, Product specification, Improve cost/performance | | Develop new products, Product modification, Evaluate competitive technology | Product Performance information, Evaluate application conditions |
| Procurement | Contract for freight delivery, Manage vendor relationships | Buy raw materials | Provide regional warehouse facilities | Provide media advertising | |
| | Receive and store material, Control raw material inventory | Materials planning, Production planning, Component manufacture sub-assembly, Final assembly, Final test, Schedule labor loading | Receive finished goods, Plan shipping schedule, Ship finished goods | Maintain customer relations, Order entry, New product pricing, Manage internal sales | Installation, Customization, User support |

Margin

Margin

39

Porter emphasizes what he calls the **linkages** between the activities that the firm performs. No activities in a firm are independent, yet each department is managed separately. It is most important to understand the cost linkages that are involved so that the firm may get an overall optimization of the production rather than departmental optimizations. A typical linkage might be that, if more is spent in procurement, less is spent in operations. If more testing is done in operations, after-sales service costs will be lower. Multi-functional coordination is crucial to competitive advantage, but it is often difficult to see. Insights into linkages give the ability to have overall optimization. Any strategic information system must be analyzed across all departments in the organization.

### 2.3.1    COST AND COMPETITIVE ADVANTAGE

Cost leadership is one of Porter's two types of competitive advantage. The cost leader delivers a product of acceptable quality at the lowest possible cost. It attempts to open up a significant and sustainable cost gap over all other competitors. The cost advantage is achieved through superior position in relation to the key cost drivers.

Cost leadership translates into above-average profits if the cost leader can command the average prices in the industry. On the other hand, cost leaders must maintain quality that is close to, or equal to, that of the competition. Achieving cost leadership usually requires trade-offs with differentiation. The two are usually incompatible.

Note that a firm's relative cost position cannot be understood by viewing the firm as a whole. Overall cost grows out of the cost of performing discrete activities. Cost position is determined by the cumulative cost of performing all value activities.

To sustain cost advantage, Porter gives a number of **cost drivers** which must be understood in detail because the sustainability of cost advantage in an activity depends on the cost drivers of that activity. Again, this type of detail is best obtained by classical systems analysis methods. Some of the cost drivers which must be analyzed, understood, and controlled are:

| | |
|---|---|
| **Scale:** | The appropriate type of scale must be found. Policies must be set to reinforce economies of scale in scale-sensitive activities. |
| **Learning:** | The learning curve must be understood and managed. As the organization tries to learn from competitors, it must strive to keep its own learning proprietary. |
| **Capacity Utilization:** | Cost can be controlled by the leveling of throughput. |
| **Linkages:** | Linkages should be exploited within the value chain. Work with suppliers and channels can reduce costs. |
| **Interrelationships:** | Shared activities can reduce costs. |
| **Integration:** | The possibilities for integration or de-integration should be examined systematically. |

**Timing:**            If the advantages of being the first mover or a late mover are understood, they can be exploited.

**Policies:**          Policies that enhance the low-cost position or differentiation should be emphasized.

**Location:**          When viewed as a whole, the location of individual activities can be optimized.

**Institutional Factors:** Institutional factors should be examined to see whether their change may be helpful.

Care must be taken in the evaluation and perception of cost drivers because there are pitfalls if the thinking is incremental and indirect activities are ignored. Even though the manufacturing activities, for example, are obvious candidates for analyses, they should not have exclusive focus. Linkages must be exploited and cross-subsidies avoided.

Porter gives **five steps** to achieving cost leadership:

1.    Identify the appropriate value chain and assign costs and assets to it.

2.    Identify the cost drivers of each value activity and see how they interact.

3.    Determine the relative costs of competitors and the sources of cost differences.

4.    Develop a strategy to lower relative cost position through controlling cost drivers or reconfiguring the value chain.

5.    Test the cost reduction strategy for sustainability.

## 2.3.2    DIFFERENTIATION ADVANTAGE

Differentiation is the second of Porter's two types of competitive advantage. In the differentiation strategy, one or more characteristics that are widely valued by buyers are selected. The purpose is to achieve and sustain performance that is superior to any competitor in satisfying those buyer needs.

A differentiator selectively adds costs in areas that are important to the buyer. Thus, successful differentiation leads to premium prices, and these lead to above-average profitably if there is approximate cost parity. To achieve this, efficient forms of differentiation must be picked, and costs must be reduced in areas that are irrelevant to the buyer needs.

Buyers are like sellers in that they have their own value chains. The product being sold will represent one purchased input, but the seller may affect the buyer's activities in other ways. Differentiation can lower the buyer's cost and improve the buyer's performance, and thus create value, or competitive advantage, for the buyer.

The buyer may not be able to assess all the value that a firm provides, but it looks for **signals of value,** or perceived value.

A few typical factors which may lower the buyer's costs are:

a.   Less idle time

b.   Lower risk of failure

c.   Lower installation costs

d.   Faster processing time

e.   Lower labor costs

f.   Longer useful life

**Figure 2-3, Representative Sources of Differentiation,** shows a number of typical examples of activities that should be considered.  It indicates the breadth and detail that must be involved in the study.

Porter points out that differentiation is usually costly, depending on the cost drivers of the activities involved.  A firm must find forms of differentiation where it has a cost advantage in differentiating.

Differentiation is achieved by enhancing the sources of uniqueness.  These may be found throughout the value chain, and should be signaled to the buyer.  The cost of differentiation can be turned to advantage if the less costly sources are exploited and the cost drivers are controlled.  The emphasis must be on getting a sustainable cost advantage in differentiating.  Efforts must be made to change the buyer's criteria by reconfiguring the value chain to be unique in new ways, and by preemptively responding to changing buyer or channel circumstances.

Differentiation will not work if there is too much uniqueness, or uniqueness that the buyers do not value.  The buyer's ability to pay a premium price, the signaling criteria, and the segments important to the buyer must all be understood.  Also, there cannot be over reliance on sources of differentiation that competitors can emulate cheaply or quickly.

Porter lists **seven** steps to achieving differentiation:

1.   Determine the identity of the real buyer.

2.   Understand the buyer's value chain, and the impact of the seller's product on it.

3.   Determine the purchasing criteria of the buyer.

4.   Assess possible sources of uniqueness in the firm's value chain.

5.   Identify the cost of these sources of uniqueness.

6.   Choose the value activities that create the most valuable differentiation for the buyer relative to the costs incurred.

7.   Test the chosen differentiation strategy for sustainability.

Figure 2-3

## REPRESENTATIVE SOURCES OF DIFFERENTIATION

**Firm Infrastructure**
- Top management support
- Image-enhancing facilities

**Human Resource Management**
- Stable work force
- Optimal size work force
- QWL
- Delivery incentives
- Sales incentives
- Retention of superior personnel
- Extensive service force training

**Technology Development**
- Superior materials handling technology
- Unique product features
- Unique process
- Unique vehicle scheduling Software
- Applications engineering support
- Superior market research
- Advanced service techniques

**Procurement**
- Reliable transportation companies
- Highest quality raw materials
- Well located warehouse space
- Special purpose vehicles
- Most desirable media placements
- Wide variety of replacement parts

| Inbound Logistics | Operations | Outbound Logistics | Marketing and Sales | Service |
|---|---|---|---|---|
| Handling that minimizes damage | Attractive product appearance | Timely delivery | High advertising levels | Rapid installation |
| Timeliness of supply | Low defect rate | Accurate order processing | Extensive sales force coverage | High service quality |
| | Short time to manufacture | Handling that minimizes damage | Superior sales aids | Wide service coverage |
| | Conformance to specifications | | Generous credit | Extensive buyer training |

*Margin*

43

### 2.3.3    FOCUS STRATEGIES FOR ADVANTAGE.

Porter's writings also discuss **focus strategies.** He emphasizes that a company that attempts to completely satisfy every buyer does not have a strategy. Focusing means selecting targets and optimizing the strategies for them. Focus strategies further segment the industry. They may be imitated, but can provide strategic openings.

Clearly, multiple generic strategies may be implemented, but internal inconsistencies can then arise, and the distinctions between the focused entities may become blurred.

Porter's work is directed towards competitive advantage in general, and is **not** specific to strategic information systems. It has been reviewed here at some length, however, because his concepts are frequently referred to in the writings of others who are concerned with strategic information systems. The value chain concept has been widely adopted, and the ideas of low cost and differentiation are accepted. This section, therefore, is an introduction into a further discussion of strategic information systems. The implementation of such systems tends to be an implementation of the factors elucidated by Porter.

## 2.4     WISEMAN'S "STRATEGIC PERSPECTIVE VIEW"

Charles Wiseman has applied the current concepts of Strategic Information Systems in work at GTE and other companies, and in his consulting work as President of Competitive Applications, Inc. His book extends Porter's thinking in many practical ways in the Information Systems area, and discusses many examples of successful strategic systems.[4]

Wiseman emphasizes that companies have begun to use information systems strategically to reap significant competitive advantage. He feels that the significance of these computer-based products and services does not lie in their technological sophistication or in the format of the reports they produce. Rather, it is found in the role played by these information systems in the firm's planning and implementation in gaining and maintaining competitive advantage.

Wiseman points out that, although the use of information systems may not always lead to competitive advantage, it can serve as an important tool in the firm's strategic plan. Strategic systems must not be discovered haphazardly. Those who would be competitive leaders must develop a systematic approach for identifying strategic information systems (SIS) opportunities. Both business management and information management must be involved.

He emphasizes that information technology is now in a position to be exploited competitively. A **framework** must be developed for identifying SIS opportunities. There will certainly be competitive response, so one should proceed with **strategic thrusts** based on information technology. These moves are just as important as other strategic thrusts, such as acquisition, geographical expansion, and so on. It is necessary to plan **rationally** about acquisitions, major alliances with other firms, and other strategic thrusts.

IBM's Business Systems Planning (BSP) and MIT's Critical Success Factor (CSF) methodologies are ways to develop information architectures and to identify **conventional** information systems, which are primarily used for planning and control purposes. To identify SIS, a new model or framework is needed. The conventional approach works within the perceived structure of the organization. An effective SIS approach arises from the forging of new **alliances** that expand the horizon of expectation. Such an approach is most difficult to attain, and can only work with top management support. **Innovations,** however, frequently come from simply a new look at existing circumstances, from a new viewpoint. Information Services personnel must start to look **systematically** at application opportunities related to managers.

Wiseman believes that the range of opportunities is limited by the framework adopted. He contrasts the framework for **Conventional IS Opportunities (Figure 2-4)** with the framework for **Strategic IS Opportunities (Figure 2-5).**

In the **conventional view,** there are two information system thrusts: to automate the basic processes of the firm, or to satisfy the information needs of managers, professionals, or others. There are three generic targets: strategic planning, management control, and operational control. In this perspective, there are, thus, six generic opportunity areas.

---

[4] Charles Wiseman, **Strategy and Computers:   Information Systems As Competitive Weapons,** (Dow Jones - Irwin, 1985).

**Figure 2-4**

### CONVENTIONAL IS OPPORTUNITIES

| CONVENTIONAL THRUSTS | Strategic Planning | Management Control | Operational Control |
|---|---|---|---|
| Automate Basic Process | | | |
| Satisfy Information Need | | | |

**Figure 2-5**

### STRATEGIC IS OPPORTUNITIES

| STRATEGIC THRUSTS | Supplier | Customer | Competitor |
|---|---|---|---|
| Differentiation | | | |
| Cost | | | |
| Innovation | | | |
| Growth | | | |
| Alliance | | | |

In the **strategic view** of IS opportunities, there are five strategic information thrusts and three strategic targets. This gives fifteen generic strategic opportunity areas. This opens up the range and perspective of management vision.

Sustainable competitive advantage can mean many things to different firms. Competitive advantage may be with respect to a supplier, a customer, or a rival. It may exist because of a lower price, because of desirable features, or because of the various resources that a firm possesses. Sustainability is also highly relative, depending upon the business. In established businesses, it may refer to years, and the experience that the firm develops may be quite difficult to emulate. In other industries, a lead of a few weeks or months may be all that is necessary.

There is an advantage in looking at Figure 2-5 as a study group, and brainstorming through it to find out what information may be needed to do a job better. One can find competitive advantage in information systems when the subjects are broken down to specifics.

## 2.4.1   STRATEGIC THRUSTS

Wiseman uses the term **strategic thrusts** for the moves that companies make to gain or maintain some kind of competitive edge, or to reduce the competitive edge of one of the strategic targets. Information technology can be used to support or to shape one or more of these thrusts. Examining the possibilities of these thrusts takes imagination, and it is helped by understanding what other firms have done in similar situations. This is why so many examples are presented in the literature. Analogy is important.

There is no question that there is considerable overlap between conventional information systems and strategic information systems. Systems are complex and a great deal of data is involved. The idea is to look at this complexity in a new light, and see where competitive advantage might possibly be gained. Note that Wiseman takes Porter's three generic categories: low cost producer, differentiation, and focus, and extends them to five categories: differentiation, cost, innovation, growth, and alliance.

- **Differentiation** can work two ways. First, it can be used to distinguish the product from the offerings of competitors. Secondly, there may be opportunities to use information technology to **reduce** the differentiation advantage of your strategic targets. There are various differentiation opportunities in different industries. The development of marketing systems to help firms segment their markets is another form of differentiation. Whether the methods adopted are sustainable or significant can usually only be discovered over time.

- <u>Cost</u> may be a move that not only reduces the costs, but also reduces the costs of selected strategic targets so that you will benefit from preferential treatment. A strategic cost thrust may also aim at achieving economies of scale. The examples always seem obvious when they are described, but the opportunities can usually only be uncovered by considerable search.

- **Innovation** is another strategic thrust that can be supported or shaped by information technology in either product or process. In many financial firms, the innovative product is really an information system. Innovation requires rapid response to opportunities to be successful, but this carries with it the question of considerable risk. There can be no innovation without risk, whether information systems are included or not. Innovation, however, can achieve advantage in product or process that results in a fundamental transformation in the way that type of business is conducted.

- **Growth** achieves an advantage by expansion in volume or geographical distribution. It may also come from product-line diversification. Information systems can be of considerable help in the management of rapid growth.

- **Alliance** gains competitive advantage by gaining growth, differentiation, or cost advantages through marketing agreements, forming joint ventures, or making appropriate acquisitions.

## 2.4.2    THE STRATEGIC PLANNING PROCESS

Wiseman advocates brainstorming and the systematic search for SIS opportunities. He has had considerable success with a formalized framework for surfacing ideas. He describes his SIS Planning Process in five phases:

**Phase A:**  Introduce the Information Services management to SIS concepts. Give an overview of the process and describe cases. Gain approval to proceed with an idea-generation meeting in Information Services.

**Phase B:**  Conduct an SIS idea-generation meeting with Information Services middle management. Test the SIS idea-generation methodology. Identify significant SIS areas for executive consideration.

**Phase C:**  Conduct an SIS idea-generation meeting with senior Information Services management. Identify SIS ideas, and evaluate them together with the ideas from the previous meeting.

**Phase D:**  Introduce the top business executives to the SIS concept. Discuss some of the SIS ideas that were considered for the business. Gain approval to proceed with the SIS idea-generation meetings with business planners.

**Phase E:**  Conduct an SIS idea-generation meeting with the corporate planners. Identify some SIS ideas and evaluate them together with the ideas that have emerged from the previous meetings.

Wiseman points out that the whole idea is designed to introduce the strategic perspective on information systems, stimulate the systematic search for SIS opportunities, and evaluate and select a set of projects that are expected to secure the greatest competitive advantage for the firm. In the idea-generation meetings of Phases B, C, and E of the process, there are always **seven explicit steps:**

1. **Give a Tutorial on Competitive Strategy.** Introduce the concepts of strategic thrusts, strategic targets, and competitive strategy.

2. **Apply SIS Concepts to Actual Cases.** Develop an understanding of SIS possibilities and their strategic thrusts and targets.

3. **Review the Company's Competitive Position.** Try to understand its present business position and its strategies.

4. **Brainstorm for SIS Opportunities.** Generate SIS ideas in small groups.

5. **Discuss the SIS Opportunities.** Use the experience of the group to correlate and condense the SIS ideas.

6. **Evaluate the SIS Opportunities.** Consider the competitive significance of the SIS ideas.

7. **Detail the SIS Blockbusters.** Select the best SIS ideas, and detail their competitive advantages and key implementation issues.

Wiseman says that typical SIS idea-generation meetings will last for days. Each step takes about two hours, at least. The process generates many good SIS ideas, and a few will always be considered well worth implementation. Top management begins to focus their attention on SIS opportunities. The ideas that are generated can produce significant competitive advantage.

## 2.5    MCFARLAN'S "INFORMATION TECHNOLOGY AND COMPETITIVE STRATEGY"

Dr. F. Warren McFarlan, Professor of Business Administration, Harvard Business School, has done a variety of research in the competitive strategy area. With Professor James McKenney he wrote **Corporate Information Systems Management: The Issues Facing Senior Executives.** He also wrote **Information Technology Changes the Way You Compete,** Harvard Business Review.

Information systems technology is having a marked effect on the way organizations do business. They are beginning to use this technology in competitive strategy. Information systems technology includes computing, telecommunications, office automation, and remotely connected devices associated with end-user computing.

Some of the factors that have accelerated the use of computers in corporate strategy are:

- A shift in the use of computing, particularly end user computing, to gain competitive advantage rather than to simply reduce costs or gain efficiency.

- The ability of a firm to introduce systems that differentiate it from the competition.

- A major shift in the economics of technology as hardware becomes considerably cheaper, with increased power.

- The excruciating problem of shortages of Information Services support staff, despite the new productivity aids that are available.

- The general management focus of the next generation of technology.

- The general decline in the capability of school graduates arriving in business.

The systems with the greatest impact have been those that develop computer communications links between suppliers and their customers. These links offer the opportunity of competitive advantage. At the same time, they create a strategic vulnerability, as the improved operational systems cause vastly greater interdependence. For example, it becomes much harder for manufacturers to change suppliers. If such computing is effectively managed, however, there is a potential for forging new offensive tools which can enable significant and lasting gains to be achieved in the market share.

**Figure 2-6, Strategic Impact - Information Systems,** is a strategic grid, developed and described in "The Information Archipelago" article.[5]    It shows the position of Information Systems in various types of companies.  In a number of organizations, there may be agreement that their firm is located on the left-hand side

---

[5]  F. W. McFarlan, J. L. McKenney, P. Pyburn, **"The Information Archipelago - Plotting the Course,"** Harvard Business Review, January-February 1983.

of the grid in either the support or factory quadrants. They have handled their staffing, organization, and planning activities accordingly. However, the dramatic changes in information technology and the evolving competitive conditions in the industry may pose a danger that this categorization is wrong. In the new conditions, the competition may have developed new ideas using information technology that are superior in the market. It may well be very difficult and expensive to rapidly match these new approaches, yet the whole game has been changed. It may well be that a firm can comfortably and profitably remain in the support and factory boxes. There have been dramatic and sudden technical changes recently, however, particularly with the possibilities of end-user computing, and Information Systems should periodically review their position and the competitive strategy of the firm. This is a subject which needs regular review.

**Figure 2-6**

## STRATEGIC IMPACT - INFORMATION SYSTEMS

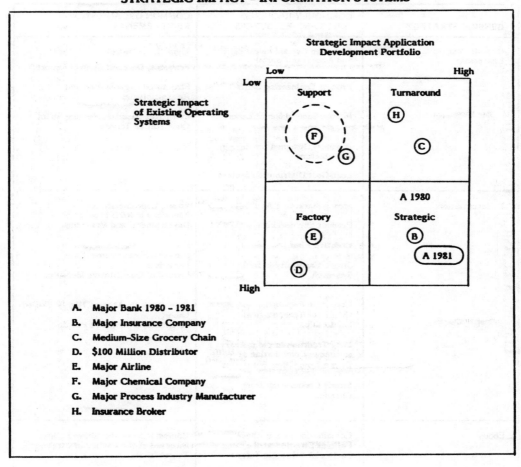

A.   Major Bank 1980 - 1981
B.   Major Insurance Company
C.   Medium-Size Grocery Chain
D.   $100 Million Distributor
E.   Major Airline
F.   Major Chemical Company
G.   Major Process Industry Manufacturer
H.   Insurance Broker

The three types of strategy that were described by Michael Porter are listed below. These are:

- Low cost

- Product differentiation

- Focus

Figure 2-7, Requirements for Generic Strategies, lists some of the commonly required skills and resources and some of the common organizational requirements for following such strategies.

Figure 2-7

## REQUIREMENTS FOR GENERIC STRATEGIES

| GENERIC STRATEGY | COMMONLY REQUIRED SKILLS AND RESOURCES | COMMON ORGANIZATIONAL REQUIREMENTS |
|---|---|---|
| Overall Cost Leadership | Sustained Capital Investment and Access to Capital<br><br>Process Engineering Skills<br><br>Intense Supervision of Labor<br><br>Products Designed for Ease in Manufacture<br><br>Lost-Cost Distribution System | Tight Cost Control<br><br>Frequent, Detailed Control Reports<br><br>Structured Organization and Responsibilities<br><br>Incentives Based on Meeting Strict Quantitative Targets |
| Differentiation | Strong Marketing Abilities<br><br>Product Engineering<br><br>Creative Flair<br><br>Strong Capability in Basic Research<br><br>Corporate Reputation for Quality or Technological Leadership<br><br>Long Tradition in the Industry or Unique Combination of Skills Drawn from Other Businesses<br><br>Strong Cooperation from Channels | Strong Coordination Among Functions in R&D Product Development, and Marketing<br><br>Subjective Measurement and Incentives Instead of Quantitative Measures<br><br>Amenities to Attract Highly Skilled Labor, Scientists, or Creative People |
| Focus | Combination of the Above Policies Directed at the Particular Strategic Target | Combination of the Above Policies Directed at the Particular Strategic Target |

Information Systems can be strategic and affect the profitability of the organization. There are several ways listed below in which IS can enable cost reductions that could be strategic. There are also several ways listed in which IS could have the ability to provide necessary product differentiation:

**Information Systems can be low cost if they:**

- Enable major reduction production/clerical staff.

- Enable better utilization plant/fixed assets scheduling, better maintenance.

- Enable sharp reduction in inventory levels, accounts receivable, etc.

- Enable material efficiency, improvement.

- Can change the basis of competition from cost to sustainable product differentiation.

**Information Systems can provide product differentiation if they have:**

- Ability to deliver unique product features.

- Ability to sharply reduce development cycle.

- Ability to deliver radically more customized product.

- Ability to open new channels and uncover new market niches.

- Ability to produce significant higher quality levels.

**Figure 2-8, Resource Allocation Grid,** shows an analysis of the resource allocation priorities by Strategic Business Unit. This type of analysis should be one of the end products of IS planning. It can be used to communicate the overall competitive impact of expenditures to senior management. **Figure 2-8** helps identify appropriate priorities for guiding the allocation of staff and financial resources. There are several notions that underline this exhibit. First, a large amount of existing development effort is merely to simply repair worn-out systems and to do the necessary maintenance to meet changed business conditions. Second, there is often neglected expenditure for research and development to stay on top of the evolving IS technology and to be assured that the company understands the full range of possibilities. It should be made clear whether money is spent for pure competitive advantage, or to regain or maintain competitive parity because of previous developmental oversights. Also, those items where investment is defined for ROI should be kept separate.

**Figure 2-8**

## RESOURCE ALLOCATION GRID

| Category of IS Expenditure | Business Units in Growing, Highly Competitive Industries | Business Units in Relative Stable Industry, Known Ground Rules | Business Units in Static or Declining Industries |
|---|:---:|:---:|:---:|
| Necessary System Rehabilitation and Maintenance | ① | ① | ① |
| Research in New Technology | ② | ③ | ③ |
| Gain Competitive Advantage | ② | ② | ③ * |
| Maintain or Regain Parity | ② | ③ | ④ |
| Define ROI Justification** | ③ | ③ | ④ |

Note:  The numbers indicate the relative attractiveness of the investment.

\*   Assuming the change is not so dramatic as to revolutionize the industry's overall performance.

\*\*  In an environment characterized by intense competition, defined ROI is the same as gaining competitive advantage.

It is obvious that the potential for such end-user services will vary widely between organizations and industries. It will depend on the basic rules of competition in the industry, the firm's geographical location, size, and implicit product technology, and the potential for Information Services applications. Technologies such as Computer Aided Design and Manufacturing (CAD/CAM) can have a profitable effect for even the smallest firms. In some situations, it may be appropriate for a firm to be a leader, or close to it. Since the stakes can be high, the decisions can be critical.

There are a vast number of opportunities. Some of these may be in the so-called "expert type" of systems, using the new findings of artificial intelligence research. Others may be in financial services, an area that has been widely developed. Still other opportunities may be in the sales force. They can carry "expertise in a briefcase." This approach is excellent for the complicated types of sales processes.

There are new planning notions that have evolved since 1971 which must be considered in planning.  These include:

- **The Breadth of Technologies:**

  Data processing, teleprocessing, office automation, and the use of microcomputers now have a much wider span of technological complication, capabilities, and potential uses.

- **The Phases of Technology Assimilation:**

  This has been discussed in the literature.  It is crucial to understand the relationships between the individual learning curves and the problems of organizational learning.

- **The Strategic Role of IS Technology:**

  No longer should IS planning be driven by the internal estimates of machine size and systems analysts required for planned projects.  It must be driven by the strategic needs of the organization to accomplish objectives and meet competition.

- **The Competitive Role of IS Technology:**

  The rapid developments in IS technology will frequently present new possibilities for competitive use, if handled rapidly and appropriately.

- **The Corporate Culture and Values:**

  New competitive approaches can only be introduced if the corporate culture allows room for the rapid assimilation of innovation.   End users can only be introduced to end-user computing for their own advantage if they place a high value on the new possibilities of analysis and reporting approaches.

- **Generic Competitive Strategy:**

  Is the organization primarily concerned with low cost, product differentiation, product focus, or support to market research?  If the competitive environment is based on **cost,** the question is whether a firm can offer a significantly better price for its products than the competition through IS capabilities, such as end-user computing.  If the environment is based on **product differentiation,** the question is whether the firm can offer an attractive mix of product features, service, quality, and delivery that is better than the competitors.  Many firms are using end-user computing for this purpose.  If the environment is based on **product focus,** where a firm specializes in only a niche of the market, the question is whether it can distinguish itself in that niche by either unusual product features or cost features.  In some cases, this approach is handled effectively with the aid of computing analysis.

There are six strategic questions that must be asked.  Clearly, all aspects of information systems technology may be directed to have an impact on the firm's profitability.  If the answer to any of these six questions is affirmative, then the technology represents a strategic resource which should be explored.

### 1.    Can information technology be used to build barriers to entry?

One approach to building a defensible barrier to entry is to develop a complex, value-added system, including user computers and software, that is capable of further refinement and response to demand.  The first successful system that is developed can effectively tie up the future ordering relationships of the customers.  The complexity and difficulty of replication of the system can create a barrier to the competition.  It is a process of selective entrapment that can be called inoculation.

This approach can start with relatively simple models and then respond with new features as the demand is created.  The best examples of this approach are the American Airlines Sabre system and the United Airlines Apollo system in the airline industry.  For example, in Denver, 75% of the airline agents have the United Apollo computer terminals.  Since all systems have biases, this must affect the market share.  The leaders in the industry started on-line systems in 1962.  In fact, they had Information Systems reporting to their marketing organization. They now offer such sophistication in the service that they have created an effective barrier against the entry of others, and the systems continue to work to their advantage.

### 2.    Can information technology strengthen customer relationships?

This potential is also exhibited by the successful airline systems. There are numerous other examples of encouraging customers to rely more and more on the computer services provided.  End-user computers in the customers' offices are simple to start using.  As the increasingly complex and helpful procedures on the system are then understood and used, there is a continuously unfolding dependence that develops.  The customer begins to use the on-line computers as part of the routine, daily operating procedures. There are many examples of the successful use of such an approach.    Many suppliers provide value-added electronic services that support the firm's basic product line, and quickly build in effective switching costs, thereby holding the customer to the advantage of both.  There are a number of manufacturers and distributors who have taken this route.  Home electronic banking is another good example.  Once a person has coded his banking needs into a system, he becomes locked in as a customer because of the considerable difficulty and switching costs to change.

### 3.    Can information technology change the intra-industry competitive balance?

IS technology can be used to change competition from one of product differentiation to that of low cost.  On-line computers and access to files can provide dramatic cost reductions and can significantly alter the basis of competitive balance. One approach can supply major cost reductions by allowing customers to reduce their staffs, and by improving the material distribution and utilization through lowering inventories and better scheduling. Another approach is to change the basis of the competition by differentiating the product. This can be obtained through better service performance, customized product features, and faster delivery.

The introduction of computers may dramatically change the industry ground rules and bring in new market segmentation. Success is obtained by the firm which first identifies the potential new rules of competition and implements a usable program that delivers the features desired. Once again, the pioneering of the airlines reservation services brought a significant increase in market share. Today, this is widely recognized, and there is fierce competition by airlines to get their computer terminals and their flight recommendations into the end-user offices - the travel agents. The management problems are difficult; it is hard in the early stages to sort out whether intriguing new ideas are ephemeral frills or potentially major structural innovations.

**4.   Can information technology change the basis of competition from low cost to product differentiation?**

A good example of success in using information technology to change the base of competition from low cost to product differentiation was in the approach taken by ARA Newsstands. They supplied the same low cost, but also added computer profit models for magazine sales. They analyzed the profit of the use of limited space. They then gave value-added recommendations to the newsstand owners.

**5.   Can information technology change supplier relations?**

Systems that connect organizations, with end-user computers in the customers' offices connected to suppliers' computers, can be a powerful asset. Major cost savings can be obtained by both parties by the dramatic reduction of inventory levels along the pipeline and the rapid delivery of required goods. The automotive industries have found such systems to be indispensable. Some major retailers have electronic ordering systems linked to their major suppliers' order entry systems. They can automatically check for particular orders, consider shipping costs and delivery times, and take the best result. Suppliers who do not cooperate with such a system soon find their orders dropping.

Such interorganizational systems soon redistribute the power in the buyer/supplier relationship. They create greater dependence on particular suppliers, create arrangements that are hard to discontinue, and introduce new problems in the handling of price increases by the supplier or price demands by the dominant customer.

6.    **Can information technology be productized?**

The information technology itself, and the use of end-user computing, can become a new product that will meet customer
needs.  This may sharply increase the value-added of a product
or supply a completely new approach.  One cosmetics firm has
10,000 registered consultants.  The consultants pay about $750
for the service and buy the products.  The firm knows the
consultants, but does not know the end customers.  They,
therefore, paid for the names of the customers who made
purchases and created a large base for telemarketing.  If a
customer now pays over $50 for her products, she gets a
magazine via direct mail.  They also have systems to key in
individual analyses.  A few days later, a beauty care recommendation is automatically sent out.  This includes customized,
individually prepared beauty care creams, with the customer's
name engraved on the glass, at about one third the price of
competitive offerings.

If it is clear that IS technology could offer significant competitive advantage,
then IS management and users should work together and explore imaginative approaches.  It is certainly not easy to verify the advantages of IS approaches, such as
end-user computers with customers, at an early study stage.  On the other hand, a
strong ROI focus by management at the early stages may also greatly limit the
possibilities of IS technology.

A categorization such as shown in **Figure 2-8** can significantly aid in allocating
resources to those areas where the most significant upside potential exists.  It is
important not to use simplistic rules of thumb.  The ratio of IS expenditures is widely
varied and is changing rapidly.  It is also important to examine the hidden second-order
effects of IS systems and end-user computing.  Inter-organization IS systems pose new
opportunities for shifts in the relative balance of power between firms.  Second-order
effects may include sourcing inflexibility, pricing, vulnerability, potential system
inefficiencies, and excess expense.  Finally, use careful, creative analysis rather than
excessive orientation to efficiency and IS resource allocation procedures.

## 2.6    PARSONS' "STRATEGIC INFORMATION TECHNOLOGY MANAGEMENT"

Dr. Gregory L. Parsons, Professor of Business Administration, Harvard Business School, presented a multi-level framework for assessing the competitive impact of information technology on a firm in **Information Technology: A New Competitive Weapon,** Sloan Management Review. This paper provided a guide for integrating information systems with a firm's strategy.

Dr. Parsons states that the objective of strategic information technology is to use information technology as a competitive resource. The management process itself involves analytical frameworks and approaches for achieving strategic competitive advantage with the use of information technology. The family of existing, emerging, and potential information technologies are in the areas of:

- Data Processing

- Telecommunications

- Office and Professional Support

- Decision Support Analysis and Decision-Making

- Production Control

Dr. Parsons accepted Michael Porter's work in industry and competitive analysis, and started with the following assumptions:

a. The goal of competitive strategy for a firm is to earn above-average returns within a particular competitive environment or industry.

b. All firms face a set of competitive forces which define the industry structure. These competitive forces determine the profitability of an industry and shape the potential successful strategies for a firm in the industry.

c. Competitive strategy operates in a broad, organizing framework. It is shaped by competitive forces. It guides both offensive and defensive actions. It is executed through the functional resources of a firm.

Information technology supports, enhances, and may even enlarge the competitive strategy of the organization. It should be executed through the functional areas of the organization, rather than being a part of administration, which is the traditional view of data processing. When information technology is integrated into the organization, it has the potential for aiding the competitive strategy and supporting the various functional areas of the firm. It is then an area to look to for competitive advantage.

Information technology becomes a competitive advantage in a number of ways, which can be divided into three different levels for creating competitive opportunities and threats:

### INDUSTRY LEVEL:

Information technology can impact the entire industry structure. For example, in the banking industry with deregulation, information technology has become one of the major components of change.

### FIRM LEVEL:

Information technology will impact the specific competitive environment of the firm. It occurs when a company looks out at the specific competitive forces that it faces, and realizes that technology is changing these forces for that firm.

### STRATEGY LEVEL:

Information technology impacts the firm's competitive strategy by allowing it to either change, enhance, or further its own strategy.

These three levels are, of course, related. Obviously, if a firm is in an industry where the entire environment is changing due to technology, that firm's specific competitive environment will change. Bank managers, for example, cannot ignore the fact that information technology is becoming the key competitive advantage in the industry. This understanding must be translated into a particular strategy that involves computers. Some industries may not be affected by information technology, but they must go through McFarlan's analysis to perceive the elements for their particular company and determine the role which they should adopt.

## 2.6.1    INFORMATION TECHNOLOGY AT THE INDUSTRY LEVEL

Information technology can change an entire industry by:

- **Changing the Nature of its Products and Services:**

    In the publishing area, for example, paper will soon be simply an alternate form of distribution of published materials and information. This changes the nature of the product life cycle and affects the speed of distribution.

- **Changing Markets:**

    In an industry where the whole competitive nature is changing because of information technology, the focus must be more external, to predict where the new products are going to come from, what the new markets are going to be, where the profitability is going to be in that industry, and what the implications are of competing in an industry where information technology is changing the industry. Management must review the critical dimensions of competition to see if they are changing. Other extra-industry forces, such as regulation, will also be impacted. Strategies may have to be rearranged for foreign marketplaces.

New information technology services can change the overall demand, the degree of possible segmentation, and the geographic distribution possibilities.

● **Changing the Economics of Productions:**

Management must determine the capabilities of available information technology resources relative to the new industry baseline requirements. This means that if technology is going to be a key component, it is necessary to assess how much is going to be required even to play the game. A lot of regional banks are running into problems in the area of financial services. It appears that there is no way that they can invest the money to pay for the major new systems required.

The relevant range for scale economies must be evaluated. There is a trade-off to be made between flexibility and standardization. The economics of production must be analyzed by considering Porter's Value-Added Stream.

Thus, to understand the implications of industry-level impact, management must review the critical dimensions of competition to determine if they are changing, and assess how information technology change will impact other extra-industry forces. There is a need for each firm to determine the capabilities of its information technology resources relative to the baseline industry requirements. The critical industry level decisions are:

● Will the firm have technological leadership or followership?

● What degree of vertical integration of information technology is desired?

● Should the market be enlarged to national or global?

## 2.6.2    INFORMATION TECHNOLOGY AT THE FIRM LEVEL

At this level, the specific firm sees specific information technology changing the relationship between itself and its buyers, suppliers, new entrants, substitutes, and rivalry; the five competitive forces of the environment. For buyers, the factors are switching costs and buyer selection. For suppliers, the factors are avoiding switching costs and backwards integration. For new entrants, the considerations are entry barriers and entry deterrents. In substitution, the relative price/performance and product features must be considered. For rivalry, the factors are setting a new base of competition, or using shared information technology.

All firms in all industries face these competitive forces. When senior management makes decisions, they do so with regard to these competitive forces. Therefore, it is a great advantage to anticipate where the firm will be going. They may then see how systems can be used to leverage a particular position against one of these competitive forces.

**Entry barriers,** for example, are the structural components that a firm uses to keep new entrants out. Entry barriers make it more difficult to get into a market. Information technology may create or undo entry barriers. A major insurance company built an on-line network to its 500 agencies. This created a massive barrier for new entrants when considering the high end of the insurance market. A regional bank in the Boston area developed a large ATM network which effectively overcame the branch office entry barriers of its competitors.

**Switching costs** is another way that a firm can get competitive advantage. Switching costs has its roots in the relationship between a particular business and its customers. If you can hook up your buyers and make it difficult for them to switch to an alternate vendor, or make it difficult for them to beat down prices because there is nowhere else for them to go, you have a real competitive advantage. Information technology can be used to increase switching costs between a firm and its competitors. The classical example in this area is American Hospital Supply, the large medical supply company which installed on-line terminals at its customer's sites for order entry and inventory control. This introduced substantial costs to those hospitals if they wished to consider another supplier.

**Product differentiation** can be obtained through the use of information technology by many firms who wish to differentiate their products or services from their rivals. A financial company developed a new financial product based on a sophisticated information technology system which allowed the combination of multiple product features.

### Searching for These Opportunities:

As an example of searching for strategic advantages, one can use  a **strategic map** as illustrated in **Figure 2-9, An Impact of Competitive Forces Matrix - 1986.** It shows the impact of information technology along the vertical axis, and the impact of competitive forces on strategy along the horizontal axis. This example was a distribution company. Senior management thought that the biggest issue to be dealt with was new entrants. Another big problem was suppliers; where they got all their inventory. Rivalry was not intense, and substitution was not an issue.

Figure 2-9

## AN IMPACT OF COMPETITIVE FORCES MATRIX - 1986

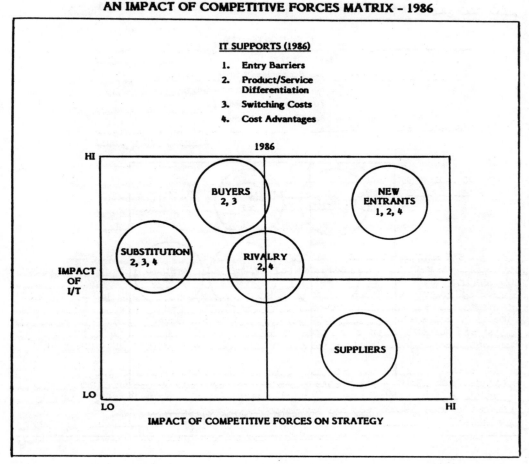

**IT SUPPORTS (1986)**

1. Entry Barriers
2. Product/Service Differentiation
3. Switching Costs
4. Cost Advantages

They were fairly innovative, and the impact of information technology seemed to represent a barrier to new entrants. They intended to get even more sophisticated, and they were differentiating their products and services. They did not have any system for suppliers, yet it was a major force, so it was low on the grid. The differentiation introduced switching costs to the buyers.

Looking ahead ten years to where they thought the industry was going, they expected major change **(Figure 2-10, An Impact of Competitive Forces Matrix - 1995).** They expected the industry to consolidate, which would be a barrier to new entrants, but which would introduce more powerful rivalry. The suppliers would continue to be strong. After this type of analysis, management was able to consider the impact of information technology. They could see the key factors, and plan their key information strategy. The analysis gave them a road map for their information systems.

Figure 2-10

## AN IMPACT OF COMPETITIVE FORCES MATRIX - 1995

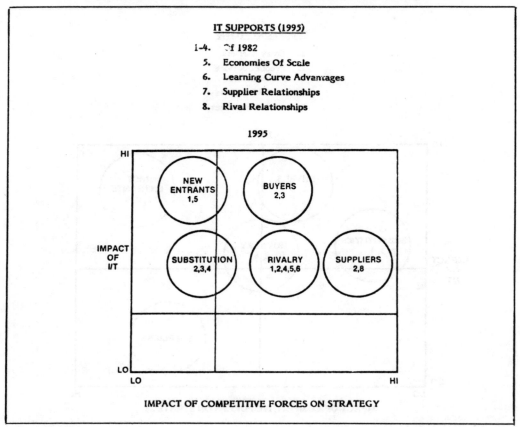

**IMPACT OF COMPETITIVE FORCES ON STRATEGY**

### 2.6.3    INFORMATION TECHNOLOGY AT THE STRATEGY LEVEL

Information technology does have the potential for giving competitive advantage.  Management has to determine the changes in the power of the existing competitive forces.  These forces are constantly shifting, and it is necessary to understand what their importance will be in the future.  Potential must be assessed, and opportunities must be scanned.   Strategy is a broad framework, responsive to the competitive environment, which serves to guide individual offensive and defensive actions. There are three general ways that companies are successful over time in a particular industry:

1.   **Overall low cost producer:** Information technology can reduce
the  overall  cost  directly.   It  enhances  the  ability  to  reduce
overall cost through other functions.

2.  **Overall differentiation:** Information technology adds unique features directly to products and services. It enhances the ability to differentiate products and services through other functions.

3.  **Focusing on niche:** Information technology can identify and create market niches directly. It enhances the ability to create market niches through other functions.

Information technology affects the firm's ability to execute strategy. A key factor is to notice the big difference between the general systems that will support and aid cost leadership, as opposed to the systems that will support and aid a differentiation strategy. The idea is not to say that all possible systems should be put in place, but to use the analysis as a checklist to ascertain whether the company is doing any of these things. Information systems analysis provides a way of bringing together what the corporation needs in order to be successful in the marketplace, and what the systems can do to provide support and enhancement.

## 2.7    LOVE'S "ALIGNING IS WITH CORPORATE STRATEGY"

Gerald Loev, Vice President of Index Systems, Inc., in a presentation of the experiences of Index Systems in practical techniques for aligning Information Services with Corporate strategy, clearly pointed out that the reasons to invest in automation include both improving competitive position and improving business operations. Both may be involved in strategic planning, depending upon the current position of the corporation. Loev bridged the gulf between the older paradigm, of MIS strategic planning for technology strategy and planning process states, and the new paradigm of joining with business strategic planning.

He used a representation of business types shown in **Figure 2-11, A Method Of Segmenting a Business,** that was designed by Bruce Henderson, of the Boston Consulting Group, in the early 1970's. The "star" business has a dominant market share in a high-growth business. The "question mark" business has a small market share in a high-growth business. The "cash cow" business has a dominant market share in a low-growth business. The "dog" business has a small market share in a low growth business. The concept of segmentation is important to strategic planning. You can break the corporation off into either strategic business units or clusters of products, depending upon how the organizational philosophy and the culture of the company operates. The important dimensions are the relative market share of the business unit and the potential growth rate of the industry. Efforts at strategic planning will depend strongly upon the type of business, although a good strategic idea could move the business from one label to another.

**Figure 2-11**

## A METHOD OF SEGMENTING A BUSINESS

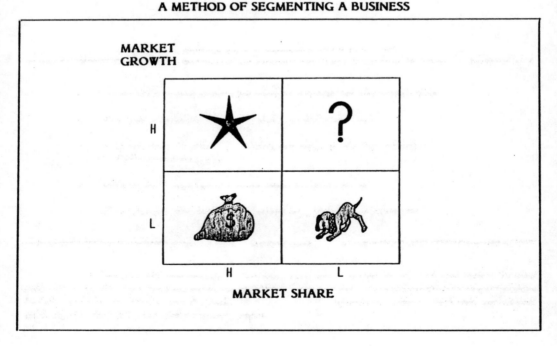

There is a continuum of business behavior. MIS operations start with a control orientation when business managers are constantly concerned about return on investment. Problems of cost escalation in MIS are of great importance to them. When MIS starts to match the business thrust, and becomes market-oriented, there are possibilities of high growth.

Loev spoke from experience with the older paradigm of strategic planning, where "strategic" meant more than five years, but he has clearly bridged the gap to the new paradigm by showing how MIS needed to interpret business strategy. **Figure 2-12, Systems Planning Overview,** shows that the older questions of cost reduction are important, but the real business question is, "What are the major opportunities for a strategic breakthrough in my business, that will enable the business unit to succeeed in a dramatic fashion?"

A strategic systems planning effort, therefore, has **two main phases. Phase I** is the strategic systems opportunity analysis, which examines the business thrust and asks what should be done with automation. **Phase II** is the strategic systems planning work, which finds out how to position the systems resources to aid the business thrust, or how the EDP momentum can be moved from operational effort to business growth effort.

The significant problem is that the "why" of automation has become clouded. The questions that should be asked are:

- How do we identify the really attractive automation opportunities ahead of the crowd?

- Have we already exploited the significant opportunities?

- What is left to do, and how much business impact will it have?

- How can we recognize and avoid marginal investments?

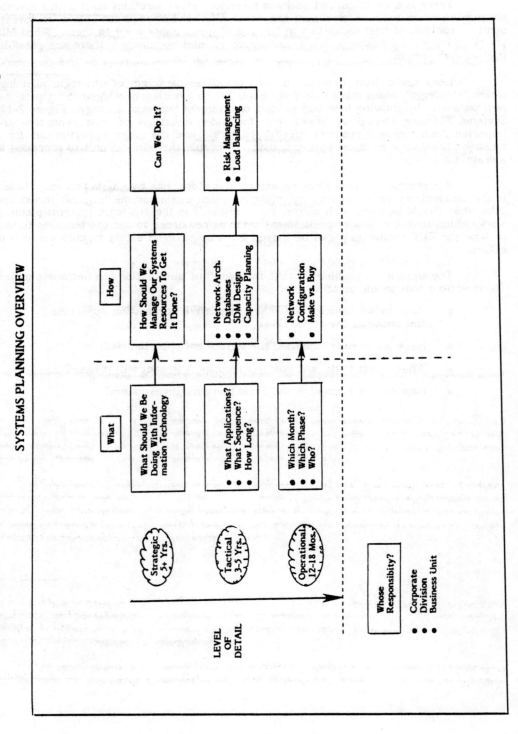

Figure 2-12

SYSTEMS PLANNING OVERVIEW

An example brings out the basic issues in strategic planning. This is the case of a company that has a number of local plants and had a central spare parts warehouse and a parts customer base. Top management asked Information Systems if they could achieve some sort of significant reduction in inventory levels. They came up with the standard solution, which was a **large inventory system** on the computer that had substantial savings and a 42% ROI. **(See Figure 2-13)** This was the wrong thing to do, however. By broadening their horizons, and looking at the problem strategically, they saw that they could build an **inventory management network** among the local plants. **(See Figure 2-14)** This made many improvements in the company, and the resulting gain was $40 million rather than $5 million. What is needed, therefore, is a planning process which provides a strategic view of the potential business impact of automation.

**Figure 2-13**

## STANDARD SOLUTION – LARGE INVENTORY SYSTEM

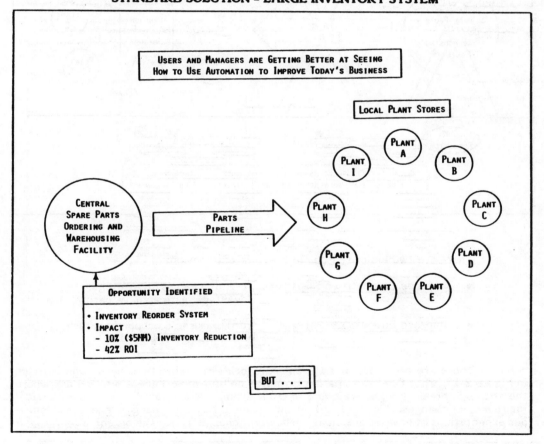

Figure 2-14

## INVENTORY MANAGEMENT NETWORK

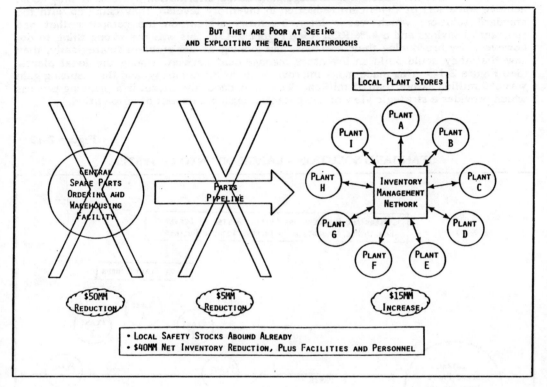

There are two major reasons to invest in automation:

- **Improve Competitive Position:**   To gain meaningful strategic advantage or to achieve parity.

- **Improve Business Operations:**   For measurable economic return or for intangible benefits.

There are a number of different categories of business changes. One is listed in **Figure 2-15, What Does Automation Do?** It is helpful to sort these out and ask where the strategic breakthroughs are going to come from. We are familiar with the classical improvement changes. We need to find the dynamic business changes, and a problem is our expectations of how we anticipate behavioral change within the organization.

Index Systems evolved a technique for strategic systems planning from strategic business planning. It is called the concept of the value-added change, and is especially useful in identifying where the real strategic plays are likely to be. It pinpoints where important business changes will have a significant impact upon the

Figure 2-15

## WHAT DOES AUTOMATION DO?

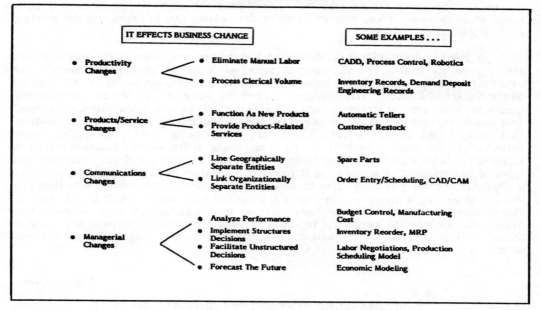

| IT EFFECTS BUSINESS CHANGE | | SOME EXAMPLES... |

- **Productivity Changes**
  - Eliminate Manual Labor — CADD, Process Control, Robotics
  - Process Clerical Volume — Inventory Records, Demand Deposit Engineering Records

- **Products/Service Changes**
  - Function As New Products — Automatic Tellers
  - Provide Product-Related Services — Customer Restock

- **Communications Changes**
  - Line Geographically Separate Entities — Spare Parts
  - Link Organizationally Separate Entities — Order Entry/Scheduling, CAD/CAM

- **Managerial Changes**
  - Analyze Performance — Budget Control, Manufacturing Cost
  - Implement Structures Decisions — Inventory Reorder, MRP
  - Facilitate Unstructured Decisions — Labor Negotiations, Production Scheduling Model
  - Forecast The Future — Economic Modeling

business unit's ability to achieve its strategic business objectives. This approach to strategic opportunity analysis is in four steps:

**Step 1:** Break the business down for analysis.

**Step 2:** Test the impact of business changes.

**Step 3:** Assess the kind of business benefits the changes will yield.

**Step 4:** Assess the role of technology in implementing the change.

There is no doubt that information technology is becoming one of the key vehicles for implementing business change. The idea is to first segment the business, then manage the segments. Why not think of automation as a vehicle for accomplishing desired business change?

The business analysis technique should vary with the business change orientation. If the change orientation is to improve the competitive position, the business analysis focus must be on products and markets, and useful techniques are the value-added chain and CSF's. If the change orientation is to improve the business operations, then the business analysis focus must be on those operations, and the useful techniques are the traditional business process planning approaches, as well as CSF's.

For example, a competitive focus for the analysis of business components can be found in a detailed analysis of the value-added chain of typical manufacturing/distribution companies. Their advantages derive from scale, which is market share, in each of the functions in the value chain. You look for opportunities within this value-added chain to identify some business change that will have a significant impact on the whole business. If we introduce a business change by raising the volume for a **part** of the value-added chain, there may be a significant reduction in the final unit cost. Automation can play a key role in handling the volume and in improving the existing factory utilization.

The key to an effective strategic planning process, then, is the way it makes the organization think. The old way was thinking: What are my systems needs? For exactly the same system that is being proposed, we should begin to think: What would be the impact of a productivity change in part of the value chain? We can then ask the question: What are the strategic automation opportunities throughout the corporation? This can be represented as shown in **Figure 2-16, Summarizing Across the Corporation.** This figure shows the amount of discretionary dollars being spent on new applications systems. As you start to look at what you are doing in the various business units you support, you have a profile for the business units, and you can see if you have the right types of expenditures. For example, if you have a question mark business unit, you have a small market share in a high growth area. You are primarily concerned with finding a niche, and getting a breakthrough that will establish your business unit in the market. Money spent on productivity improvement, or the reduction of cost, is absolutely irrelevant. We need to merge the top-down strategic view with the parochial view of the unit. This is a way of thinking that is important in a strategic sense in business units.

**Figure 2-16**

## SUMMARIZING ACROSS THE CORPORATION

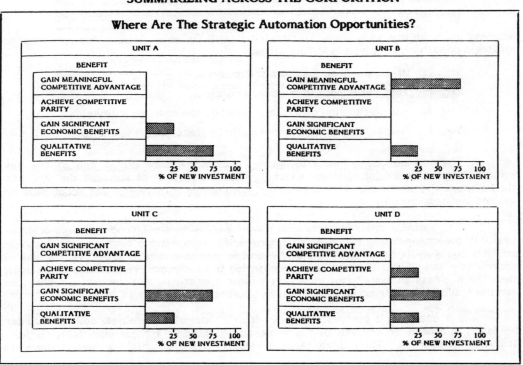

Figure 2-17, illustrates the combined Perspective Yields From Overall Investment Priorities. This is a way of establishing some sort of a priority when there are multiple strategic business units. This is not necessarily a step to take in the planning process, but it illustrates the concept of choosing from amongst a complex of projects. Simply following ROI's and ranking them, would be making a mistake. Businesses do not have to be segmented as dogs, cows, stars, and question marks, but the principle of the segmentation is necessary to decide where to go after a meaningful competitive advantage.

Figure 2-17

## COMBINED PERSPECTIVE YIELDS FROM OVERALL INVESTMENT PRIORITIES

| Dominant Automation Benefit | Business Profile | | | |
|---|---|---|---|---|
| | ★ | 💰 | ? | 🐕 |
| Gain Meaningful Competitive Advantage | 1 | 3 | 1 | 5 |
| Achieve Competitive Parity | 1 | 2 | 3 | 4 |
| Measurable Economic Return | 2 | 2 | 2 | 3 |
| Intangible Benefits | 3 | 4 | 4 | 5 |

The suggested approach is to think in terms of **business** changes, such as those shown in **Figure 2-15,** and the kinds of benefits they will bring about. Ascertain whether the changes improve competitive position or improve business operations. In this decade, information technology will be a primary vehicle for effecting business change.

Phase I, strategic systems opportunity analysis thus asks what we should be doing with automation, and tries to determine the business thrust. Phase II: strategic systems planning then determines how to position our systems resources to align the EDP momentum with the business thrust that is indicated. How do we get the strategic systems accomplished? These are structural issues, and there are a host of questions that can be asked, **(See Figure 2-18).** Some of the questions in the area of **applications** are, "When should I build an application on a shared basis across business units, as opposed to building it in a single instance?" "When does it make sense to purchase packaged systems?" What amount of risk is worth taking in the project?" **Figure 2-19** shows how to attempt to answer those three questions systematically. It gives a visual picture of the application posture.

**Figure 2-18**

## STRATEGIC PLANNING FOR DP RESOURCES - APPLICATIONS

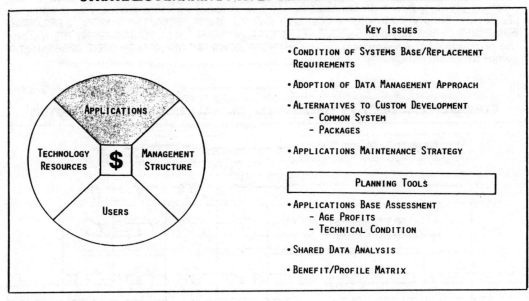

KEY ISSUES

• CONDITION OF SYSTEMS BASE/REPLACEMENT
  REQUIREMENTS

• ADOPTION OF DATA MANAGEMENT APPROACH

• ALTERNATIVES TO CUSTOM DEVELOPMENT
  - COMMON SYSTEM
  - PACKAGES

• APPLICATIONS MAINTENANCE STRATEGY

PLANNING TOOLS

• APPLICATIONS BASE ASSESSMENT
  - AGE PROFITS
  - TECHNICAL CONDITION

• SHARED DATA ANALYSIS

• BENEFIT/PROFILE MATRIX

**Figure 2-19**

## APPLICATIONS POSTURE

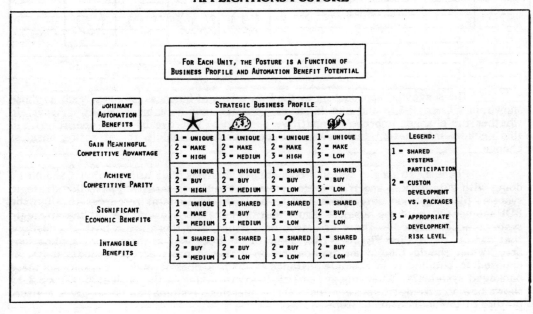

FOR EACH UNIT, THE POSTURE IS A FUNCTION OF
BUSINESS PROFILE AND AUTOMATION BENEFIT POTENTIAL

| DOMINANT AUTOMATION BENEFITS | STRATEGIC BUSINESS PROFILE | | | |
|---|---|---|---|---|
| | ★ | (💰) | ? | 🏹 |
| GAIN MEANINGFUL COMPETITIVE ADVANTAGE | 1 = UNIQUE<br>2 = MAKE<br>3 = HIGH | 1 = UNIQUE<br>2 = MAKE<br>3 = MEDIUM | 1 = UNIQUE<br>2 = MAKE<br>3 = HIGH | 1 = UNIQUE<br>2 = MAKE<br>3 = LOW |
| ACHIEVE COMPETITIVE PARITY | 1 = UNIQUE<br>2 = BUY<br>3 = HIGH | 1 = UNIQUE<br>2 = BUY<br>3 = MEDIUM | 1 = SHARED<br>2 = BUY<br>3 = LOW | 1 = SHARED<br>2 = BUY<br>3 = LOW |
| SIGNIFICANT ECONOMIC BENEFITS | 1 = UNIQUE<br>2 = MAKE<br>3 = MEDIUM | 1 = SHARED<br>2 = BUY<br>3 = MEDIUM | 1 = SHARED<br>2 = BUY<br>3 = LOW | 1 = SHARED<br>2 = BUY<br>3 = LOW |
| INTANGIBLE BENEFITS | 1 = SHARED<br>2 = BUY<br>3 = MEDIUM | 1 = SHARED<br>2 = BUY<br>3 = LOW | 1 = SHARED<br>2 = BUY<br>3 = LOW | 1 = SHARED<br>2 = BUY<br>3 = LOW |

LEGEND:

1 = SHARED
    SYSTEMS
    PARTICIPATION

2 = CUSTOM
    DEVELOPMENT
    VS. PACKAGES

3 = APPROPRIATE
    DEVELOPMENT
    RISK LEVEL

**Figures 2-20 and 2-21** show the same sort of analytical approach for **strategic planning for DP technology resources.** This helps to answer the questions of whether we should lead, match, or lag the competition, and how much technology risk is appropriate.

**Figures 2-22 and 2-23** show the same sort of planning relative to the user roles and involvement, the levels of user ability, and the they types of training that may be required. There should be an analysis of the ability of the users and managers to recognize opportunities, participate in projects, lead programs, and use systems. There can then be a determination of what can be done to correct any deficiencies in terms of education and assistance.

Finally, **Figures 2-24 and 2-25** illustrate the planning problems in what the management structure should be for accomplishing the strategic plans. It is a question of organization, and whether the IS function should be centralized or decentralized to accomplish the strategic plans. Some groups may be very market-oriented, some may be control-oriented, and some may be in-between. Do the groups fit the types of strategic system development that is being considered? Different users have different demands and trying to support everyone on a centralized basis is frequently difficult. Some applications are better centralized, while others are better decentralized.

Questions must be asked about the corporate role, and how it best meets the strategic business profile of the units being served:

- Can a strong corporate role achieve meaningful competitive advantage, or must control be closer to the business unit?

- Should corporate be the manager of shared activities, such as systems development, data center management, and training?

- Can planning tools be developed and managed from corporate that will identify funding needs, and do justice to a strategic funding model?

In summary, the key issues involve the assessment of the organization's IS capabilities in moving the EDP momentum to align with the corporate business strategic thrust:

- Can the needed capabilities be acquired in time?

- What alternative strategies are available?

- What are the consequences of each?

- Which one should we choose?

These are all excellent planning questions. The payoff comes in deciding them in a way that emphasizes efforts for obtaining competitive advantage.

**Figure 2-20**

## STRATEGIC PLANNING FOR DP RESOURCES - TECHNOLOGY RESOURCES

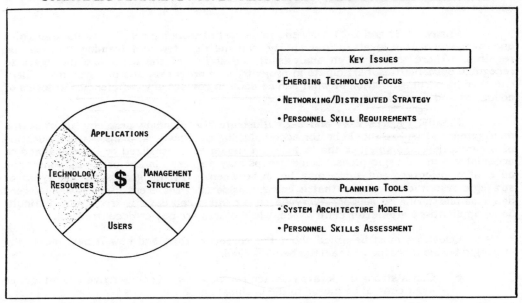

**Figure 2-21**

## SHOULD WE LEAD, MATCH, OR LAG THE COMPETITION?
## HOW MUCH TECHNOLOGY RISK IS APPROPRIATE?

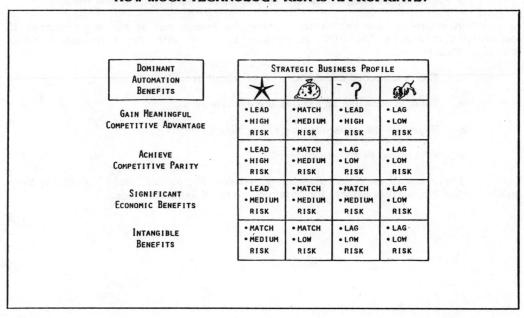

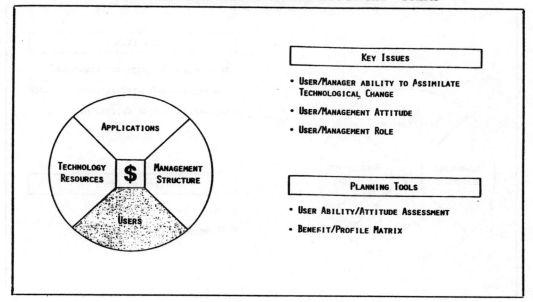

**Figure 2-22**

## STRATEGIC PLANNING FOR DP RESOURCES – USERS

**KEY ISSUES**

- USER/MANAGER ABILITY TO ASSIMILATE TECHNOLOGICAL CHANGE
- USER/MANAGEMENT ATTITUDE
- USER/MANAGEMENT ROLE

**PLANNING TOOLS**

- USER ABILITY/ATTITUDE ASSESSMENT
- BENEFIT/PROFILE MATRIX

APPLICATIONS

TECHNOLOGY RESOURCES  $  MANAGEMENT STRUCTURE

USERS

**Figure 2-23**

## USER ROLE WITHIN A BUSINESS SEGMENT

WITHIN A BUSINESS SEGMENT, USER ROLE VARIES ACCORDING TO USER LEVEL AND I.S. BENEFITS

| DOMINANT I.S. BENEFITS | MANAGEMENT LEVEL | | |
|---|---|---|---|
| | SENIOR | MIDDLE | LINE USER |
| GAIN MEANINGFUL COMPETITIVE ADVANTAGE | HEAVY PROGRAM REVIEW | DEEP PROGRAM INVOLVEMENT & PARTICIPATION | |
| ACHIEVE COMPETITIVE PARITY | HEAVY PROGRAM REVIEW | DEEP PROGRAM INVOLVEMENT & PARTICIPATION | DEEP PROGRAM INVOLVEMENT & PARTICIPATION |
| MEASURABLE ECONOMIC RETURN | PLANNING CYCLE REVIEW | PROGRAM PROGRESS REVIEWS | |
| INTANGIBLE BENEFITS | PLANNING CYCLE REVIEW | PROGRAM PROGRESS REVIEWS | |

**Figure 2-24**

## STRATEGIC PLANNING FOR DP RESOURCES – MANAGEMENT STRUCTURE

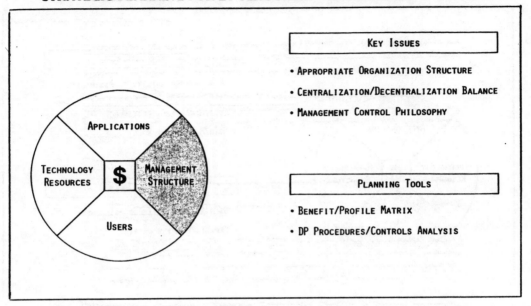

**Figure 2-25**

## SHOULD DEVELOPMENT RESOURCES BE CENTRALIZED OR DECENTRALIZED <u>WITHIN</u> A BUSINESS SEGMENT?

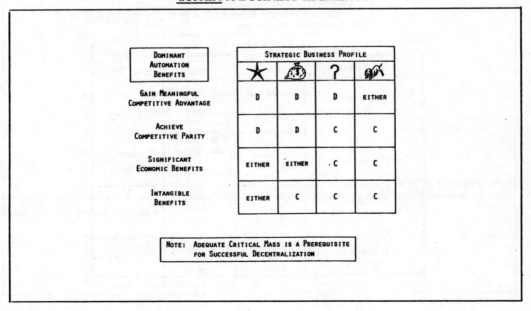

## 2.8      STRASSMAN'S "VALUE-ADDED"

Paul Strassman is a leading authority on white-collar productivity and on strategic planning for information resources management. The following are extracts from a lecture. His latest book is **Information Payoff,** published by MacMillan.

Strassman contends that the measurement of information and technology planning are required for budgeting computer investments. There has been an inability to measure effectiveness and to quantify benefits. There have also been problems in productivity measurement because you cannot measure what cannot be defined. Conventional ratio-analysis methods are misleading. Critical Success Factors only give partial answers.

The **value-added approach** is the best way of looking at productivity. It makes diagnostic comparisons possible. Strassman advocates a new ratio, Return on Management (ROM) as a means of benchmarking management productivity and information technology. It is management value-added divided by the costs of management. It can be compared to labor value-added, which is revenues, less purchases, less capital value-added. There is then a method of profiling companies which is analogous to the medical profiles of humans. This leads to a variety of productivity measures, and the ability to compare similar companies.

A value-added database has been created by Strassman for comparisons. With the value-added method, it can be applied to assessing overall funding and strategic priorities for information technology investments.

Strassman has shown that there is no point in comparing your MIS budget with other companies as a percentage of sales, or a percentage of employee cost, or so on. One should not compare organizations by just examining internal variables. The external marketplace is the competitive equalizer, and must be included in all evaluations.

The first thing you have to do before you start analyzing information on technology expenditures is to remove external purchases, which are somebody else's labor and capital. You then get a value of measurement called the **value-added approach (See Figure 2-26)** to determine the value-added of the company. Ratios based on sales are misleading. The next step is to take out the capitalization **(See Figure 2-27).** Capital is the result of past streams of decisions. It is really contributed from the balance sheet. Productivity, however, is a measure of labor contribution. We have to evaluate the effects of information technology on operations in transaction-driven kinds of systems. Management is always considered broadly, including all professionals and the overhead kinds of functions. Strassman takes apart the financial statement, and arrives at a value-added financial statement **(See Figure 2-28).** In a simplified way you arrive at labor productivity, the benchmark, by taking revenue minus purchases, minus cost of capital, and dividing it by labor costs, including fully-loaded benefits, to arrive at **labor productivity.**

You can then look at year-to-year changes in labor productivity. In **Figure 2-29,** there is the **"true economic labor productivity change",** which in this case is negative. These are self-adjusting, or self-indexing, numbers, because you are always dividing dollars by dollars. There is no problem of base period indexing.

**Figure 2-26**

## TOTAL VALUE-ADDED

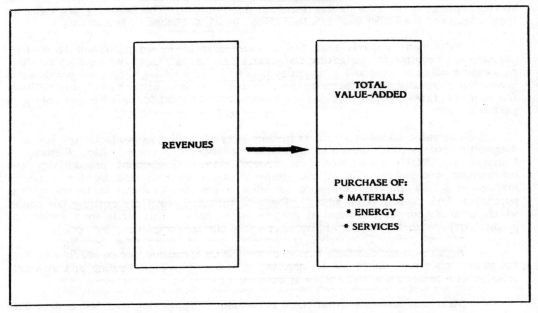

**Figure 2-27**

## LABOR VALUE-ADDED

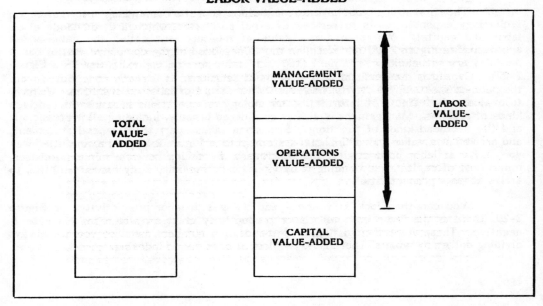

Figure 2-28

## LABOR PRODUCTIVITY

| | 1980 |
|---|---|
| **OUTPUT ($M):** | |
| REVENUE | $9,411 |
| Less: PURCHASES | 6,961 |
| VALUE-ADDED | $2,450 |
| Less: COST OF CAPITAL | 472 |
| LABOR VALUE-ADDED | $1,978 |
| **INPUT ($M):** | |
| LABOR COST | $1,499 |
| **LABOR PRODUCTIVITY:** | 1.3196 |

Figure 2-29

## PRODUCTIVITY CHANGE

| | 1980 | 1979 | 1978 |
|---|---|---|---|
| **OUTPUT ($M):** | | | |
| LABOR VALUE-ADDED | $1966 | $1989 | $1662 |
| **INPUT ($M):** | | | |
| LABOR COST | $1499 | $1513 | $1251 |
| **LABOR PRODUCTIVITY:** | | | |
| | 1.3115 | 1.3146 | 1.3285 |
| **PRODUCTIVITY CHANGE:** | | | |
| | -0.24% | -1.05% | |

The way to get to the greatest problem, which is the application of information technology to management and the overhead cost, is to calculate a Return-on-Management (ROM), which is comparable to Return-on-Assets (ROA) and Return-on-Equity (ROE). This ratio has some interesting properties for measuring productivity because it divides something living called management value-added by something living called cost of management. It is counter to the old ideas that returns to an enterprise are due to its capital, which is the basis of ROA and ROE. Capital gets all the credit. Strassman's theory indicates that **capital is a commodity** and, therefore, capital can be purchased at market price. Then what really matters about the performance of a business is its management. Since management gets the blame or the credit, ROM is the index that you are trying to measure, and are trying to influence by information technology.

**Management productivity,** then, is the same as Return-on-Management (ROM), which is (Management Value-Added) divided by (Costs of Management).

With that construct, you can compute the productivity of the information sector of your company. As shown in **Figure 2-30, Management Productivity Change,** it is labor value-added minus cost of operations. If management over pays operations by negotiating an unfavorable labor contract, management value-added will be less. If management buys commodities extensively, management value-added will be less, and so on. In this case, when management value-added is divided by management cost, the labor productivity of management, or management productivity, is declining. In this case also, for every dollar's worth of management, you get only 1.59 dollars worth of value-added, which is quite unspectacular for management.

This is the methodology which establishes a new measure, or a new way, of looking at productivity. ROM can be used as a way of benchmarking information technology. The multi-variate statistics used in drug research and insurance profiling can be used. A profile must be developed for each organization. There are a variety of **factors** that can then be realistically compared. These include:

- Absolute market share and relative market share (your share versus your next three competitors)

- Marketing divided by sales, and new products divided by sales

- Information technology costs divided by salary of management employees (This factor is higher for those with higher ROM)

- Information technology costs divided by value-added (This factor is lower for the winners)

The costs of information technology, including telecommunications, software, and all other aspects, is at very heavy capitalization rates. But the people who spend the money and are successful buy the money very cheaply because they generate value-added rather than cost reduction. Therefore, they spend less for information technology as a percentage of value-added than those who do not. You have to make sure, when you install information technology, that you generate value-added rather than cost reduction.

Figure 2-30

## MANAGEMENT PRODUCTIVITY CHANGE

| | 1980 | 1979 | 1978 |
|---|---|---|---|
| **OUTPUT ($M):** | | | |
| LABOR VALUE-ADDED | $1966 | $1989 | $1662 |
| Less: OPERATIONS | 719 | 756 | 650 |
| MANAGEMENT V-A | $1247 | $1233 | $1012 |
| **INPUT ($M):** | | | |
| MANAGEMENT COST | $780 | $757 | $601 |
| **MANAGEMEMENT PRODUCTIVITY:** | | | |
| | 1.5987 | 1.6288 | 1.6839 |
| **PRODUCTIVITY CHANGE:** | | | |
| | -1.8% | -3.3% | |

## 2.9     PASSINO'S "PROCESS AND ISSUES"

Jacques H. Passino, Jr., a Partner in the Management Information Consulting Division of the Detroit office of Arthur Andersen & Company, pointed out in a speech that businesses are increasingly challenged with intense competition and rapid change. This is an important link to technology decisions.  As information systems personnel plan and manage for this inevitable change,  they must translate their plans into successful competitive strategy.  There are specific competitive factors and changes in each major industry that must be understood for businesses to be successful.  The three major factors in driving these changes are globalization of markets, deregulation or denationalization, and technology advances.

Some of the facets of this subject are further developed in an article by Harold S.  Bott, Jacques H. Passino, and Jeff Hamilton.[6]

The following are all contributing to an increase in **global competition:**

• Reduced differences between countries

• Aggressive national industrial policies

• More open flow of technology

• Emergence of new large-scale markets (e.g., China and Russia)

• Emergence of newly developed countries (e.g., Taiwan, South Korea, Singapore and Brazil)

Nearly every marketplace in the world is now open and is more competitive than it was five years ago.  Famous ones, like the Japanese home market, are opening up (although not as quickly as U.S. marketers would like), and one way or another companies are finding ways to compete throughout the world and in new marketplaces.

Companies are much more sophisticated today in their ability to compete globally and in their market sensitivity to cultural differences between countries. Toyota and Nissan gained a significant competitive advantage over GM and other U.S. automakers by employing a coordinated global strategy.  Historically, GM in Europe has operated quite separately from GM in the U.S.

The second factor is **deregulation** or **denationalization,** depending on which country you are in.  Obviously, this had a significant impact on transportation and energy in the United States.  In the United Kingdom, there is very quick privatization of major industries, automotive, British aerospace.  There are a lot of things happening that have moved the public sector employment from 10.5% to around 6.5% in a very short period of time.  France is going the same way and even Africa is moving to privatize entrepreneurial programs in an effort to improve productivity.

The differences between countries are not really reducing, but the ability of the organization trying to market in the different countries is getting better.  We see a much more sophisticated message being delivered, depending on the country that we are trying to sell something in, and this is enhancing people's ability to compete globally.

---

6    Harold S. Bott, Jacques H. Passino, and Jeff Hamilton **"How To Make A Move With Information Systems",** Information Week, May 26, 1986.

The third factor, **technology,** has a broad impact on competitive position because it:

a. changes industry structure;

b. can act as an equalizer among businesses; and

c. spawns new business.

Technology is playing a major role in almost every business. It has changed the rules and the structure of a lot of industries. It has acted as an equalizer in many cases allowing people to get into a market they could not get into before. It has driven a lot of focus marketers to be able to serve a niche market without a lot of capital. We can think of the whole mail order business, for example, as being one that has significantly reduced the capital costs of being able to market consumer goods. We don't need any inventory. It is having a dramatic impact and, again, we are all more expert in how technology is impacting our business, but it is a major force.

An interesting thing to consider is that these three forces are linked. As an industry becomes deregulated, there is greater interest in applying technology so that we can take advantage of our deregulated status. Also, companies are looking for markets all over the world through the use of technology, and are better able to access the demand in a marketplace and then attack it. Globalization is made possible, to a certain extent, by technology which helps to overcome barriers to global competition.

One can make a distinction between continuous (evolutionary) and discontinuous (revolutionary) change in how technology impacts an industry.

The three major trends in technology are:

1. The increased use of computer-integrated manufacturing

2. Enhanced communications

3. Emphasis on information

It is on this last item, the use information in business, that we are going to focus. The idea is to try to find and sort through all the changes and the events going on that are pertinent to your business, and to devise a plan so that you can use change to gain and sustain a competitive advantage, rather than just observing it happen.

Information systems should not be planned without an analysis of the changes and events that are pertinent to a business. To sort out these changes and events, Passino applies Michael Porter's ideas on Value Chain Analysis. He suggests that the only three approaches to gain real competitive advantage are:

• Alter the industry structure: that is, re-structure the value system.

• Improve your strategic position within the industry: differentiate your product or lower your cost.

• Create new business opportunities: by understanding your value system and the available technology.

It is clear that, from many examples, information can be, and has been, used to gain and sustain competitive advantage. Information, itself, has a lot of competitive uses:

- Influence buyers and suppliers

- Differentiate products

- Lower product and process costs

- Raise industry entry barriers

- Exploit linkage in the value system

The first four uses amount to the final point; understanding the value system and exploiting the linkages between your company and suppliers, channels and buyers.

The uses of information can vary widely. You can **link yourself to customers** through an order processing system, such as the Sabre System of American Airlines. To listen to their analysis, the Sabre System is a very understandable, and not a particularly strategic evolution from a big felt board that was in a room where they used to keep track of reservations. The evolution has been important to that company. Once you understand that distribution channel, you can see why it would be very useful to have such a system. Other ways of using information are **by differentiating your product,** and adding information to your product as most of the food manufacturers have done, so that now the nutrition information on a package of cereal is more prominent than anything else. Putting on-board diagnostics in a product ranging from a machine tool to a vehicle are all things that are happening very fast. You can drive your car in and there is a computer diagnostic to tell you what is wrong with it. All of these things are really technology at work differentiating the product.

**Lowering the cost** is the traditional way that we have used data processing to make things more efficient within an organization. All of us in the computer business think about telecommunication linkages, and there are a lot of opportunities that people are moving very fast on. Putting compatible computer-aided design equipment in a capital goods supplier so that engineering changes can be moved back and forth very quickly is another. That CAD equipment becomes part of the RFP. You must have it to propose your machine tool. That is happening in both aerospace and the automobile industry quickly. The person who thinks of that first, and has an advantage in understanding the technology and moving it ahead, can end up with a competitive advantage.

- ## The Information Planning Process

In relation to information planning, or systems planning, it is important to focus on the **business strategy** as a driver for the information planning process. This is not necessarily easy, but it is very important. One of the reasons that it is not very easy is that a lot of companies do not have very well-articulated strategies. It is difficult to do this if we don't have strategy to base it on, but the concept is right. The planning process should try to do this. Based on the assessment and an understanding of competitive strategy of the organization, or a set of working assumptions about what it probably is, we can then start to answer three simple questions: Where are we? What are the opportunities (or where do we want to go)? How are we going to get there? It is a multi-dimensional problem.

The following points represent a high-level planning process for a company that wants to use information for competitive advantage. Again, the underlying assumption is that you understand your business and industry (the value system) and that your firm has a clearly defined strategic plan.

- Consider the firm's information intensity.

- Determine the role of information technology in industry structure.

- Identify and prioritize the opportunities for using information to gain competitive advantage.

- Develop a plan for implementing information technology opportunities.

First, consider your firm's information intensity. This deals with identifying those activities within your company that do or could rely heavily on information.

Second, determine the role of information technology in the industry structure, and examine how information might be used to alter that structure in your favor.

Third, identify and prioritize the uses of information that will benefit your organization the most. Finally, plan for and implement your information technology opportunities.

Don't start with **applications.** Instead, talk about **functions.** When we think about applications, we tend to replicate something that we are doing already.

When going through the planning process, there are three issues that should be considered:

- Organization
- Scope
- Change Management

## 2.9.1    THE ORGANIZATION ISSUE

The **organizational issue** is very important and needs to be dealt with as soon as possible in the process and very rigorously. It it one of the difficult parts but it is very important. It has many dimensions:

- Relationship of Information Strategy to Business Objectives

- Centralization vs. Decentralization

- End-User Computing

- Employee Education

- Position of CIO

First of all, are the business objectives clearly defined and what is their tie to the information strategy? This is an upfront issue, as is the last point, the position of the CIO in the planning process.

Other organizational issues arise as the result of implementing a plan and these include centralization vs. decentralization of the data processing facility, the use of end-user computing, and the big issue of how to train employees in the new systems and technology.

It is critical to get a good look and a good understanding of what the strategy is and have that drive the rest of the process. The present status assessment is important: identify those opportunities, develop an overall technology strategy, and then move that into specific organizational plans, functional or applications plans, and the underlying support technology. This is where we are -- down to the point where we can have an actionable plan. It has to get to the level where we can identify resources, how many, at least on an approximation basis, and something that we can get resources allocated to.

## 2.9.2    THE SCOPE ISSUE

The **scope issue** is a big problem that companies are confronted with when going through the planning process. All too often, planning teams go off on tangents and end up addressing issues that are not relevant or are not of concern to senior management. These rules of thumb should be kept in mind:

- Clearly define the scope of the effort before starting the plan, and stick to it.
- Identify key management concerns upfront.
- Maintain focus on those critical areas.
- Control level of detail.

The scope of the effort is always a problem, and is especially so as you try to put a business strategy element into it. People will say that they have a strategic plan, but many of them are not very well articulated for the rest of the organization. As you ask and try to get a handle on what the strategy really does mean to you and information processing for the rest of the organization, those answers don't come quite as easily. As you find a weakness or question at the strategy level, it is very tempting to move off into that and to explore that further. If you have a project team starting to deal with who the competitors really are and what the market segments are like, it is very possible to get a group coming back to you saying that they want to do some consumer research, a customer survey in your technology planning exercise. Sometimes that is appropriate, but it is very important to keep a lid on the scope of it so that you know where the project is and what is going on.

## 2.9.3    THE CHANGE MANAGEMENT ISSUE

The last issue, which is really an organizational issue as well, is the **change management** implications. If you really are going to make a significant change in the organization, don't underestimate the impact and the time it takes to change a lot of people's jobs.  We are learning this with a lot of modern systems that have distributed terminals all over the place and have a broader impact on the organization than the traditional batch systems did, when maybe two or three people really needed to change the way that they did their work based on the system.  Now when we put terminals everywhere, we realize that the training impact and the change management impact of doing that is significant.  That is true of any distributed system.  It is particularly true if you are also going to change those people's view of the organization and their role in it.  It can't be underestimated and it takes a lot of preparation and effort during the development process to keep track of that.

Change management is needed in three areas:

● New Technology

● Information Security and Control

● Application Portfolio

New technology can have a broad impact on an organization, and it needs to be skillfully managed.  This includes handling the current technology of a business as well as introducing new ideas.  Another factor is the security and control of information, which becomes a more complicated issue with new distributed systems and the move toward end-user computing.  Finally, you may want to consider managing your applications in a way similar to the way an investment portfolio is handled.  Of all your applications, some should be in the development stage, others in the maintenance stage, while others are being phased out.

## SECTION 3


## STRATEGIC SYSTEMS PLANNING - A CONTINGENT APPROACH


## SECTION OVERVIEW

This section begins with an essay on the need for contingent planning at the strategic planning level. Cornelius Sullivan Jr., an authority in the field, emphasizes the changing business and technology environment, and the need for flexible, issue-oriented planning. He describes the varied technology environments to point out the need for contingent planning. The information age issues are outlined as information networking, information technology architecture, end-user computing, competitive edge applications, and artificial intelligence.

The three dominant styles in contingent planning are: educational (for management), analytical (considering a variety of solutions), and benchmarking (to provide comparisons with external norms).

A key feature of contingent planning is allowing the process to vary from one instance to the next. The distinguishing traits are: responsiveness, forward linkage, backward linkage, and a corporate view. The continued relevance of traditional planning, and managing the process of contingent planning are discussed.

Three representative strategic plans are given to show how some of the most timely issues are currently being treated. They also demonstrate the broad range of styles in practice.

The first case, Wystan Retailing, illustrates the serial approach to planning, where a specific key issue is chosen to be the focus of planning efforts each year. The second case is Gotham Insurance. The form of contingent planning adopted by Gotham was largely to negotiate agreements on roles and responsibilities with diverse business units. The third case is Federated Manufacturing. Federated has chosen to pursue full contingent planning, where a unique set of planning modules is annually selected for each business unit.

## 3.1      STRATEGIC SYSTEMS PLANNING - A CONTINGENT APPROACH

In response to a changing business and technology environment, **strategic systems planning** is currently going through a significant transition at many companies. Traditionally a routine and somewhat bureaucratic exercise preceding the budget cycle, planning is now becoming highly visible, issue-oriented, flexible, and didactic. Companies are seeking a planning process which can be adapted to meet needs which not only vary from one year to the next, but vary considerably from one business unit or function to another. Requiring a dramatic change in roles and responsibilities for systems planners, the new approach is admittedly risky and difficult to implement. Still, the advantages of **contingent planning** make it an attractive alternative for exploiting technology in the information age.

After analyzing the reasons for the emergence of this new planning approach, an analytical framework of the type that often governs contingent planning efforts is presented here.[7] Advantages and difficulties associated with this kind of planning are weighed, and practical guidelines for developing and using a contingent planning focus are discussed. Finally, three case studies are presented to illustrate different kinds of contingent planning currently in use.

### 3.1.1      WHY CONTINGENT PLANNING?

The evolution of strategic planning for information technology is closely tied to the evolution of the technology itself. Twenty years ago, computers were used primarily for accounting, payroll, and a modest amount of repetitive and highly structured reporting. Now, of course, systems are employed for a great variety of purposes. They have insinuated themselves into the fabric of the corporation. And, to mix the metaphor, computer links have become a nervous system to transport and manage a broad variety of corporate information - voice, data and image. Serving as a basis for competitive advantage, information technology is becoming **strategic** in its business applications.

Numerous examples of firms that have begun to use information technology as a strategic weapon have been documented and discussed in business journals during the past few years. Many of these firms, such as American Hospital Supply, American Airlines, and Foremost McKesson, basically extended their order entry systems onto the customer site, placing some kind of terminal in front of their customers, making it as easy as possible for individuals to do business with their firms. Customers found that information about the product - its availability, price options - was an important element in their evaluation of the product itself. For these firms, information technology has become a crucial element in their marketing mix.

Another trend, just as significant, is that computer technology is now being deployed and controlled in a much different fashion. The single word that explains what is happening is **decentralization.** Whereas a company may have had only one computer twenty years ago, centrally operated and controlled by a data processing function, that same firm may now have hundreds, even thousands of computer systems. Systems are

---

7    This framework to help strategic planners choose a methodology that will best suit their organization is described in Cornelius Sullivan's article in the Winter 1985 edition of **Sloan Management Review.**

scattered throughout the corporation, affecting all departments and business units. Sometimes they are not under the direct control of a central authority. Functional and business unit managers have often taken a considerable degree of responsibility for the planning, development, and even the operation and maintenance of their own information systems.

Of course, the rate at which, and the extent to which, information technology is becoming strategic varies from one firm to another. The same is true for decentralization. At some companies, the levels of both strategic impact and decentralization are still low, and may remain so indefinitely. At most firms, however, there has been considerable movement.

If we label strategic impact of information technology "infusion," and call decentralization "diffusion," then high and low levels of infusion and diffusion may be taken as the determinants of several different information technology environments, as shown in **Figure 3-1, Technology Environments.**[8] Firms with low levels of both infusion and diffusion exist in what might be called a **traditional** environment. When a company finds that information technology is becoming more strategic, but is still centrally operated and controlled, then that firm is what may be called a **backbone** environment. But many firms are also experiencing decentralization. If diffusion takes place in the absence of strategic impact, then the environment may be characterized as a **federation.** Some loosely connected conglomerates fall into this category. The fourth environment, where technology is both important and scattered, is a **complex** environment. This is the most interesting one. Not only is this where many companies are headed, but high levels of infusion and diffusion may be taken as a practical working definition of the information age.

What is important to note is that the best way to plan for information technology seems to vary characteristically depending on the levels of strategic impact and decentralization. This was the finding of a research study in late 1982 and early 1983 into the factors which make planning successful at large corporations.[9] Technicians, users, and management representatives from over sixty firms were interviewed over a four month period about how they felt about the quality of their systems planning process. A variety of additional facts about the firm, its marketplace, organization, performance, and management, were also collected.

It turns out that it is not possible to say what kind of information systems planning large firms should use, or manufacturing firms, or profitable ones. Companies that liked their planning process, and thought it was successful and effective, could not be predicted on the basis of factors such as size, industry, management style, or any of several other factors.

However, there is substantial correlation between satisfaction with the planning methodology used and these twin factors of the strategic impact of technology and the degree of its decentralization. Multiple regression analysis revealed that firms tend to use a certain methodology, depending on these two variables - infusion and diffusion. This means that each systems environment - traditional, backbone, federation, and complex - has a characteristic planning technique which seems to work best.

---

[8]   Cornelius H. Sullivan, Jr., **"Systems Planning in the Information Age,"** Sloan Management Review 26:2 (Winter 1985), pp. 3-12.

[9]   **Ibid.**

Figure 3-1

## TECHNOLOGY ENVIRONMENTS

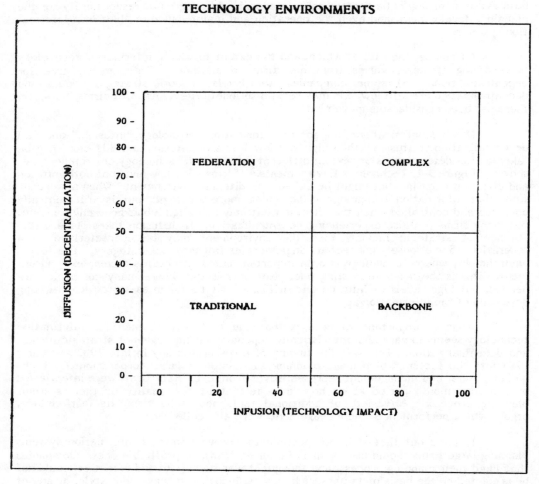

At a time when technology was of more tactical significance and centralized in the manner of its deployment, the most pressing management issue was understanding and controlling the unfamiliar enterprise of data processing. Companies were developing their first computer systems at this point, and the features and functions of those individual systems were the focus of attention. Significantly, the major systems planning process from that era, called the **stages of growth,** endeavored to make that process seem more orderly by suggesting that all firms go through a similar trajectory, or learning curve, in their attempt to identify and prioritize new applications development ideas.

With the increasing importance of information technology, a new planning idea arose. This is the notion that data, rather than computers and their applications, are the critical resource to manage. The data resource management perspective suggests that by viewing a corporation's overall storehouse of information as a key asset, it will become possible for the corporation's computer applications to share that resource and develop much better management information systems than if the data were stored in separate files.

This idea found methodological expression in the planning approach from IBM called Business Systems Planning, or BSP, which as helped to promote the idea that systems plans must be linked to business organization strategy and structure. There are many extensions and derivatives of the BSP process offered by independent consulting and accounting firms.

More recently, firms that have experienced a high degree of decentralization in their use of technology, as well as strategic impact, do not find that either the stages of growth, or BSP, is well suited to their needs. Some have turned to Jack Rockart's notion of planning based on critical success factors. This approach seems to work best at companies where technology is more decentralized that it is important.

What about the case where infusion and diffusion are both high? Under these circumstances, the information age environment, research shows that none of the major commercially available approaches does a very good job. Instead, companies in this environment are responding to a new set of issues, and devising new approaches to resolve those issues.

## 3.1.2    ISSUES

Among the many information age **issues** which strategic systems planning must begin to address are the following:

### Information Networking:

In the original strategic systems planning approaches, computers and their applications were viewed as the core of the investment in information technology. Over time, many firms have come to view data as the key resource. During this period, communications was viewed as something of an afterthought, a peripheral element in the overall investment. More recently, however, some firms are coming to see their many systems and databases as peripheral. Now it is the network that seems to be at the heart of their overall investment in technology. Accordingly, information networking has become a key issue for many systems strategies.

### Information Technology Architecture:

Diffusion of data processing, office automation, and telecommunications throughout the organization can make systems far more responsive to business needs, but the countervailing threat is that they will simultaneously become hopelessly incompatible. At most organizations, a certain degree of integration is necessary. It is generally provided through standards, utilities, and other infrastructural elements of the systems resource. Identifying the nature and extent of that necessary integration is a new job of strategic systems planners.

### End-User Computing:

Fourth generation languages, personal computers, and a growing confidence and desire among users to take responsibility for certain of their own computing needs has created a considerable challenge for information services departments. Making corporate data available to users, providing technical support to users in many different locations, establishing the procedures and guidelines that will guarantee the integrity and security of the data resource, are among the issues that the planning process has been called upon to address.

### Competitive Edge Applications:

Perhaps the most highly visible issue in planning today is the search for ways to use information technology to gain a competitive advantage. Although there are many well known cases where this has happened, there are far fewer cases where a company has been able to develop such an application in a deliberate fashion. Yet this is precisely what planners are now being asked to accomplish.

### Artificial Intelligence:

An emerging planning task is to choose areas of expertise within an organization that can be emulated with the heuristic modeling technologies and techniques of expert and advisory systems. As these systems begin to move into production mode, a host of additional management issues will come to the attention of strategic systems planners. Quite possibly, the successful exploitation and management of knowledge technologies will become one of the overriding strategic systems planning issues within the next ten to fifteen years.

## 3.1.3    STYLES

The planning processes that companies are devising to respond to these information age issues also differ from traditional planning in the **techniques** used to collect data and add value. If these techniques may be collectively called a planning "style," then it is important to point out that new planning approaches also differ from their predecessors in terms of style as well as substance.

Planning organizations have traditionally operated as a part of a control organization within a centralized data processing function. With responsibilities significantly decentralized, and with control frequently overshadowed by the desire to find creative uses for new technology, most of the new styles have lost their control focus. Three dominant styles in contingent planning are the following:

### a.    Educational:

As line managers take more responsibility for information systems, education of these "paraprofessionals" often becomes a new job for the central systems function. Frequently it is integrated into the planning function. Symposiums, seminars, workshops, clearinghouses, hot lines and help lines, computer conferences, and numerous other techniques are being incorporated into planning processes. The idea is to distribute information about the opportunities that technology offers, bring diverging points of view together for corporate purposes, and monitor advances in the field. It is a radical departure from the kind of planning that consisted of an annual distribution of a sheaf of forms, followed (at some great distance) by the publication of a voluminous summary report.

**b.   Analytical:**

Traditional systems planning processes do not consider alternatives in any systematic matter. Emerging planning approaches will now sometimes use computer models to consider a wide variety of solutions and match the capabilities of different technologies to the business needs. With this capability, planning can play a more active role in the initial stages of individual systems design.

**c.   Benchmarking:**

This style bears more resemblance to the control-oriented style of traditional systems planning processes than do the educational and analytical styles. However, an important difference is that a characteristic of the benchmarking style is to provide comparisons of performance to external norms and competitors, rather than to budgets or other internal goals. As information technology becomes more strategic to a business, a natural question for senior managers to ask is how the organization's exploitation of technology compares to that of other companies.

## 3.1.4    THE CONTINGENT PLANNING FRAMEWORK

The key fact to remember about planning in the information age is that needs will vary from one company to another. One firm may have systems in each of several hundred locations, for example, and the key planning issue is how to link them back together in a network. Another company may be particularly interested in finding a competitive use for information technology. Yet another organization may be primarily concerned with generating and analyzing new information systems application ideas.

Similarly, needs will vary from one year to the next. If a firm addresses its infrastructure one year, and makes progress, then it will be likely to focus on a different issue the following year. If one issue is introduced to a company through an educational program at first, it may be dealt with through more detailed analysis of alternatives in subsequent years. If a firm is able to resolve an issue, that issue may simply not surface at all in subsequent planning efforts.

In addition to variation from one firm to another, and changes over time, many companies are diversified enough in their use and management of technology that they will also experience significantly different needs **within** the firm, from one business unit or functional department to another. A new, but growing division will often have needs that vary considerably from those of a more established part of the business. Similarly, the manufacturing, marketing, and personnel departments will have diverging uses for information technology and, therefore, different needs for planning services.

Accommodating this diversity becomes, itself, a paramount goal of planning. No longer is it possible to assume what will be important or how to approach the planning endeavor. Rather, these questions must be answered anew each time the planning process is applied. Then, the process must be adjusted to accommodate these special needs. Otherwise, planning risks may become a burden to, rather than a facilitator of, appropriate management action.

How can strategic systems planners ensure that their efforts will accommodate these diverse needs? Any relevant framework for strategic systems planning must be based upon this new planning imperative. One consideration should be the set of systems planning issues already summarized. A second consideration should be a set of divergent planning styles such as the ones cited previously.

A third consideration pertains to the **intensity** or level of effort with which the planning endeavor is carried out. Traditional approaches not only addressed different issues from those which become paramount in the information age, and did so with a planning style that is different from what is now necessary, but also tended to be highly **structured.** The steps of the process - the set of interviews, analyses, and the format of the deliverables - were the same during each planning effort. Now an organization may want to dwell on an issue in great detail, or pass over it with only a modest amount of attention.

Taken together, the alternative issues, styles, and levels of effort constitute a new, three dimensional conceptual framework for planning in the information age. These elements of contingent planning are summarized in **Figure 3-2, Elements of Contingent Planning.** Each planning endeavor - not just each company, but each instance of planning within a firm - is likely to be a unique selection from this set of planning issues, styles, and degrees of effort.

**Figure 3-2**

### ELEMENTS OF CONTINGENT PLANNING

<u>**Information Age Issues**</u>

- Information networking
- Information technology architecture
- End-user computing
- Finding competitive advantage
- Artificial intelligence

<u>**Emerging Planning Styles**</u>

- Educational
- Analytical
- Benchmarking

<u>**Alternative Levels of Intensity**</u>

- Introductory
- Moderate
- Intense

In one instance, strategic systems planning may focus on developing an information technology architecture, and do so by carefully considering the relative merits of alternative designs in great detail. In another instance, strategic systems planning - even at the same company and in that same year - may dwell on organizational change, approaching the subject largely by holding a single conference with outside speakers discussing the human resource considerations associated with decentralizing responsibility for information systems. In yet another instance, planning may divide attention among a wide variety of management disciplines.

## 3.1.5    KEY FEATURES OF CONTINGENT PLANNING

Under these circumstances, strategic systems planning is difficult to define with precision. The whole purpose is to allow the process to vary from one instance to the next. Certainly it is far less routine and standardized than traditional planning packages. However, like all planning processes, contingent planning in practice is some combination of data collection, value-added analysis, and change management. Nevertheless, there does seem to be a set of distinguishing traits which most contingent approaches to systems planning share:

### a.  Responsive:

The hallmark of contingent planning is that it seeks to make the planning process appropriate to the needs of those for whom the planning is undertaken. This means that the issues addressed can vary, the planning techniques can be negotiated, and the extent of the planning effort can be set at a level equal to the occasion.

### b.  Forward Linkage:

Most traditional planning processes were developed prior to the advent of interest in linking systems and business planning. Contingent planning generally has a clear linkage. It is interesting to note that many contingent planning processes explicitly contradict the traditional belief that systems plans should flow from business plans and try, instead, to make the linkage a two way information exchange.

### c.  Backward Linkage:

Contingent planning should have some way tying into the more tactical layers of planning, such as long-range systems planning and operational planning.

### d.  A Corporate View:

Because contingent planning seeks to make the process as appropriate as possible for the users, it is generally necessary to have some mechanism in place to ensure that the corporation as a whole will be able to acquire and disseminate the information that it must in order to make the overall planning process a rational exercise.

### 3.1.6    THE CONTINUED RELEVANCE OF TRADITIONAL PLANNING

Are the earlier planning approaches now irrelevant?  Not at all.  Information technology may be fairly tactical at some companies, or it may be centrally managed, or both.  In these cases, the research shows that the traditional planning tools can perform well.  The primary appeal of contingent planning is the case of a company where technology is strategic in importance, and a considerable degree of decentralization has taken place.

It is also worth pointing out that each of the earlier methodologies had strong points, well worth preserving in a new planning era.  The stages of growth approach, for example, was developed by behavioral scientists.  It had a useful respect for change management.  Change management here refers to the process of unfreezing current behavior and value systems with an assessment, then developing a realistic but challenging strategy for the future, and finally refreezing behavior with tactical plans.  Unfortunately, the stages of growth in practice tended to dwell on the assessment portion of the planning process interminably:  its weakness was that it **admired** the problem.   Too often a stage assessment never moved on to the development of a strategy.

Another weakness of the stages of growth was that it tried to impose a model of how all companies would assimilate technology, rather than allow for variety and uniqueness.  In this respect, the stages of growth is the very antithesis of contingent planning.  BSP, however, took a major step in the direction of creating a model of how each organization uses technology, and tried to use that unique model to drive subsequent analysis.  Although BSP has a weakness that the stages of growth did not have (it fails to take the installed base into account before developing a strategy), BSP does recognize the uniqueness of each organization.

A strength of critical success factors planning is that it makes an effort to deal with the inter-system problems of integration and synthesis that become paramount in cases where systems have become considerably decentralized.  However, CSF planning was originally designed for individual executives, and is less successful when applied to the corporate problem of re-integration.

Although the traditional approaches fail to meet all needs in the information age, each made an advance in the practice of strategic systems planning.  These valuable lessons should be added to the new features of a contingent approach, resulting in an eclectic blend of the strengths of all ideas, an ensemble.

### 3.1.7    USING THE FRAMEWORK

The contingent planning framework is useful not only in understanding the wide variety of planning processes that the information age has begun to call forth, but can also be used as a way to structure a planning process at one particular organization.  With varying degrees of formality, some companies have endeavored to institutionalize contingent planning by following a set of basic steps similar to the following ones taken by a large manufacturing organization.

First, a set of preliminary assessment tools were developed, to pinpoint what kind of systems environment each business unit was in, or ought to be headed.   The systems environments were paired with the four business environments into which strategic business units were annually classified by the corporate planning department, producing a total of sixteen possible systems/business environments.

Next, a set of alternative planning modules and levels of effort were developed for all of the issues which the strategic planning process was charged to address. Planning modules were grouped around such categories as financial analysis, applications plans, operations, data resource management, communications, use of emerging technologies, role of corporate standards and utilities, and organizational development. Three alternative levels of effort were specified: intense, regular, and minimal.

Then a map was constructed to link each potential systems/business environment to a specific set of planning modules and levels of effort. For example, a business unit that was growing and had a high degree of technology infusion would plan more intensively for the data resource than for financial control. A rapidly growing business in a complex systems environment would focus planning effort on the development of new products and architecture. A traditional systems organization in a business unit that might be slated for divestiture would not do much at all.

After executing the preliminary departmental environmental assessments, the intermediary of the map yielded an appropriate set of planning activities that would constitute the bulk of the actual planning process. Finally, for each business unit, a planning book was assembled, distributed, and administered. As it turned out, no two businesses ended up planning in precisely the same way.

By developing the alternative planning activities at each level of effort in a modular fashion, but under a central authority, it was possible to assemble and execute a uniquely tailored planning package for each unit without sacrificing the corporation's understandable desire to keep overall tabs on the use (and cost) of information technology. Certain key indicators were summed in the end, despite the dissimilarity of the actual planning effort at different groups.

Differential planning of this kind is able to achieve the best of both worlds - it maximizes responsiveness to business and technological change throughout the corporation without sacrificing the need to see the big picture. In a word, contingent planning resolves the irony of the information age - it overcomes the gnawing fact that focused management of technology is disappearing (diffusion) just as its strategic importance is peaking (infusion).

### 3.1.8    MANAGING THE PROCESS

Contingent planning reflects the lessons of traditional approaches and frequently relies on parts of them as components of a new process. The stages of growth, BSP, and planning based on Critical Success Factors are all valuable contributions to the growing legacy of planning. However, contingent planning is very different from these traditional "packages." Combining alternative issue orientation with flexible styles, contingent planning is better suited to the needs of many corporations, particularly those where information technology has become more important and where it is decentralized in the way it is organized and managed.

In practice, the contingent approach does have its drawbacks. In particular, contingent planning places a heavy burden on the planners themselves. In cases where the planning function has been traditionally a weak portion of the control function, it is possible that new planning professionals will be needed to accomplish the difficult task of developing and executing a contingent planning process.

On balance, contingent planning appears to be a realistic approach to planning, certainly at those companies whose variety or changing business makes the standardized approaches seem too rigid and narrow. When linked to business strategies on the one hand, and to more tactical and operational systems planning on the other, the new approach can position strategic systems planning in a pivotal role in a well balanced information technology management program.

**3.2      CONTINGENT PLANNING - CASE A, WYSTAN RETAILING,**
**ISSUE FOCUSED PLANNING IN A DECENTRALIZED ENVIRONMENT**

## 3.2.1    BACKGROUND

Wystan Retailing is a large chain of over 200 stores nationwide. Most stores contain a wide variety of clothing, gifts, and housewares. Wystan also has specialty stores for shoes and sporting goods. Like many firms in its industry, its sales and profitability are volatile. However, Wystan has been expanding since the late 1970's, and plans to compete in all major metropolitan areas.

The systems organization had been a traditional functional department of the corporate office until 1983. In that year, responsibility for applications design, development, operations, and enhancement were all decentralized to a series of eight other business units and departments.

The decentralization of information systems reflected the growing role of information technology in day-to-day operations. All stores have point of sale networks, with some degree of automated inventory tracking. Wystan began to experiment with electronic order entry with major suppliers in 1982, and expects to close the loop from point of sale to merchandise ordering shortly.

By 1983, it was becoming clear at Wystan that information systems were far more crucial than they had been in the past. Wystan management endorsed the decentralization plan because it seemed to offer the best way to ensure that new information systems would be highly responsive to user department needs in this new era.

Aware of the requirements to provide a considerable amount of integration across systems serving particular business units and departments, however, senior management did not totally disband the centralized corporate systems organization. Instead, a series of corporate systems functions were collected into a new **"Corporate Systems Group" (CSG)**. These centralized functions included research and development, office automation, telecommunications, procurement engineering and contracting, and planning.

## 3.2.2    PLANNING GOALS

The traditional systems planning effort at Wystan had been bureaucratic. A set of forms were distributed annually for user managers to complete. These forms documented the application development priorities for the coming year. Systems managers estimated costs associated with each development effort, and the planning group summarized the information for review by a steering committee. Consisting of representatives from each user department, the committee was charged with allocating the budgeted resources of the systems department for the coming year. Generally about one half of the projects were assigned each year. The others were deferred.

After decentralization, the traditional mission of the planning group became less important. Each department or business unit was free to spend as much on new development as was consistent with its business priorities. Furthermore, the new planning group was quite small. Beginning with only one manager and one staff analyst, the planning unit lacked the resources to coordinate and manage a complex annual planning process effectively.

Rather than risk doing a superficial job of traditional planning, the new planning group developed a set of planning goals consistent with the emerging mission of the CSG. Initially, these goals were the following:

1.    Develop a list of corporate planning issues, and make each business unit aware of these issues. Each planning issue should be chosen on the basis of its importance to the business and its corporate scope.

2.    Select one overriding issue each year for the corporation's focus of attention.

3.    Develop and execute an appropriate planning response for that issue.

## 3.2.3    APPROACH

### STEP 1:  Planning Issue Canvass

Informal discussions with business and systems managers throughout the corporation are relied upon each year to produce a list of candidate issues. A form is then produced, listing those issues and asking participants in the canvass to rank the importance of each. For each issue, participants are also asked whether the issue has been satisfactorily dealt with so far, and what planning assistance, if any, is appropriate for the corporate planning unit to consider providing. See **Figure 3-3, 1986 Wystan Retailing Planning Canvass.** The results of the canvass are given in **Figure 3-4, 1986 Wystan Retailing Planning Canvass, Summary of Results.**

### STEP 2:  Choosing The Annual Planning Issue

Results of the canvass are analyzed to answer the following questions:

•    What planning issues do business and systems managers feel are most important to consider?

•    What issues have not been adequately addressed by individual units on their own?

•    What issues do business and systems managers feel is appropriate for the corporate planning unit to address?

The analysis should lead to a recommended planning focus for the coming year. If no single issue emerges from this analysis, the planning unit has the option of recommending to pursue more than one issue, or it may ask its oversight committee to help it to choose one issue to pursue. During the three years that this planning process has been in operation, Wystan has focused on the issues of data resource management, personal computing, and telecommunications.

Figure 3-3
(Page 1 of 4)

## 1986 WYSTAN RETAILING PLANNING CANVASS

**Department:** _____

**Form Completed by:** _____

**Date:** _____

### PLEASE RANK EACH CANDIDATE ISSUE

**ISSUE #1:** **Distributed Database Administration**

    **a.** Importance of this issue to your unit:
      ___ Not an issue ___ Minimal ___ Moderate ___Crucial

    **b.** Extent of previous planning efforts:
      ___ None ___ Recognized ___ Moderate Progress ___ Resolved

    **c.** How appropriate is corporate assistance?
      ___ Not ___ Acceptable ___ Desirable ___ Highly desirable

**ISSUE #2:** **Information Centers**

    **a.** Importance of this issue to your unit:
      ___ Not an issue ___ Minimal ___ Moderate ___Crucial

    **b.** Extent of previous planning efforts:
      ___ None ___ Recognized ___ Moderate Progress ___ Resolved

    **c.** How appropriate is corporate assistance?
      ___ Not ___ Acceptable ___ Desirable ___ Highly desirable

**ISSUE #3:** **Packet Switching And Developing A Corporate Network**

    **a.** Importance of this issue to your unit:
      ___ Not an issue ___ Minimal ___ Moderate ___Crucial

    **b.** Extent of previous planning efforts:
      ___ None ___ Recognized ___ Moderate Progress ___ Resolved

    **c.** How appropriate is corporate assistance?
      ___ Not ___ Acceptable ___ Desirable ___ Highly desirable

**ISSUE #4:** **New Office Automation Technologies**

    **a.** Importance of this issue to your unit:
      ___ Not an issue ___ Minimal ___ Moderate ___Crucial

    **b.** Extent of previous planning efforts:
      ___ None ___ Recognized ___ Moderate Progress ___ Resolved

    **c.** How appropriate is corporate assistance?
      ___ Not ___ Acceptable ___ Desirable ___ Highly desirable

**Figure 3-3**
**(Page 2 of 4)**

### 1986 WYSTAN RETAILING PLANNING CANVASS

Department: _____

Form Completed by: _____

Date: _____

### PLEASE RANK EACH CANDIDATE ISSUE

**ISSUE #5:**   **Productivity Tools For Systems Professionals**

    **a.**   Importance of this issue to your unit:
      ___ Not an issue   ___ Minimal   ___ Moderate   ___Crucial

    **b.**   Extent of previous planning efforts:
      ___ None   ___ Recognized   ___ Moderate Progress   ___ Resolved

    **c.**   How appropriate is corporate assistance?
      ___ Not   ___ Acceptable   ___ Desirable   ___ Highly desirable

**ISSUE #6:**   **Point of Sale System Enhancements**

    **a.**   Importance of this issue to your unit:
      ___ Not an issue   ___ Minimal   ___ Moderate   ___Crucial

    **b.**   Extent of previous planning efforts:
      ___ None   ___ Recognized   ___ Moderate Progress   ___ Resolved

    **c.**   How appropriate is corporate assistance?
      ___ Not   ___ Acceptable   ___ Desirable   ___ Highly desirable

**ISSUE #7:**   **Electronic Order Entry and Data Links To Suppliers**

    **a.**   Importance of this issue to your unit:
      ___ Not an issue   ___ Minimal   ___ Moderate   ___Crucial

    **b.**   Extent of previous planning efforts:
      ___ None   ___ Recognized   ___ Moderate Progress   ___ Resolved

    **c.**   How appropriate is corporate assistance?
      ___ Not   ___ Acceptable   ___ Desirable   ___ Highly desirable

**ISSUE #8:**   **Using Systems For Competitive Advantage**

    **a.**   Importance of this issue to your unit:
      ___ Not an issue   ___ Minimal   ___ Moderate   ___Crucial

    **b.**   Extent of previous planning efforts:
      ___ None   ___ Recognized   ___ Moderate Progress   ___ Resolved

    **c.**   How appropriate is corporate assistance?
      ___ Not   ___ Acceptable   ___ Desirable   ___ Highly desirable

Figure 3-3
(Page 3 of 4)

## 1986 WYSTAN RETAILING PLANNING CANVASS

Department: _____

Form Completed by: _____

Date: _____

### PLEASE RANK EACH CANDIDATE ISSUE

**ISSUE #9:**   **Telecommunications Systems For Individual Stores**

    **a.**  Importance of this issue to your unit:
      ___ Not an issue    ___ Minimal    ___ Moderate    ___Crucial

    **b.**  Extent of previous planning efforts:
      ___ None    ___ Recognized    ___ Moderate Progress    ___ Resolved

    **c.**  How appropriate is corporate assistance?
      ___ Not    ___ Acceptable    ___ Desirable    ___ Highly desirable

**ISSUE #10:**   **Store Management Systems**

    **a.**  Importance of this issue to your unit:
      ___ Not an issue    ___ Minimal    ___ Moderate    ___Crucial

    **b.**  Extent of previous planning efforts:
      ___ None    ___ Recognized    ___ Moderate Progress    ___ Resolved

    **c.**  How appropriate is corporate assistance?
      ___ Not    ___ Acceptable    ___ Desirable    ___ Highly desirable

**ISSUE #11:**   **Opportunities In Artificial Intelligence**

    **a.**  Importance of this issue to your unit:
      ___ Not an issue    ___ Minimal    ___ Moderate    ___Crucial

    **b.**  Extent of previous planning efforts:
      ___ None    ___ Recognized    ___ Moderate Progress    ___ Resolved

    **c.**  How appropriate is corporate assistance?
      ___ Not    ___ Acceptable    ___ Desirable    ___ Highly desirable

**ISSUE #12:**   **Store Security Systems**

    **a.**  Importance of this issue to your unit:
      ___ Not an issue    ___ Minimal    ___ Moderate    ___Crucial

    **b.**  Extent of previous planning efforts:
      ___ None    ___ Recognized    ___ Moderate Progress    ___ Resolved

    **c.**  How appropriate is corporate assistance?
      ___ Not    ___ Acceptable    ___ Desirable    ___ Highly desirable

**Figure 3-3**
**(Page 4 of 4)**

### 1986 WYSTAN RETAILING PLANNING CANVASS

**Department:** _____

**Form Completed by:** _____

**Date:** _____

### PLEASE RANK EACH CANDIDATE ISSUE

**OTHER ISSUE:** _____

    **a.** Importance of this issue to your unit:
        ___ Not an issue   ___ Minimal   ___ Moderate   ___Crucial

    **b.** Extent of previous planning efforts:
        ___ None   ___ Recognized   ___ Moderate Progress   ___ Resolved

    **c.** How appropriate is corporate assistance?
        ___ Not   ___ Acceptable   ___ Desirable   ___ Highly desirable

**OTHER ISSUE:** _____

    **a.** Importance of this issue to your unit:
        ___ Not an issue   ___ Minimal   ___ Moderate   ___Crucial

    **b.** Extent of previous planning efforts:
        ___ None   ___ Recognized   ___ Moderate Progress   ___ Resolved

    **c.** How appropriate is corporate assistance?
        ___ Not   ___ Acceptable   ___ Desirable   ___ Highly desirable

**Figure 3-4**
**(Page 1 of 2)**

### 1986 WYSTAN RETAILING PLANNING CANVASS
### SUMMARY OF RESULTS - 29 RESPONSES

**(THE RECOMMENDED ISSUE FOR 1986 PLANNING IS ISSUE #8)**

**ISSUE #1:**    **Distributed Database Administration**

| | | |
|---|---|---|
| Importance rating | (Scale 1-4): | 2.3 |
| Status | (Scale 1-4): | 1.4 |
| Desire for assistance | (Scale 1-4): | 2.6 |

**ISSUE #2:**    **Information Centers**

| | | |
|---|---|---|
| Importance rating | (Scale 1-4): | 3.5 |
| Status | (Scale 1-4): | 3.1 |
| Desire for assistance | (Scale 1-4): | 2.2 |

**ISSUE #3:**    **Packet Switching And Developing A Corporate Network**

| | | |
|---|---|---|
| Importance rating | (Scale 1-4): | 2.5 |
| Status | (Scale 1-4): | 1.1 |
| Desire for assistance | (Scale 1-4): | 2.3 |

**ISSUE #4:**    **New Office Automation Technologies**

| | | |
|---|---|---|
| Importance rating | (Scale 1-4): | 2.7 |
| Status | (Scale 1-4): | 3.0 |
| Desire for assistance | (Scale 1-4): | 2.5 |

**ISSUE #5:**    **Productivity Tools For Systems Professionals**

| | | |
|---|---|---|
| Importance rating | (Scale 1-4): | 2.0 |
| Status | (Scale 1-4): | 2.4 |
| Desire for assistance | (Scale 1-4): | 1.8 |

**ISSUE #6:**    **Point Of Sale System Enhancements**

| | | |
|---|---|---|
| Importance rating | (Scale 1-4): | 3.4 |
| Status | (Scale 1-4): | 2.7 |
| Desire for assistance | (Scale 1-4): | 2.7 |

Figure 3-4
(Page 2 of 2)

### 1986 WYSTAN RETAILING PLANNING CANVASS
### SUMMARY OF RESULTS - 29 RESPONSES

**(THE RECOMMENDED ISSUE FOR 1986 PLANNING IS ISSUE #8)**

**ISSUE #7:**   **Electronic Order Entry And Data Links To Suppliers**

| | | |
|---|---|---|
| Importance rating | (Scale 1-4): | 3.5 |
| Status | (Scale 1-4): | 2.1 |
| Desire for assistance | (Scale 1-4): | 3.4 |

**ISSUE #8:**   **Using Systems For Competitive Advantage**

| | | |
|---|---|---|
| Importance rating | (Scale 1-4): | 3.6 |
| Status | (Scale 1-4): | 1.6 |
| Desire for assistance | (Scale 1-4): | 3.7 |

**ISSUE #9:**   **Telecommunications Systems For Individual Stores**

| | | |
|---|---|---|
| Importance rating | (Scale 1-4): | 2.1 |
| Status | (Scale 1-4): | 1.4 |
| Desire for assistance | (Scale 1-4): | 1.2 |

**ISSUE #10:**   **Store Management Systems**

| | | |
|---|---|---|
| Importance rating | (Scale 1-4): | 1.3 |
| Status | (Scale 1-4): | 1.3 |
| Desire for assistance | (Scale 1-4): | 1.4 |

**ISSUE #11:**   **Opportunities In Artificial Intelligence**

| | | |
|---|---|---|
| Importance rating | (Scale 1-4): | 2.2 |
| Status | (Scale 1-4): | 1.0 |
| Desire for assistance | (Scale 1-4): | 1.8 |

**ISSUE #12:**   **Store Security Systems**

| | | |
|---|---|---|
| Importance rating | (Scale 1-4): | 2.7 |
| Status | (Scale 1-4): | 3.1 |
| Desire for assistance | (Scale 1-4): | 2.0 |

**(No other issues were mentioned by more than one respondent)**

### STEP 3: Developing The Planning Response

Once an issue has been selected, a unique planning response must be developed. The planning activities for the following year are always highly dependent on the nature of that specific issue, work-to-date on that issue, and the kind of planning activities that business and systems managers feel is appropriate for that issue. Sometimes the planning unit will restrict itself to providing educational materials, but it frequently endeavors to help the business units develop a common strategy for resolving the issue.

## 3.2.4    DELIVERABLES

Each year, the planning unit commits itself to the following deliverables:

a.    **Corporate Issue Canvass:**    Each business unit is asked for its sense of the key planning issues for the coming year.

b.    **Analysis of Canvass Results, With Recommendation:**    Here a key planning issue is selected.

c.    **A Program Plan for the Selected Issue:**    The planning response to the selected issue is developed.

d.    **Execution of the Program Plan:**    The planning response is provided to each business unit.

In addition to these annual new deliverables, the results of previous planning cycles are collected into a workbook. The workbook is provided as part of an orientation package to new employees. On some occasions, the process from a previous year is used again at a newly formed or recently acquired business unit.

## 3.2.5    ILLUSTRATION

The best way to describe the planning process at Wystan is by using the illustration of a recent planning cycle. In 1986, the "call" for planning issue priorities was issued in May to a total of 29 managers. The form in **Figure 3-3** was used for the canvass. A dozen planning issues were included on the form, and space provided to add new issues.

The canvass produced data on key issues, their current status at Wystan, and opinions about what assistance line managers felt was appropriate for the corporate organization to provide. This information was summarized for management consumption in the table in **Figure 3-4**. Analysis of results led the planning unit to recommend the issue of achieving competitive advantage with information systems to be the focus of corporate planning for 1987. This idea was presented to unit managers in September of 1986, and approval for this focus of attention was obtained.

Research into the ways that other companies dealt with this interesting issue showed that most firms were at the point where senior managers were being educated about the opportunity. Some were currently trying to implement new systems that would provide competitive edge. Many of the pioneers in the field had actually not relied on planning to reach this new goal. In fact, in many cases, the pioneers had really been trying to accomplish something else. Some of the firms which had created new electronic links with customers were actually only trying to get their customers to enter data for them and take responsibility for its accuracy.

Considering that Wystan management was already familiar with the need to pursue competitive advantage with information technology, it did not seem appropriate to limit the planning process to educational efforts. Yet the objective at Wystan was quite different from the objectives of the pioneers. Those companies had achieved their competitive edge almost accidentally, as a byproduct of other objectives. Wystan's overt goals was to look deliberately for a new technology or application that could provide an advantage in their industry.

The way that the planning unit pursued this objective was with a technique they called "reasoning by analogy." The planning unit first collected a large number of documented case histories or examples of competitive edge systems in all industries. Next the planning unit profiled the precise circumstances that made each application "work" for that firm. For example, if one application only made sense because the company's customers needed to track orders and wanted their supplier to reveal its inventory position on all products, then those factors became part of the profile for that application.

The overall list of factors for all cases was then shared with each unit of Wystan Retailing in a series of workshops. These sessions also tried to document the critical success factors of each unit. The critical success factors of each unit were then compared to those underlying each "success story." In certain cases, there existed a close match between the needs of a Wystan Unit and the circumstance facing one of the companies that had been a pioneer in achieving competitive advantage with a certain information technology.

These close fits were highlighted for management review. In each case, it was possible to explain at length just why it seemed to make sense to emulate a pioneer. The profile comparison also revealed the subtle differences faced by the pioneer and the Wystan unit. Generally, the pioneer was in a totally different industry, so there was still an opportunity to be first in retailing with an analogous system.

The standard workshop agenda may be found in **Figure 3-5, Wystan Retailing, Competitive Advantage Planning Workshop Agenda.** Some of the workshop sessions failed to produce clear commitment to pursue a new application. Others led to several ideas, but ones that were not necessarily truly strategic in impact. One of the most productive sessions led immediately to a major development project for a retail demand forecasting model. Significantly, the application was not precisely the same as the one originally uncovered by the corporate planning unit's process of reasoning by analogy, but user management still credited the process with being the original inspiration for their idea.

Figure 3-5

## WYSTAN RETAILING
## COMPETITIVE ADVANTAGE PLANNING WORKSHOP
## AGENDA

8:15 a.m.    **Introduction**
- Includes discussion of purpose and objectives of this meeting.

8:30 a.m.    **Pioneers In Competitive Advantage**
- Survey of cases and their critical success factors.

10:00 a.m.    **Coffee Break**

10:30 a.m.    **Business Unit Critical Success Factors**
- Roundtable discussion of the factors at this Wystan business unit that would lead to competitive advantage.

12:00 noon    **Lunch**

1:30 p.m.    **Analysis Of Close "Fits"**
- Which cases have profiles that closely resemble the situation at Wystan?

2:30 p.m.    **Coffee Break**

3:00 p.m.    **Discussion Of Candidate Applications**
- How many close "fits" are realistic and desirable to pursue?

4:00 p.m.    **Action Items**
- Next steps - Commitment building

4:30 p.m.    **Adjourn**

**3.3    CONTINGENT PLANNING - CASE B, GOTHAM INSURANCE GROUP,
        ORGANIZATIONAL DEVELOPMENT**

### 3.3.1    BACKGROUND

Gotham Insurance Group is a large multi-line carrier.  Although affected by the industry-wide downturn in profits, particularly in property/casualty operations, Gotham remains profitable, and anticipates growth.  Nevertheless, Gotham is aware of the fact that the broader financial services industry is changing, and expects its traditional businesses to be changed to a considerable extent.

A new Chief Executive initiated a business planning task force in 1983.  After several months of study, the task force recommended no drastic changes in products.  However, the task force members concluded that the market would continue to be very competitive, with low mark-ups.  Service and product innovation appeared to be the keys to non-price competition.  The single most important factor in winning new business or retaining existing accounts appeared to be responsiveness to the customer.  The task force also suggested more unbundled services, and innovative arrangements with third parties, including other financial institutions, retail establishments, and franchise operations.

The major recommendation of the task force was to make a corporate transition from a product orientation to a customer focus.  This seemed necessary to be able to differentiate the company's product from the competition, solidify relationships with customers, and become more responsive to marketplace needs.  Two key elements of this strategy were organizational change and information systems.

Traditionally, insurance companies have had two classes of line professionals.  Field agents have been customer-oriented, but had no responsibility or authority to make underwriting decisions.  Home office underwriters, on the other hand, have been analysts who made financial commitments, but had little or no contact with the marketplace.  So ingrained has this tradition been in insurance that personality stereotypes have even grown up around these two categories of professional employees (Field agents are former football players with firm handshakes who joined the company right after college; underwriters are introverted statisticians with spectacles and advanced degrees).

Like all stereotypes, these were largely false, yet the historical organizational dichotomy did, in fact, exist at Gotham.  The task force recommended a major change here through the creation of a new job called the field underwriter.  Also known facetiously as the "renaissance man," because of his or her versatility (firm handshake **and** MBA degree), this field underwriter would call on customers, but would also be authorized to underwrite several classes of insurance.  Complex or unusual policies would still be sent to the home office for underwriting review by "desk underwriter" specialists.  Each field underwriter would have complete responsibility for a set of customer or supplier relationships.

Besides the amalgamation of field and home office functions, the other major operational change implied by the new strategy was a different systems philosophy.  Information systems at Gotham had always been a centralized corporate staff function.  Although numerous systems were now on-line, the basic operating mode was little changed from the days when claims and other transactions were processed  in batches.

This meant that most transactions, such as applications for insurance and claims forms, were all sent to corporate headquarters. Outputs, such as policies and payment authorizations, were sent after processing from headquarters back to the field. Communications between the field and headquarters was vast, yet the communication technology relied upon for most of this information movement was the U. S. Mail.

The task force identified automation as a key marketing opportunity, but recommended that each field underwriter be equipped with a full function management workstation. This workstation should be tied to all systems needed for marketing, sales, claims, renewals, and other aspects of customer relationships for all product lines handled by the field underwriter. In effect, the goal was to equip the field underwriter with access to all processing power now available to home office personnel. Users in the field would view a single processing system.

## 3.3.2   PLANNING GOALS

Needless to say, this business strategy was a radical departure of the Information Services Department. In discussions with their users, it appeared that different departments and units of the company were planning to proceed at widely varying rates of speed toward the goal of field underwriting. Not all processing systems were currently set up to accommodate long distance networking with users. Additionally, the Information Services Department found that different user areas planned to implement the field underwriter concept differently. One group expected to use all existing systems, and simply access them remotely. Another group planned to migrate to totally new applications specifically designed to accommodate the field underwriter.

Although the business needs, preferred rates of change, and technical competence of different units varied, the overriding corporate need of Gotham Insurance was to develop a common interface between the home office and the field in a coherent fashion and without interrupting day-to-day operations. The systems planning challenge was, therefore, to orchestrate this corporate migration. More specifically, its goals were the following:

a. Coordinate the interdepartmental effort to specify the field underwriter workstation and communications network.

b. Identify those tasks which would remain the responsibility of the corporate Information Services area.

c. Identify those tasks which would become the responsibility of separate departments.

d. Assist in negotiating an annual agreement on objectives and changing responsibilities.

### 3.3.3    APPROACH

Several concurrent and interwoven planning tasks had to be pursued:

a.    Systems planning took overall responsibility for the technical job of specifying the field underwriter workstation and its associated architecture.  The workstation and its local database and telecommunications capabilities were viewed by all applications as standardized utilities.

b.    The planning group also developed an extensive task list and responsibility matrix.  The task list broke down the overall field underwriter support effort into several hundred discrete activities.  The responsibility matrix showed what organizational unit would be responsible for the activity, or would contribute to it, approve it, or be kept informed of progress toward completion of the activity.   A pert chart was also created to show the interrelationship and dependencies of these activities.

c.    Working with different corporate systems units, as well as the business units, the planning group helped to negotiate agreement on roles and responsibilities for all activities on the task list.

d.    The planning group provided or made arrangements to provide assistance to business units taking on new systems responsibilities.  One technique that the planning group used successfully was a series of workshops on systems management disciplines.

e.    The planning group established milestones for the overall field underwriter project, and monitored achievements by all organizational units.   Recommendations were made in a series of memos to correct signs of uneven or incompatible development.


### 3.3.4    DELIVERABLES

The corporate systems planning group developed and maintained the following tangible deliverables:

●    Master Task and Responsibility Worksheet

●    Completed Worksheets for each business unit

●    Signed Systems/User Contracts

●    Updated Gotham Insurance Field Underwriter Architecture and Migration Plan Summary

●    Management Disciplines Workshops

●    Progress Reports to management

### 3.3.5 RESULTS

The field underwriter workstation and systems architecture were specified, a variety of projects needed to migrate to that environment were initiated, and several applications are now complete. Others are scheduled for implementation over the next two years.

At least as important as these systems developments efforts, however, has been the organizational change throughout Gotham Insurance Group. Virtually all business units are now better informed and more active participants in information technology management. As the president of Gotham put it, "The field underwriter project served as a catalyst for line managers to take responsibility for their systems. The result has been better systems, better operations, better products, and better service to customers."

In order to achieve these results, the systems planning group relied on a full array of new planning styles. Organizing workshops on systems management disciplines, the planning group used an educational planning style. Designing workstations and interfaces for the corporation, the planning group used an analytical style. Monitoring and reporting implementation progress in different business units, the planning unit also used a benchmarking style. Only by using this versatile set of techniques were their goals achievable.

**3.4      CONTINGENT PLANNING – CASE C, FEDERATED MANUFACTURING CORP., MODULAR PLANNING SERVICES**

### 3.4.1    BACKGROUND

Federated Manufacturing is a diversified manufacturer of heavy equipment and chemicals. Its largest business units include trucks, military equipment, agriculture fertilizer, and petrochemicals. Federated has grown rapidly over the past fifteen years, partly through internal growth, but also because of an active program of acquisitions. However, Federated is also becoming equally active in divestitures. Five units have been sold over a five year period.

Federated's senior management read a series of articles in Harvard Business Review and Sloan Management Review about the ability of information technology to change business competition. Based on the strength of those arguments, Federated management decided to solicit input from its Information Systems division into its business planning process. This responsibility was then assigned to the Information Systems Planning Department.

### 3.4.2    PLANNING GOALS

The immediate goal of the Planning Department was to satisfy the senior management request for information and participation in the business planning process. However, a longer term goal was to forge an ongoing linkage between systems planning and business planning. The difficulty that the Planning Department anticipated was that different business units of Federated had such widely varying needs that the linkage might become too generic to be particularly valuable to any one group.

### 3.4.3    APPROACH

For the first goal – education – the Planning Department quickly provided a brief set of readings and case study materials for senior managers to use in order to gain more insight about how other companies are making strategic use of information technology. Only articles written for general management audiences were chosen. This reading list may be found in **Figure 3-6, Information Technology Management.**

The Planning Department followed up with a series of technology briefings for line managers. Here the dual objective was to supply information about new technologies that might be of interest to a particular business unit, along with an opportunity to discuss the role that information technology should play in helping the unit achieve its goals. The typical agenda for one of the briefings may be found in **Figure 3-7, Federated Manufacturing Corporation, Technology Awareness Briefing.**

To meet the longer term goal of assisting Federated's diverse business units in their systems planning, the Planning Department decided to begin by performing an initial assessment on each business unit. The purpose of this quiz was to find out how, in general terms, each unit used and managed information technology.

Figure 3-6

## INFORMATION TECHNOLOGY MANAGEMENT

### Introductory Publications For A General Management Audience

Michael E. Porter and Victor E. Millar, **"How Information Gives You Competitive Advantage,"** Harvard Business Review (July - August 1985), pp. 149-160.

John Wyman, **"Technical Myopia - The Need to Think Strategically About Technology,"** Sloan Management Review 26:4 (Summer 1985), pp. 59-64.

Robert E. Cole, **"Target Information for Competitive Advantage,"** Harvard Business Review (May-June 1985), pp. 100-109.

James I. Cash and Benn R. Konsynski, **"IS Redraws Competitive Boundaries,"** Harvard Business Review (March-April 1985), pp. 134-142.

John Naisbitt and Patricia Abudrene, **"Re-inventing the Corporation: Transforming Your Job and Your Company for the New Information Society,"** New York: Warner Books, 1985).

John F. Rockart and Adam D. Crescenzi, **"Engaging Top Management in Information Technology,"** Sloan Management Review 25:4 (Summer 1984), pp. 3-16.

F. Warren McFarlan, **"Information Technology Changes the Way you Compete,"** Harvard Business Review (May-June 1984), pp. 98-103.

Robert I. Benjamin, John F. Rockart, Michael S. Scott Morton, and John Wyman, **"Information Technology: A Strategic Opportunity,"** Sloan Management Review 25:3 (Spring 1984), pp. 3-10.

Gregory L. Parson, **"Information Technology: A New Competitive Weapon,"** Sloan Management Review 25:1 (Fall 1983), pp. 3-13.

F. Warren McFarlan, James L. McKenney, and Philip Pyburn, **"The Information Archipelago - Plotting A Course,"** Harvard Business Review (January-February 1983), pp. 145-156.

Brandt Allen, **"An Unmanaged Computer System Can Stop You Dead,"** Harvard Business Review 60:6 (November - December 1982), pp. 77-87.

Daniel Bell, **"Communications Technology - For Better or for Worse,"** Harvard Business Review (May-June 1979), pp. 20-42.

Cornelius H. Sullivan, Jr., **"Systems Planning in the Information Age,"** Sloan Management Review 26:2 (Winter 1985).

Figure 3-7

### FEDERATED MANUFACTURING CORPORATION
### TECHNOLOGY AWARENESS BRIEFING
### AGENDA

| | |
|---|---|
| 8:30  a.m. | Introduction - Objectives |
| 8:45  a.m. | Recent trends in information technology |
| 10:00  a.m. | Coffee Break |
| 10:15  a.m. | Current uses of emerging technologies in other industries, and by competitors |
| 11:00  a.m. | Future developments in advanced technology |
| 11:30  a.m. | Potential applications at Federated Manufacturing |
| 12:00  noon | Lunch |
| 1:00  p.m. | Roundtable discussion - Applications |
| 2:30  p.m. | Action Plan |

This was accomplished with the preliminary environmental assessment package that may be found in **Figure 3-8, Preliminary Environmental Assessment.** This assessment package enabled Federated systems planners to plot each business unit in terms of how important information technology was to the business **(infusion),** and how decentralized its operation and management of technology had become **(diffusion).** The results are shown in **Figure 3-9, Preliminary Environmental Assessment Results.**

Not surprisingly, different Federated units appeared in all quadrants of the resulting infusion/diffusion was **(See Figure 3-9, Page 6).** The planning group was working on the theory that key planning issues in each of the quadrants would vary. For example, units in a traditional environment (low infusion/low diffusion) tend to focus on managing the computer resource efficiently, while units in the backbone quadrant (high infusion/low diffusion) generally are beginning to focus on the data resource. Decision support systems are frequently a key issue in the federation environment, while networking and architecture predominate in the complex quadrant. Knowing which quadrant a business unit falls into enables the Planning Department to tailor its offerings appropriately.

The next step was to decide that kind of planning made the most sense for units in each quadrant. Because some businesses were growing fast, others were stable but profitable, and still others were slated for divestiture, the Planning Department solicited information from the business planners about the status of each unit. This enabled the systems planners to categorize the intensity of planning that was warranted for each unit.

**Figure 3-8**
**(Page 1 of 7)**

### FEDERATED MANUFACTURING CORPORATION

### PRELIMINARY ENVIRONMENT ASSESSMENT
### INFUSION/DIFFUSION QUESTIONNAIRE

As computers and information technology become more integral to business operations, and users become more comfortable with the technology, systems architecture and applications become increasingly idiosyncratic to each organization. Planning for more effective use of technology under these circumstances must, therefore, be modified or tailored to unique and specialized needs.

Studies have shown that the kind of information systems planning that works best in an organization is closely related to answers to the following two fundamental questions:

  1.  **How strategic are information systems and technology to the business?**

  2.  **How decentralized or dispersed is the deployment and control of the technology?**

The attached environment assessment questionnaire is a way of identifying or documenting answers to these questions. Responses to questions about the strategic importance of information systems, and responses to questions about decentralization of systems, are tallied to provide the basis for a plot of an organization's position on a two-dimensional matrix. The assessment, for example, may tell us that an organization makes strategic use of computers, but that the deployment and control of them is highly centralized. This is the "Factory" environment on the matrix. Each quadrant of the matrix has certain management issues associated with it, and a most appropriate planning response.

The intent of this preliminary assessment is to provide useful input to the subsequent planning process - it helps us to differentiate our approach in an appropriate manner. Additionally, the exercise can be conducted from different points of view. For example, different parts of the organization can be separately rated. When each function or business unit is plotted, the diversity of the organization becomes clear. Likewise, a company and its competition can be compared, or a company's position today can be compared to its position at some point in the past, or to some goals it sets for itself in the future.

**Figure 3-8**
**(Page 2 of 7)**

### PRELIMINARY ENVIRONMENT ASSESSMENT

**The purpose of this questionnaire is to gather data about your organization's information systems environment. It will help determine what kind and extent of strategic planning for information systems is most appropriate for the organization.**

-------------------------------------------------------------------------------

1. What is the current (fully loaded) expenditure on information systems as a percentage of sales? Include data processing, office automation, and communications.

   3% _____    3%-7% _____    7%-11% _____    11%-15% _____    15% _____

2. What is the expenditure of new systems development as a percentage of the total systems budget?

   10% _____    11%-20% _____    21%-30% _____    31%-40% _____    40% _____

3. To whom does the senior Information Systems executive report?

   To Middle Mgmt. _____    To Divisional Mgmt. _____    To Senior Mgmt. _____

4. On a scale of 1 to 5 (1 is weak and 5 is strong), rate the strength at your firm of the following arguments for automation:

   _____    Reduce costs
   _____    Increase productivity
   _____    Differentiate or improve products and services.
   _____    Support new forms of organizational design, such as matrix management, or more decentralized field support.

5. Characterize your firm's overall stance toward new information technologies (Check one):

   _____    Conservative (wait and see)
   _____    Actively monitor (occasionally test)
   _____    Actively test and prototype
   _____    Try anything and everything

6. How much of the total systems effort is devoted to direct support for products and services?

   10% _____    11%-20% _____    21%-30% _____    31%-40% _____    40% _____

Figure 3-8
(Page 3 of 7)

## PRELIMINARY ENVIRONMENT ASSESSMENT

7. How much of the total systems effort is devoted to conventional support, such as payroll and accounting?

    40% _____    30%-39% _____    20%-29% _____    10%19% _____    10% _____

8. How many business units or functional areas at your company have responsibility for their own systems design, development, and operations? (Check one range on each line).

    **Design:**

    20% _____    20%-39% _____    40%-60% _____    61%-80% _____    80% _____

    **Development:**

    20% _____    20%-39% _____    40%-60% _____    61%-80% _____    80% _____

    **Operations:**

    20% _____    20%-39% _____    40%-60% _____    61%-80% _____    80% _____

9. What proportion of total company computing is done on mainframes?

    80% _____    61%-80% _____    40%-60% _____    20%-39% _____    20% _____

10. What is the current annual growth rate of personal computers and desktop professional workstations at your firm?

    20% _____    20%-39% _____    40%-60% _____    61%-80% _____    80% _____

11. What is the current annual growth rate of word processors:

    20% _____    20%-39% _____    40%-60% _____    61%-80% _____    80% _____

12. On a scale of 1 to 5 (where 1 means negligible and 5 means crucial), how important are the following technologies to your business?

    _____    Office Automation
    _____    CAD/CAM, Process Automation, Robotics
    _____    Laboratory and Scientific Computing
    _____    Point of Sale, Other Transaction Devices

**Figure 3-8**
**(Page 4 of 7)**

### PRELIMINARY ENVIRONMENT ASSESSMENT

#### Scoring The Environment Assessment

The completed assessment should contain twenty answers. The first ten answers pertain to the strategic impact of information systems and technology (Questions 1 through 7). The second ten answers pertain to the deployment or diffusion of technology (Questions 8 through 12).

Each answer can be directly or indirectly assigned a value ranging from 1 to 5. The circled numbers on the attached "Scoring Guidelines" show what value to assign to an answer to each question. Maximum infusion or diffusion, after multiplying by 2, is 100.

The following worksheet can help tabulate the infusion and diffusion scores:

| Infusion | | Diffusion | |
|---|---|---|---|
| Question | Score | Question | Score |
| 1 | | 8a | |
| 2 | | 8b | |
| 3 | | 8c | |
| 4a | | 9 | |
| 4b | | 10 | |
| 4c | | 11 | |
| 4d | | 12a | |
| 5 | | 12b | |
| 6 | | 12c | |
| 7 | | 12d | |
| Total Score: | | Total Score: | |
| X 2 | | X 2 | |
| Total Infusion: | | Total Diffusion: | |

Now plot these scores on the attached matrix. Infusion, the strategic impact of technology, is plotted on the x-axis. The quadrant in which the organization falls can be used as a guideline for shaping the subsequent strategic planning process.

**Figure 3-8**
**(Page 5 of 7)**

## PRELIMINARY ENVIRONMENT ASSESSMENT

### SCORING GUIDELINES

The purpose of this questionnaire is to gather data about your organization's information systems environment. It will help determine what kind and extent of strategic planning for information systems is most appropriate for the organization.

--------------------------------------------------------------------------------

1. What is the current (fully loaded) expenditure on information systems as a percentage of sales? Include data processing, office automation, and communications.

   3% ①   3-7% ②   7-11% ③   11-15% ④   15% ⑤

2. What is the expenditure of new systems development as a percentage of the total systems budget?

   10% ①   11-20% ②   21-30% ③   31-40% ④   40% ⑤

3. To whom does the senior information systems executive report?

   Middle Mgmt. ①   Divisional Mgmt. ③   Senior Mgmt. ⑤

4. On a scale of 1 to 5 (1 is weak and 5 is strong), rate the strength at your firm of the following arguments for automation:

   ①-⑤   Reduce costs

   ①-⑤   Increase productivity

   ①-⑤   Differentiate or improve products and services

   ①-⑤   Support new forms of organizational design, such as matrix management, or more decentralized field support.

5. Characterize your firm's overall stance toward new information technologies (Check one).

   __1__   Conservative (wait and see)

   __2__   Actively monitor (occasionally test)

   __4__   Actively test and prototype

   __5__   Try anything and everything

6. How much of the total systems effort is devoted to direct support for products and services?

   10% ①   11-20% ②   21-30% ③   31-40% ④   40% ⑤

## PRELIMINARY ENVIRONMENT ASSESSMENT

### SCORING GUIDELINES
#### (Continued)

7. How much of the total systems effort is devoted to conventional support, such as payroll and accounting?

   40% ①    30-39% ②    20-29% ③    10-19% ④    10% ⑤

8. How many business units or functional areas at your company have responsibility for their own systems design, development, and operations? (Check one range on each line).

   **Design:**

   20% ①    20-39% ②    40-60% ③    61-80% ④    80% ⑤

   **Development:**

   20% ①    20-39% ②    40-60% ③    61-80% ④    80% ⑤

   **Operations:**

   20% ①    20-39% ②    40-60% ③    61-80% ④    80% ⑤

9. What proportion of total company computing is done on mainframes?

   80% ①    61-80% ②    40-60% ③    20-39% ④    20% ⑤

10. What is the current annual growth rate of personal computers and desktop professional workstations at your firm?

    20% ①    20-39% ②    40-60% ③    61-80% ④    80% ⑤

11. What is the current annual growth rate of word processors:

    20% ①    20-39% ②    40-60% ③    61-80% ④    80% ⑤

12. On a scale of 1 to 5 (where 1 means negligible and 5 means crucial), how important are the following technologies to your business?

    ①-⑤  Office Automation
    ①-⑤  CAD/CAM, Process Automation, Robotics
    ①-⑤  Laboratory and Scientific Computing
    ①-⑤  Point of Sale, Other Transaction Devices

Figure 3-8
(Page 7 of 7)

## PRELIMINARY ENVIRONMENT ASSESSMENT

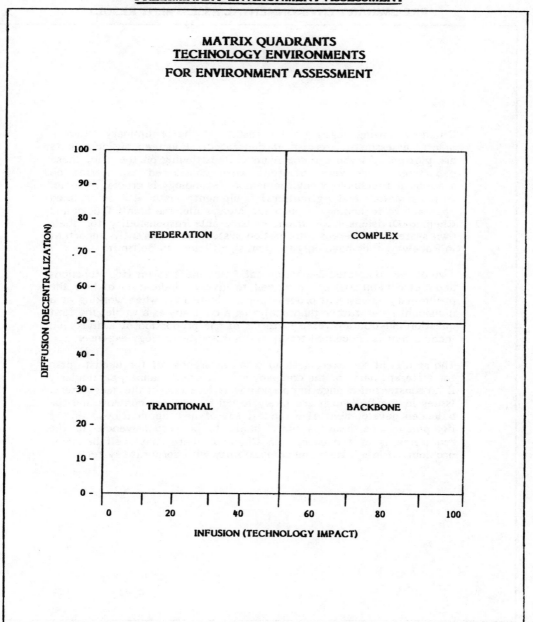

### MATRIX QUADRANTS
### TECHNOLOGY ENVIRONMENTS
### FOR ENVIRONMENT ASSESSMENT

Figure 3-9
(Page 1 of 6)

### FEDERATED MANUFACTURING CORPORATION
### PRELIMINARY ENVIRONMENTAL ASSESSMENT RESULTS

On the following pages are the results of the preliminary environmental assessment exercise at Federated.  Fourteen business units
are plotted.  As you can see from the positioning on the grid, these
departments are very different when considered as information
systems and technology environments.  Technology is crucial in some,
such as Motors and Agricultural Equipment, but here a centralized
approach to technology is pursued.  Meanwhile, the Small Trucks and
Chemco Divisions have taken considerable responsibility for their
own systems.  Whereas information systems are currently important
in Raceway, they have only tactical significance in Bellsmith.

Two of the completed Departmental Assessment forms (for Munitions
and Petrochemicals) are provided to give an indication of how the
preliminary assessment process works.  Note that when working at a
divisional level, rather than analyzing a company as a whole, the first
question must be answered in terms of the proportion of a divisional
income that is accounted for by systems and technology expense.

The results of the exercise lead to an awareness of the need to plan
for different parts of the company in a different manner, particularly
if no substantial change in positioning is foreseen in the near future.
Issues in the Bellsmith are likely to center on cost controls and the
balanced development of a modest set of new applications.  In Ag
Equipment, the issue is more likely to be responsiveness to the
requirements of the users.  In Chemco, there may well be some
problems of integration and compatibility with corporate systems.

**Figure 3-9**
**(Page 2 of 6)**

**FEDERATED MANUFACTURING CORPORATION**
**PRELIMINARY ENVIRONMENTAL ASSESSMENT RESULTS**

The purpose of this questionnaire is to gather data about your organization's information systems environment. It will help determine what kind and extent of strategic planning for information systems is most appropriate for the organization.

-------------------------------------------------------------------------------------

1.  What is the current (fully loaded) expenditure on information systems as a percentage of sales? Include data processing, office automation, and communications.

    3% ⊗    3-7% ____    7-11% ____    11-15% ____    15% ____

2.  What is the expenditure of new systems development as a percentage of the total systems budget?

    10% ⊗    11-20% ____    21-30% ____    31-40% ____    40% ____

3.  To whom does the senior information systems executive report?

    To Middle Mgmt. ⊗    Divisional Mgmt. ____    Senior Mgmt. ____

4.  On a scale of 1 to 5 (1 is weak and 5 is strong), rate the strength at your firm of the following arguments for automation:

    ⑤    Reduce Costs
    ③    Increase Productivity
    ①    Differentiate or improve products and services
    ①    Support new forms of organizational design, such as matrix management, or more decentralized field support.

5.  Characterize your firm's overall stance toward new information technologies (Check one).

    ⊗    Conservative, wait and see
    ____    Actively monitor, occasionally test
    ____    Actively test and prototype
    ____    Try anything and everything

6.  How much of the total systems effort is devoted to direct support for products and services?

    10% ⊗    11-20% ____    21-30% ____    31-40% ____    40% ____

**Figure 3-9
(Page 3 of 6)**

**FEDERATED MANUFACTURING CORPORATION
PRELIMINARY ENVIRONMENTAL ASSESSMENT RESULTS**

7. How much of the total systems effort is devoted to conventional support, such as payroll and accounting?

   40% ⊗　　30-39% ____　　20-29% ____　　10-19% ____　　10% ____

8. How many business units or functional areas at your company have responsibility for their own systems design, development, and operations? (Check one range on each line).

   **Design:**

   20% ____　　20-39% ____　　40-60% ____　　61-80% ____　　80% ⊗

   **Development:**

   20% ____　　20-39% ____　　40-60% ____　　61-80% ⊗　　80% ____

   **Operations:**

   20% ____　　20-39% ____　　40-60% ____　　61-80% ⊗　　80% ____

9. What proportion of total company computing is done on mainframes?

   80% ____　　61-80% ____　　40-60% ____　　20-39% ____　　20% ⊗

10. What is the current annual growth rate of personal computers and desktop professional workstations at your firm?

    20% ____　　20-39% ____　　40-60% ____　　61-80% ⊗　　80% ____

11. What is the current annual growth rate of word processors:

    20% ____　　20-39% ____　　40-60% ⊗　　61-80% ____　　80% ____

12. On a scale of 1 to 5 (where 1 means negligible and 5 means crucial), how important are the following technologies to your business?

    ⑤　　Office Automation
    ①　　CAD/CAM, Process Automation, Robotics
    ①　　Laboratory and Scientific Computing
    ①　　Point of Sale, Other Transaction Devices

**Figure 3-9**
**(Page 4 of 6)**

**FEDERATED MANUFACTURING CORPORATION**
**PRELIMINARY ENVIRONMENTAL ASSESSMENT RESULTS**

The purpose of this questionnaire is to gather data about your organization's information systems environment. It will help determine what kind and extent of strategic planning for information systems is most appropriate for the organization.

------------------------------------------------------------------------------

1.  What is the current (fully loaded) expenditure on information systems as a percentage of sales? Include data processing, office automation, and communications.

    3% _____    3-7% _____    7-11% _____    11-15% _____    15% _(X)_

2.  What is the expenditure of new systems development as a percentage of the total systems budget?

    10% _____    11-20% _____    21-30% _____    31-40% _(X)_    40% _____

3.  To whom does the senior information systems executive report?

    To Middle Mgmt. _____    Divisional Mgmt. _(X)_    Senior Mgmt. _____

4.  On a scale of 1 to 5 (1 is weak and 5 is strong), rate the strength at your firm of the following arguments for automation:

    _(5)_    Reduce Costs
    _(5)_    Increase Productivity
    _(3)_    Differentiate or improve products and services
    _(5)_    Support new forms of organizational design, such as matrix management, or more decentralized field support.

5.  Characterize your firm's overall stance toward new information technologies (Check one).

    _____    Conservative, wait and see
    _____    Actively monitor, occasionally test
    _(X)_    Actively test and prototype
    _____    Try anything and everything

6.  How much of the total systems effort is devoted to direct support for products and services?

    10% _____    11-20% _____    21-30% _____    31-40% _____    40% _(X)_

**Figure 3-9**
**(Page 5 of 6)**

### FEDERATED MANUFACTURING CORPORATION
### PRELIMINARY ENVIRONMENTAL ASSESSMENT RESULTS

7. How much of the total systems effort is devoted to conventional support, such as payroll and accounting?

   40% _____    30-39% _____    20-29% _____    10-19% _____    10% (X)

8. How many business units or functional areas at your company have responsibility for their own systems design, development, and operations? (Check one range on each line).

   **Design:**

   20% _____    20-39% (X)    40-60% _____    61-80% _____    80% _____

   **Development:**

   20% (X)    20-39% _____    40-60% _____    61-80% _____    80% _____

   **Operations:**

   20% (X)    20-39% _____    40-60% _____    61-80% _____    80% _____

9. What proportion of total company computing is done on mainframes?

   80% (X)    61-80% _____    40-60% _____    20-39% _____    20% _____

10. What is the current annual growth rate of personal computers and desktop professional workstations at your firm?

    20% (X)    20-39% _____    40-60% _____    61-80% _____    80% _____

11. What is the current annual growth rate of word processors:

    20% (X)    20-39% _____    40-60% _____    61-80% _____    80% _____

12. On a scale of 1 to 5 (where 1 means negligible and 5 means crucial), how important are the following technologies to your business?

    (3)    Office Automation
    (1)    CAD/CAM, Process Automation, Robotics
    (1)    Laboratory and Scientific Computing
    (1)    Point of Sale, Other Transaction Devices

Figure 3-9
(Page 6 of 6)

### FEDERATED MANUFACTURING CORPORATION
### PRELIMINARY ENVIRONMENTAL ASSESSMENT RESULTS

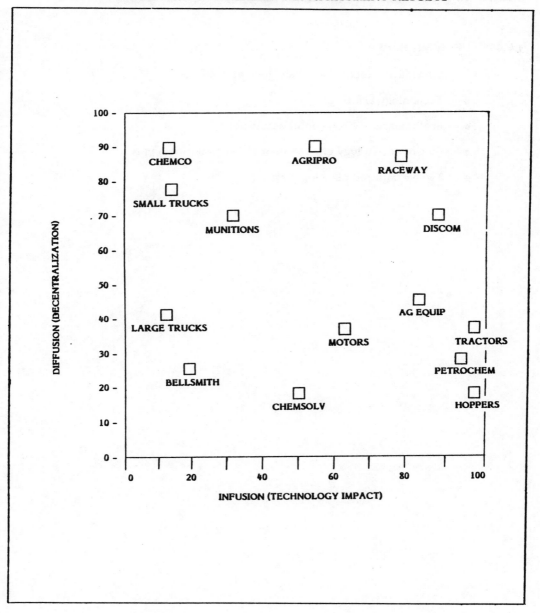

For each technology environment and each level of intensity, the Planning Department then developed what it thought would be an appropriate planning response. Given four environments and three levels of intensity, twelve planning packages were needed. The twelve program offerings for the first year are summarized in **Figure 3-10, Information Technology Planning Program Summary.**

## 3.4.4    DELIVERABLES

- Information technology management readings

- Technology briefings

- Preliminary environmental assessment

- Plot of technology environment for each business unit

- Twelve tailored planning programs.

**Figure 3-10**
**(Page 1 of 4)**

## FEDERATED MANUFACTURING CORPORATION
## INFORMATION TECHNOLOGY PLANNING PROGRAM SUMMARY

**PROGRAM 1:     Traditional Environment, Intensive Effort**

- Application identification canvass, analysis, written feedback, and follow-up workshop

- Application priority setting questionnaire, computer modeling, written feedback, and follow-up workshop

- Human resource management needs assessment, analysis, feedback report, and planning meeting

- Professional productivity assessment, benchmarks, and planning workshop

- Capacity management assessment, computer model, written feedback, and planning workshop

**PROGRAM 2:     Traditional Environment, Moderate Effort**

- Application identification canvass and follow-up workshop

- Application priority setting questionnaire, computer modeling, and follow-up workshop

- Human resource management needs assessment, analysis, and planning meeting

- Professional productivity assessment, benchmarks, and planning workshop

- Capacity management assessment, computer model, and planning workshop

**PROGRAM 3:     Traditional Environment, Minimal Effort**

- Application identification workshop

- Application priority setting questionnaire and follow-up workshop

- Human resource management needs assessment and planning meeting

- Professional productivity assessment and planning workshop

- Capacity management assessment and planning workshop

Figure 3-10
(Page 2 of 4)

### FEDERATED MANUFACTURING CORPORATION
### INFORMATION TECHNOLOGY PLANNING PROGRAM SUMMARY

**PROGRAM 4:      Backbone Environment, Intensive Effort**

- Data resource management assessment, modeling, feedback report, and planning meetings
- Capacity management assessment, computer model, written feedback, and planning workshop
- Human resource management needs assessment analysis, feedback report, and planning meeting
- End-user computing introductory workshop, needs assessment, Information Center design

**PROGRAM 5:      Backbone Environment, Moderate Effort**

- Data resource management assessment, feedback and planning meetings
- Capacity management assessment, computer model, and planning workshop
- Human resource management needs assessment, analysis, and planning meeting
- End-user computing introductory workshop, and needs assessment

**PROGRAM 6:      Backbone Environment, Minimal Effort**

- Data resource management assessment
- Capacity management assessment, computer model, and planning workshop
- Human resource management needs assessment, analysis, and planning meeting
- End-user computing introductory workshop, and needs assessment

**Figure 3-10**
**(Page 3 of 4)**

**FEDERATED MANUFACTURING CORPORATION**
**INFORMATION TECHNOLOGY PLANNING PROGRAM SUMMARY**

PROGRAM 7:　　Federation Environment, Intensive Effort

- Decision support assessment, CSF analysis, written report, and strategy session
- Office automation needs assessment, architecture planning, and productivity improvement estimates
- End-user computing status report and strategy assistance
- Distributed processing opportunity analysis and planning assistance
- Networking assessment and application identification and qualification

PROGRAM 8:　　Federation Environment, Moderate Effort

- Decision support assessment and CSF analysis
- Office automation needs assessment and planning
- End-user computing status report and strategy assistance
- Distributed processing opportunity analysis and planning assistance
- Networking Assessment and application identification and qualification

PROGRAM 9:　　Federation Environmnet, Minimal Effort

- Decision support assessment and CSF analysis
- Office automation needs assessment
- End-user computing status report
- Distributed processing opportunity analysis
- Networking assessment and application identification

Figure 3-10
(Page 4 of 4)

**FEDERATED MANUFACTURING CORPORATION
INFORMATION TECHNOLOGY PLANNING PROGRAM SUMMARY**

---

**PROGRAM 10:    Complex Environment, Intensive Effort**

- Networking assessment and application identification and qualification
- Architecture documentation and planning session
- Installed base tracking - system set-up
- Distributed processing opportunity analysis and planning assistance
- Artificial intelligence introductory session and opportunity analysis

**PROGRAM 11:    Complex Environment, Moderate Effort**

- Networking assessment and application identification
- Architecture documentation and planning session
- Installed base tracking - system set-up
- Distributed processing opportunity analysis
- Artificial intelligence introductory session and opportunity analysis

**PROGRAM 12:    Complex Environment, Minimal Effort**

- Networking assessment and application identification
- Architecture documentation and planning session
- Distributed processing opportunity analysis
- Artificial intelligence introductory session

# SECTION 4

## STRATEGIC INFORMATION SYSTEMS PLANNING

### SECTION OVERVIEW

Potential strategic information systems are usually identified by a conscious, coordinated effort of opportunity analysis. It is necessary to develop a good line of communication between the developers of information systems and the senior managers who are looking for ways to improve the business. Opportunity analysis, or the identification of strategic systems, must itself be handled systematically. Two common approaches are the use of experienced consultants and the training of capable internal staff people.

There are a number of approaches to identifying strategic information systems possibilities. It is important to move in the key operational areas of the business, where strategic successes can be highly profitable. Structured approaches offer the best solution for internal staff efforts. Pilot projects are reasonable because of the wide use of personal computers for decision-making.

Information technology has become a prime vehicle for effecting business change. Strategic thinking looks to the improvement of effectiveness, rather than efficiency.

This section describes and defines the events in the strategic planning process and the various terms that are commonly used. Issues and objectives are the keystones of Information Services strategic planning. The purpose is to help resolve the organization's business issues and attain desired objectives by setting Information Services objectives and accomplishing them.

Definitions are provided for the critical terms which describe the process of resolving business and IS issues, setting objectives, and developing strategic plans and proposals.

In this section, the strategic information systems planning process is described in six phases. They are:

- Situation Analysis
- Business Planning
- Information Services Planning
- Setting Strategic Priorities
- Strategic Planning
- Operational Planning

The steps in these phases can be combined or expanded for particular projects. They are described in some detail to illustrate the strategic planning process.

An update to Richard Nolan's familiar "Stages" theory of data processing development is included because of its fundamental position in information systems planning. Nolan describes the shifts in the computer environment that has caused the changes in data processing development, and the approaches that must be taken in the new era of strategic planning.

John Rockart's "Critical Success Factors" are discussed because of their excellent fit with the planning process for strategic information systems. He describes the central position of building a strategic data model and the planning process for the role of information technology in the competitive advantage of the firm.

Ephraim McLean's "Strategic Planning Framework" pulls all the systems planning methods that are required together in a cohesive manner. McLean speaks from the older paradigm, but the planning framework presented aptly fits the needs of professional IS planners, partly because it is the distilled experience of many organizations.

Peter Keen's "Creating the Business Vision" describes the necessity of Information Services opening their horizons if they are to participate in strategic planning. His process is based on his consulting experience in telecommunications planning, but is generally applicable. He emphasizes that the dynamics of innovation require the preparation of a formalized business "vision" to relate the technology to the business.

### Examples:

Strategic planning methodologies vary considerably, partly because of where the organization stands on the paradigm shift to strategic planning for information systems as a competitive weapon, but mainly because of the different organizational structures and the management methods in place in organizations. Several case studies described in the literature are summarized. They include both traditional strategic planning that is still proving profitable, and planning information systems as competitive weapons.

Avon Product's strategic planning approach, described by John Walsh in 1980, describes the now-familiar Pressure Point Analysis method that asks, Where are we? Why **should** we change? What **could** we do? What should we do? How can we get there? It offers a framework that is readily understood, and it provides a good "talking" paper on strategic issues.

Gordon Campbell's outline of the Diamond Shamrock approach to strategic planning is significant because it describes one of the several commercially-available strategic planning methodologies being applied in a practical way to set up a strategic planning process that may identify strategic opportunities. They used and modified the Price-Waterhouse system, Strategic Information Systems Planning (S.I.S.P.).

Robert Lief, Robert Dodge, and Ralph Ogden described Fluor Corporation's efforts to adapt their DP strategy to their corporation's management style. It evidently caught the interest of top management and was a useful means of developing specific objectives and strategies.

The Veteran's Administration ADP and Telecommunications Strategic Plan is briefly outlined. It describes their experience in relating the ADP planning strategies to the agency's programmatic objectives which, in effect, is their "competitive" posture. Policy and planning are completely linked.

A major insurance organization's strategic plan is outlined to show how the corporate mission is translated into the Information Systems Division CSFs, goals, objectives, and strategy. Corporate sets the competitive tone, and the ISD shows how it will respond in its plans.

## 4.1      IDENTIFICATION OF STRATEGIC INFORMATION SYSTEMS

Potential strategic information systems are usually identified by a conscious, coordinated effort of opportunity analysis. It is necessary to develop a good line of communication between the developers of information systems and the senior managers who are looking for ways to improve the business. Opportunity analysis, or the identification of strategic systems, must itself be handled systematically. Two common approaches are the use of experienced consultants and the training of capable internal staff people.

## 4.1.1      STRATEGIC SYSTEMS OPPORTUNITY ANALYSIS

There are two main phases to a strategic systems planning effort. The first is the opportunity analysis, or the identification of potential strategic information systems. The second is the strategic systems planning itself. Much of the literature on strategic systems is concerned primarily with the opportunity analysis, because the Information Services group has been positioned in the organization in such a way that they have little access to the decision-makers who can most readily identify strategic system possibilities. In the past, information systems have been used principally in business automation areas to reduce clerical costs, reduce inventory levels, provide operational information, computerize the company's books, and so on. Many of these systems have been most effective in saving money and in making information more readily available. Some of these systems have actually had strategic impact on the firm. There has not always been a good line of communication, however, between the developers of information systems and the senior management who are looking for business successes. Information Services generally has asked what to do with automation by talking to those with immediate operational problems that can be benefited by the use of the computer. They usually have not asked how they should position their systems resources to provide the greatest support to the business thrust.

Automation, therefore, has been invested in mainly to improve business operations. Most of the systems have shown a measurable economic return. There have also been many intangible benefits obtained from the system, mostly in the areas of providing information and control to management in a way that allows them to move strategically with the business. The problem has been that the Information Services planners have not understood management thinking, because they have not been part of management discussions, and because possible strategic thrusts have not been recognized during the development of the systems.

The purpose of strategic analysis is to find automation opportunities that will improve the competitive position of the business; to find ways to direct the Information Services staff to gain meaningful advantage for the firm, and to move into new and profitable areas. Information Services capabilities can then be planned with a strategic view of the potential business impact of the computer systems. Many computer applications are on the verge of being strategically important, if they are only recognized as containing capabilities and information that can be directly applied to business thrusts. Information is obviously a key vehicle for effecting business change. The problem in realizing the potential is usually in the mutual lack of understanding between the key business managers and the information system developers. The identification of opportunities for business advances using information systems lies in having a mutual, concerted approach by both the responsible managers and the system developers. Methodologies are available. The technology is available. Only the applied communication is normally lacking. If senior business management desires to look into the possibilities of gaining strategic advantage by the use of information systems, the first task is to organize the effort so that there is meaningful communication and systematic review of the possibilities.

Thus, the opportunity analysis, or the identification of strategic systems, must itself be handled systematically. There are two common approaches to such opportunity analysis. One of the most attractive to many has always been the use of experienced consultants. These may be the authors of papers on strategic systems and their staffs, or professional consultants who have had some successes in uncovering strategic opportunities. The advantages of the use of such consultants are that:

- They have recent experience to draw on, and many ideas already formed.

- Using them is a method of gaining access to higher levels of management, who are interested in what they might advocate.

- They have worked through their methodologies several times, and know the strong areas and the pitfalls.

- If they do not discover a strategic breakthrough, no one internally is blamed.

The other approach to opportunity analysis and strategic planning is to train capable internal staff people, and encourage them to make presentations to higher levels of management. Use the existing systems development staff, who certainly understand the present and possible capabilities of information technology, and give them a chance to work on planning critical, strategic systems. The advantages of the use of internal staff are that:

- They will likely remain with the organization and retain the experience there.

- They can train other staff members over time.

- They can apply the knowledge gained from one success directly to other systems in the organization.

- An understanding of, and a desire for, strategic information systems will be diffused throughout the organization.

Whichever approach is used, external consultants or internal staff, the first and probably most interesting part is the opportunity analysis, and the second part is the detailed planning of the strategic system and the execution of the plan.

A number of approaches to identifying strategic information systems opportunities have been described in the literature. One of the best is briefly outlined in this manual in **Section 2.4, "Wiseman's Strategic Perspective View."** If a consultant is used, clearly the methodology preferred by that consultant will be central. It is not necessary to have a single methodology, however, as a syncretic mixture of the ideas that appear to best fit the organization's culture may prove to be the best, because of the likelihood of its acceptability. There are several criteria that are important in the selection of a strategic system identification approach:

- Move in the key operational areas of the business, where strategic successes can be highly profitable.

- Adopt a **proactive,** rather than a passive style. Strategic systems are seldom found by waiting for system requests to come through the mail. It is helpful to give classes and seminars, talk up the possibilities, and go out and seek interested managers.

- Use proven techniques for systems development. Do not confuse the problem of identifying strategic opportunities with the problem of realizing their benefits. Identification requires management interaction. Realization requires proven systems development methods.

- Leave contingency room in the Information Services plans. Do not fill the allocated budget with mundane automation projects. Budget for opportunity search, and be ready to ask for other funds. Their use will be multiplied by the existing Information Services capabilities.

- Experiment with different methods for identifying strategic systems. These may be Critical Success Factors, Pressure Points Analysis, Key External Factors, or even IBM's Business Systems Planning, which has often surfaced new ideas. Any good systematic analysis can lay an excellent base for the education of management and the search for strategic opportunities.

Structured approaches offer the best solution for internal staff efforts to find possible strategic information systems. First, they can be pre-identified as the approach that will be followed, and can be funded. Second, they carry with them a degree of authenticity as having been proven elsewhere. Third, they provide understood checkpoints for supplying plan-vs-actual information to management. Fourth, the documentation is useful for training purposes. A few of the structured approaches that are available are:

- IBM's Business Systems Planning and Business System Information Planning

- McAuto's Information Systems Transition Planning

- Price Waterhouse's Strategic Information Systems Planning.

These have all had many successful users and are well documented. Unfortunately, they have less psychological appeal than consultant approaches. For example, the ideas of Charles Wiseman to have small groups brainstorming for strategic system opportunities, to discuss and evaluate the ideas, and to pick out the "blockbusters," combines training and communication with some enthusiasm for the outcome. Such enthusiasm can be equaled by any approach, of course, if a responsible operations manager comes away from the planning with a perception of gaining strategic advantage in a particular area. Obviously, the best approach to take to uncover strategic opportunities will vary according to the company culture. It will take experience to learn how to identify potential strategic system opportunities, to alert the corporation to the possibilities in such systems, and to sustain the effort required to implement them.

**Pilot projects** can be one way of introducing the strategic concepts. Frequently, such projects are already partially implemented on personal computers at the staff level. What is then needed is cooperation with the analysts who have implemented the approach, interest in its further development, and a reasonable amount of management interest. Unfortunately, pilot projects seldom offer great strategic advantage in themselves, but merely point to the possibilities. They are great training tools, and an excellent way of developing technical skills among the management staff. Since many people are using personal computers, there are many more opportunities to identify strategic systems, experimentation is encouraged, and there can be calculated risk-taking at a reasonable level. The proliferation of analytical systems of many types is teaching senior management about the real applications of technology. There is great awareness and consciousness raising, and widespread assimilation of information systems concepts. All this leads to better opportunities for identifying and pursuing strategic information systems.

The key element in thinking strategically is the development of a new way of approaching information systems planning. The operational way of thinking about a system is to pursue what labor and equipment costs can be cut, how more accurate information can be made available, and how operations can be made to run more smoothly. Exactly the same system can be looked at from a strategic point of view and the results will be different. Now the thinking is on the impact of the change. Will it increase productivity? Will it open more markets? Will it increase the business?

Not only does the thinking change, but the system itself will be designed from a different perspective. Operationally, people look for the most data processing for the dollar. Strategically, people look at the competitive and informational opportunities, then ask how much they will cost.

Those participating in the search for strategic opportunities must start thinking in terms of **business** changes. Information technology is becoming a primary vehicle for effecting business changes.

- **Productivity changes** must be in terms of reducing the overall product costs significantly. The elimination of labor and the processing of clerical volume may be involved, as it was in the older operational systems. The thinking, however, is directed toward reducing the overall market costs.

- **Product and service changes** can come from information technology in providing product-related services. The services may even function as new products.

- **Communications changes** are becoming more realizable. Separate entities can be linked geographically and organizationally. A new view of organization-wide coordination is possible.

- **Managerial changes** also come with coordinated efforts. Decisions are implemented, performance is analyzed, and the future is forecast from a whole-company viewpoint, rather than by department. When a strategic system appears to be a winner, the staff relationships may change markedly.

This sort of change can be found and planned when the overall, strategic view is taken. It is the facilitation of corporate **effectiveness** rather than efficiency. The thinking is directed to improving the competitive position to gain meaningful advantage, and improving the business operations to effect economic return and intangible competitive benefits. Information technology is used as a primary vehicle to effect business change. The momentum of the Information Services activities must be shifted from producing automation to following the thrust of the business.

## 4.1.2   ISSUES AND OBJECTIVES

All strategic systems do not come out of brainstorming sessions or consultant interviews. Many corporations have had great success by examining the possibilities systematically with their internal staff. Strategic information systems can be planned within the Information Services group if they have good communications with the operational management of the organization. A good example of the process is in the banking industry. Some of the early leaders moved swiftly towards Automatic Teller Machines and some of the many other systems that have sprung up in the last decade. Other banks have accepted the change as a strategic challenge, and have organized their staffs internally to meet it. They have opened the communications lines with their data processing staffs, hired people with appropriate experience, and have planned and executed successful strategic response. The large oil companies have long defined strategic planning within their operations, and have assigned large staffs to the problems of analyzing the issues and developing appropriate objectives.

The planning of strategic information systems should be accomplished systematically, with all participants aware of their roles. Many corporations regularly look for strategic opportunities in their planning. Those that are successful in their search have two-way discussions between the operational planners and the Information Services planners. Regular presentations to line managers about IS possibilities often spark new ideas and new thrusts. Such systematic searches will not always produce major breakthrough systems, but they maintain a goal of increasing the firm's profitability in front of all the Information Services staff participants. The result is frequently beneficial. The great war stories of the consultants are most helpful to generate management interest. The reality is that many skirmishes are won by involving all parties in a systematic planning process.

**Issues** and **objectives** are the keystones of modern IS strategic planning. Their purpose is to help resolve the organization's business issues, and attain the organization's business objectives by setting IS objectives, measuring their attainment, and accomplishing them. All other elements in the planning process, such as feasibility studies, proposals, analyses, projections, action programs, resource estimates, and so forth, are the means or the tools for attaining business objectives and resolving business issues.

The planning process is intended to be flexible so that it can be adapted to all types of companies, to the various industry groups, and to both line and staff functions. This feature of the planning process makes it particularly adaptable to organizations which are in a constant state of flux, for example, typical IS organizations that are constantly adding new technologies. However, while the overall process is flexible and parts may be added or taken away depending upon the company environments, each part of the process is itself well structured. For example, the terms "issue," "objective," and "strategy" should always mean the same thing to each participant in the process so that the planning process has a well-established methodology and is cohesive, integrated, and disciplined. In this manner, the process may be taught to others, thus lending itself to delegation and cross-training, for example, to users.

In addition, there is a regular order in which planning events should customarily occur. While it is perfectly appropriate for each company to rearrange the order of planning events to suit its own environment and management style, it is important that each organization establish its own desired order of events and adhere to this sequence in developing its issues, objectives, and planning strategies. If done properly, the sequence of events in IS planning should approximate, as closely as possible, the sequence of the company's business planning process.

**Figure 4-1,** depicts the **Relationship of Events in Strategic Planning.** Strategic planning is anticipatory planning of specific objectives in response to specific issues. Certain mandatory projects, as well as straightforward system maintenance and enhancement projects, may lend themselves more to other planning methods, since the objectives may already be well known and quantified. They will not require the full range of strategic planning steps identified in the diagram. This method should be reserved for critical issues.

The events or elements of the strategic IS planning process are:

- Mission setting
- Business objectives
- Pressure points, problem areas, and opportunities
- Impact points
- Business issues
- Strategies and targets
- IS objectives
- Implementation programs
- Performance measurement

**Figure 4-1**

**RELATIONSHIP OF EVENTS IN STRATEGIC PLANNING**

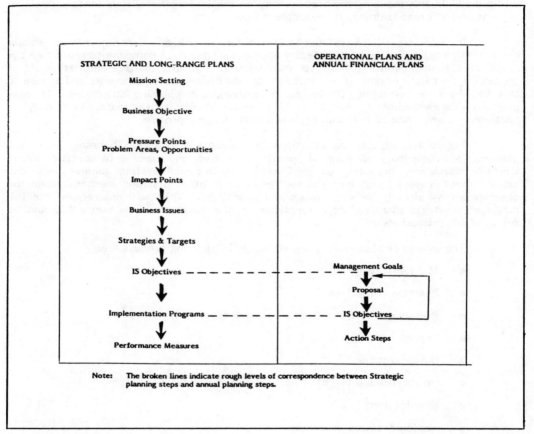

Note:    The broken lines indicate rough levels of correspondence between Strategic
         planning steps and annual planning steps.

Several factors become immediately obvious from **Figure 4-1.** For example:

**a.**    IS objectives are set only after strategic analyses are conducted
(unlike MBO, where objectives-setting is usually the first step in
the process).

**b.**    The process starts with **business objectives** and not IS objectives.

**c.**    Strategies are used to help establish objectives and work out the
implementation program.

**d.**    The strategic, long-range, and annual plans are linked by making
the operational annual plan into a refinement of the first year of
the long-range plan, with budgets, resource estimates and program action steps added, and incorporating the strategic plans
into the long-range operations plans.

**4.1.3    DEFINITIONS**

There are some commonly accepted definitions for certain critical terms which describe the process of resolving business and IS issues, setting objectives, and developing strategic plans and proposals. These terms appear, roughly, in the sequence in which they occur in the planning process.  They are:

- Mission
- Problem Area or Pressure Point
- Opportunity Area
- Impact Point
- Business Issue
- Strategy
- Sub-Strategy
- Proposal
- Implementation Program
- Relationship between Strategy, Sub-Strategy, and Implementation Program
- Objective
- Performance Measurement
- Contingency Plans
- Alternative Strategies
- Action Steps

**a.    Mission:**

The mission is a statement of business boundaries.  Mission setting specifies the sectors in which the IS unit will conduct its business, broadly describes how the unit will undertake its business, and states any other constraints.

The business is segmented into sectors such as the management group being served, the users being served, geographical areas, a mode of operation (how the business will be conducted), and a grouping of products or services.

Early in the planning process, a tentative definition of a mission should be reviewed with the executive responsible for the unit. In the corporate IS organization, this is usually a senior executive.  In divisional IS organizations, this may be the division general manager.  In any event, the executive should be one having policymaking authority. In this way, a proposed extension to business boundaries can be approved or rejected before a great deal of time is spent on its consideration.

Generally speaking, a mission statement also serves as:

1. A set of general organizational objectives.
2. A set of working or ongoing business or IS objectives.

- **Mission as a set of general organizational objectives:** An organizational objective is a statement of organizational purpose. Once set, it usually remains unchanged for some period of time. Organizational objectives should be written into the unit's charter. "To provide IS support to the Company's business plans" is an example of an appropriate organizational objective (mission) for the IS unit.

- **Mission as a set of working or ongoing objectives:** A mission can also be an objective of somewhat shorter duration than an organizational objective. When the term mission is used in this way, it can be considered a "working objective," which changes over time. For example, "To provide inventory control systems for customers" may be an appropriate working objective (mission) for the IS unit. It cannot be considered a long-term organizational objective as it may consist of simply a one-shot design and implementation effort. The statement, however, is not sufficiently refined to be considered a final objective as defined below. Therefore, this statement is considered to be a mission statement, or a statement of working objectives.

- **Confusion between mission and objectives:** Sometimes the terminology causes confusion and business and IS planners call a mission statement an objective. The term "to establish an appropriate management information system" is **not** an objective which is useful for purposes of strategic IS planning, but many people feel it is one and call it the goal that is to be reached, or how its accomplishment is to be measured. In short, if the goal cannot be reasonably measured, then an objective does not exist for purposes of strategic planning. For instance, the term "appropriate" in the preceding mission statement disqualifies it from being an objective as it leaves the specifics of "appropriate" to individual discretion. To determine the difference between a mission statement and an objective, the following should be kept in mind:

    - The word "mission" comes from a Latin root meaning "to send." Generally speaking, therefore, a mission is something that an organization is "sent to do."

    - If a statement **sounds** like a statement of objectives, but if its outcome (goal) cannot be specifically measured in quantifiable terms, it is most likely a mission statement instead.

- A mission statement must be further refined before reasonable objectives can be set. Otherwise, there is danger that the results may be disputed, no matter what the outcome of the project may be.

**b.   Problem Area or Pressure Point:**

Problem areas are defined as anticipated conditions which could adversely affect future profitability. Problem areas can be either external to the company or internal. They become the issues addressed in the planning process, provided the solutions to the problems are or can be controlled by management, and there are significant savings when such control is exercised. They may be the result of strategic initiatives by competitors. Examples are:

● **Internal problem area** - An example of an internal problem area is an anticipated continued increase in the volume of product returns for repair which might necessitate a complete change in data processing methods and equipment to support an expanded network of product service centers.

● **External pressure point** - An example of an external pressure point would be an anticipated slowdown in domestic economic growth. The expected consequent reduction in total domestic sales growth may necessitate looking for development opportunities in other countries which, in turn, might necessitate an international data communications network.

**c.   Opportunity Area:**

The converse of a problem area is an opportunity area. It is an anticipated condition which could favorably affect future profitability. Opportunity areas can also be either external to the company or internal. They, similar to problem areas, can become the issues addressed in the strategic planning process. **For example:** An internal opportunity area could be an anticipated continued increase in the training needs of the decentralized business units which might suggest the development of an in-company training group to meet the new business thrusts.

● **Turning problems into opportunities:** Some IS executives and planners have found it advisable to change problem statements into opportunity statements, and to express them as opportunities rather than problems. For instance, **the statement,** "A problem exists because the IS organization is not knowledgeable in inventory control systems, communications networks, etc.," **could be restated as,** "Further experience in inventory control systems and communication networks might afford IS the opportunity to support the business plans as well as to develop new revenue streams from outside sales activities."

Opportunity statements have advantages over problem statements. They tend to be more optimistic, progressive, and upbeat than problem statements, and are more apt to gain agreement and support of users and top management. Successful consultants have long employed the opportunities-oriented approach to their clients in order to remove the stigma of criticism from their consulting engagements.

### d.    Impact Point:

An impact point is a business element which, when changed through efforts on the part of management, can favorable affect profitability. Like problem and opportunity areas, impact points which have a significantly high dollar effect, and which have been chosen by senior management to be addressed in the planning process, become issues. Several of the **impact points** might be:

- The trend of the ratio of IS expenses to sales

- The trend of the ratio of product returns to sales

- The trend of the ratio of communications costs to sales

These would be impact points if management was able to institute programs which would reduce an unfavorable trend or improve a satisfactory one.

### e.    Business Issue:

A business issue is an aspect of the business which senior management has selected to be addressed in the planning process and which:

1.    is under the potential control of management; and

2.    can have a significant impact on the bottom line if management control is exercised.

Issues arise from problem areas, opportunity areas, and impact points identified early in the planning process or, alternatively, as a by-product of considering ways to resolve other issues.

Issues can also be described as unsettled matters of strategic importance to top management. In this regard, issues can sometimes be stated in the form of questions, and, at other times, as alternatives.

**An issue in the form of a question is:**  "To what extent can prepackaged inventory control programs be utilized to satisfy the company's business application needs in this area?"

**An issue in the form of an alternative is:**  "Should the users' terminals for the entry of product orders and inquiry of inventory status be on-line terminals to the central computer, or should they be microcomputer systems in the customer's offices?"

Strategic planning seeks to settle these unresolved issues. In order for a management topic to be a legitimate issue, worthy of strategic analysis, the IS executive and his planners should be able to answer the following three questions in the affirmative.

1. Is the matter something about which top management is really concerned?

2. Does this matter seriously impact the company in real, measurable terms? (Revenue, expense, risk, legal, jurisdiction, public image, etc.)

3. Is it a subject about which IS can do something?

If the answer to all three questions is "Yes," then the matter at hand is an issue appropriate for IS to address through strategic analysis.

f. **Strategy:**

There are two complementary definitions of strategy which will be used in discussing strategic IS planning:

1. A general statement (mission statement) of the way in which an issue will be controlled by management to achieve the desired effect on profits.

2. The method used to resolve unsettled matters (issues) into settled, or final, objectives.

- **A general statement about controlling an issue:** An issue must be turned around in a positive manner to become a strategy. Listed below are examples of issues (problem statements) that have been turned around into positive strategic statements. We call these mission statements or working objectives. They are not considered final objectives, because they do not have meaningful measurement factors applied to them as yet. Examples are:

| Issue | Strategy |
|---|---|
| Limited number of customers using our services | Offer services tailored to the needs of potential customers not yet using our services. |
| High operating costs make product not competitive | Reduce the cost of processing transactions. |

- **Method used to resolve issues into objectives:** The second definition of strategy is the method for settling issues, resolving unanswered questions, and refining the results of strategic analysis into a statement of objectives. Several steps may be required to do this analysis, including: business plans analysis, environmental analysis, forecast, trends, assumptions, internal (strengths and weaknesses) analysis, risk analysis, contingency analysis, legislative analysis, and economic analysis.

At the end of a successful strategic analysis, objectives are set (including key measurement factors) and a strategic plan (report) is prepared for top management, which may be expected to make either a go or no-go decision on the plan as presented. The scope of this management review usually covers the objectives presented, as well as a review of the various business issues and strategies leading to these objectives. Decision-oriented planning is facilitated through the use of the strategic planning process.

## g. Sub-Strategy:

If an issue can be controlled in more than one way simultaneously, these approaches are called sub-strategies. An example is:

| Issue | Strategy | Sub-Strategy |
|---|---|---|
| Limited range of services provided to existing customers | Extend range of services to existing customers. | Expand product offerings. |
| | | Add services. |
| | | Offer products tailored to particular needs. |

## h. Proposal:

A proposal is a recommendation from subordinate to senior management for a significant change or innovation in activities. A proposal is, therefore, a potential objective. Since all proposals should be reviewed by senior management within the business unit, it is important that only those changes which are regarded as significant by their originator be submitted as potential objectives in the long-range and annual business plans.

## i. Implementation Program:

An implementation program is an outline of one stage in the process of carrying out a strategy or sub-strategy, or achieving an objective, giving estimates of: expected duration, benefits, costs, resources, and performance measures.

If an implementation program is to begin in the first year of the long-range plan, it should be:

1. designated a management objective in the long-range business/IS plan; 2. fully developed and presented in more detail in the annual business/IS plan; and

**3.** its numerical designation in the long-range business/IS plan should coincide with its designation in the annual business/IS plan.

**j.** **Relationship Between Strategy, Sub-Strategy and Implementation Program:**

It would be unfortunate if new ideas were subjected to a time-consuming debate of the question: "Is this really a strategy?" What is important is that:

**1.** A strategy or a sub-strategy addresses an issue. (An issue may have a strategy plus sub-strategy, or just a strategy associated with it.)

**2.** An implementation program is at a realistic level of detail.

The fact that a strategy addresses an issue implies that it deals with an aspect of the business which senior management has decided needs attention and that, by addressing it, they can improve future profitability.

The level of detail appropriate to an implementation program is determined by when it will be implemented. If it is to be undertaken within the first year, it is a management objective. It will also be part of the annual plan and should be developed in some detail in that document. If not undertaken in the first year, less detail is required, although estimates of the following items should be made:

- expected duration

- benefits

- costs

- resources

- performance measures

Each business unit of the company should exercise its own judgment so that the result is a useful presentation of what it intends to do, showing how the various courses of action relate to each other and affect the company's profitability.

**k.** **Objective:**

An objective has one or more of the following meanings when used in the context of strategic IS planning:

- An end or objective to be gained

- A business or financial goal

- A management aim or target to be attained

- **An end or objective to be gained:** Two kinds of ends or objectives are important to the IS executive and planners:

business and IS.  In order for a business or IS end to be considered a legitimate objective for IS planning, the following four questions should be answered affirmatively:

1.  Can its achievement be measured in terms that are objective and equally understood by all parties involved (e.g., in terms of dollars, business volumes, rations, etc.)?

2.  Can the objective be reasonably attained using resources over which the company's management has, or will have, control?

3.  Can we explain, to the satisfaction of a critical third party, the various strategies that will be employed to gain the objective?

4.  Will the objective, once it is gained, succeed in resolving the issues which led to the development of the objective itself?

- **A business or financial goal:**  A business goal is one or all of the following:

  - A significant change or innovation in activities.

  - An appraisal of a potentially significant change or innovation in activities.

    In the definition, "significant" means that the change or innovation is sufficiently far-reaching in its effect to warrant senior management involvement during the course of the year.  Launching a new product or service would be a significant innovation.

  - A statement of the percentage of profit growth, contributions in earnings per share, as well as the return on investment (ROI) the company expects to achieve.

- **A management aim or target to be attained:**  This is a measure of the benefits to be received from a strategy or a sub-strategy, and of the time when the benefit will be substantially received.

| Strategy or Sub-Strategy | Hypothetical Target |
|---|---|
| Offer products tailored to the needs of young people. | Sell products to 150,000 young people between the ages of 18 and 35 by the end of the second year, thus gaining an increase in pre-tax profits of $xxx in that year. |
| Reduce the cost of processing transactions. | Reduce the level of processing cost per transaction from 9 cents in 1986 to 5 cents in 1988. |

Aims are the guidance given by the general manager to subordinates on what is planned for the coming year, such as cost reduction or an increase of sales. These plans will probably, but not necessarily, end up as management objectives in the final report.

For those units with long-range business/IS plans, the aims communicated by the general manager will probably be quite specific, spelling out in some detail the proposals for management objectives which are to back up the long-range business plan/IS strategies.

l. **Performance Measurement:**

Performance measures are the criteria for the acceptable level of achievement of implementation programs in the operating area over one or more years. The measurement must be objective, specific, and representative of objectives. For example:

| Implementation Program | Performance Measure |
|---|---|
| Reduce the percentage of documents having errors. | Cost of error correction per 1,000 documents processed will be reduced as follows: |
| | $8 per 1,000 in first year |
| | $7 per 1,000 in second year |
| | $6 per 1,000 in third year |

This performance measure has been specifically costed out, and is more useful in controlling expenses than simply measuring the percentage of errors found in documents.

m. **Contingency Plans:**

A division may choose on its own or be required by senior management to prepare a contingency plan for certain parts of its business. This may result because the timing of some probable future problem is not known or because senior management is not convinced that the problem is likely enough to warrant implementing a strategy to handle it. The contingency plan is then a "standby" plan in case the objectives are not met.

n. **Alternative Strategies:**

In some cases, a manager may have two excellent, but mutually exclusive, strategies for response to an issue. The manager may prefer one strategy over the other, but still may wish to show the alternative in order to obtain further discussion and guidance from senior management. The strategy would be designated as an alternative in the plan report, its financial implications not incorporated in the projected P&L statement.

o.   **Action Steps:**

An action step is one stage in the process of accomplishing an objective.  It is the lowest level of activity which should be described in the plan and for which responsibility would usually be assigned to one person.

**For example:**

"Introduce work measurement in operations center" may be broken down into the following action steps:

-   Select industrial engineering consultant.

-   Select and assign personnel to work with consultant.

-   Install work measurement in billing department.

-   Install work measurement in telephone order entry department.

## 4.1.4    STRATEGIC INFORMATION SYSTEMS PLANNING

The process of strategic information systems planning is inherently flexible and changeable because, by its nature, strategic planning is concerned with special situations that have differing time demands and a wide range of management interest and urgency.   Operational planning and budget planning can proceed lockstep in an orderly, planned fashion with their calendar of events predicted far in advance. Strategic planning must adapt to the requirements of unique business situations, however, and it will be driven and timed according to business necessity, as dictated by higher management.

This section presents a full schedule for strategic planning conducted in an optimum fashion for a large project.  It gives all the suggested steps that will help to assure that all facets of the problem and solution have been fully explored.   The strategic planning process that is shown is a combination of proven methodologies and approaches, leading to the best business result.  The recommended process is outlined in **Figure 4-2, Strategic Information Systems Planning,** which summarizes the six phases:

Phase I    -    **Situation Analysis:** Identifying issues and objectives.

Phase II   -    **Business Planning:**   Describing the business functions and preparing the strategic analysis.

Phase III  -    **Information Services Planning:**   Correlating IS issues with the strategic inputs.

Phase IV   -    **Setting Strategic Priorities:**   Performing analyses and ranking the options.

Phase V    -    **Reporting the Strategic Plan:**   Describing proposed architectures and strategies.

Phase VI   -    **Operational Planning:**   Entering the systems planning phase of the System Development Life Cycle.

For particular projects, the steps in these phases can be combined or expanded.  If particular steps are considered especially critical to a company's business strategy, they may be divided into two or more sub-steps for scheduling and educational purposes.  The specific combination of strategic planning steps, as well as the depth of analysis conducted, should be considered flexible so as to accommodate any of the broad range of business issues facing a particular company.  None of the planning shown here should be eliminated, however.  The various elements of the planning process all contribute to the success of the planning effort.

Figure 4-2
(Page 1 of 2)

## STRATEGIC INFORMATION SYSTEMS PLANNING

**Phase I    -    SITUATION ANALYSIS**

**A.    Identify Business Issues and Objectives**

- Describe business requirements, process, and functions
- Describe and assess current business systems

**B.    Identify Information Services Issues and Objectives**

- Describe and assess current IS capabilities
- Assess current and possible technology
- Identify Information Services issues

**C.    Develop Strategic Systems Objectives**

**Phase II    -    BUSINESS PLANNING**

**A.    Analyze Business Plans**

- Review business planning process
- Describe planned business functions to be automated
- Outline plans linkage between business and IS plans

**B.    Describe Objectives for the System**

- Identify operational business objectives
- State management goals for the system
- Make business forecasts of activity and volume

**C.    Prepare Strategic Analysis**

- Summarize strategic inputs and assumptions
- Perform strategic analyses
- Correlate strategic inputs with business issues
- Summarize the strategic issues
- Agree on the critical success factors

**Phase III    -    INFORMATION SERVICES PLANNING**

**A.    Develop IS Issues and Requirements**

- Correlate IS issues with strategic inputs
- State IS objectives and opportunities

Figure 4-2
(Page 2 of 2)

## STRATEGIC INFORMATION SYSTEMS PLANNING

B. **Propose IS Options and Alternatives**
   - Alternative system solution strategies
   - Alternative organizational arrangements
   - Alternative equipment and software strategies
   - Alternative communications strategies
   - Describe strength and weaknesses of the options

C. **Create Impact Statements**

**Phase IV** - **SETTING STRATEGIC PRIORITIES**

A. **Establish Evaluation Criteria**

B. **Perform Investment and Cost-Benefit Analysis**

C. **Establish Priority Ranking of Options**

D. **Make Funding Recommendations**

**Phase V** - **REPORTING THE STRATEGIC PLAN**

A. **Describe Proposed Architecture**
   - Business system architecture
   - Data processing systems architecture

B. **Describe Proposed Strategies**
   - Refine and tune business objectives
   - Strategic systems alternatives
   - Organizational strategy alternatives
   - Equipment and software strategy alternatives
   - Communications strategy alternatives

C. **Compare Systems to Available Resources**

D. **Develop Strategic Plan Document**

E. **Obtain Necessary Management Commitments**

**Phase VI** - **OPERATIONAL PLANNING**

A. **Enter Systems Analysis Phase of System Development Life Cycle**

B. **Proceed With System Development**

### 4.1.4.1   PHASE I - SITUATION ANALYSIS

**A.**     **Identify Business Issues and Objectives:**

Strategic information systems planning must commence with the development of a framework of business issues and objectives to properly synchronize the IS activities with the business activities. It is important that IS personnel not become so completely involved with their internal IS projects and ongoing activities that they neglect the analysis of the basic business functions. The only premise for starting IS strategic planning is a business premise. There are three main reasons for this:

1.  Business activities in most companies are becoming too complex for IS organizations to continue to expect to survive by operating in a defensive/enhancement mode.

2.  Business systems are changing faster and faster. For example, marketing programs to introduce a new product or service once took five years or longer to complete; the same programs today are typically finished in half that time, or less. Thus, the IS manager who thinks defensively, or in terms of enhancements only, finds the systems being rapidly outpaced by business change.

3.  With few exceptions, an IS organization does not require a formal strategic planning process merely to carry out internal IS projects. In these circumstances, the communications requirements (top management, users, outside organizations) are not stringent, and the traditional management-by-objectives (MBO) approach is usually sufficient.

On the other hand, IS organizations are increasingly adopting IS strategic planning in the conduct of their business systems projects. Strategic planning, along with strategic thinking, allows IS to better anticipate future changes involving top management and users, as well as critical environmental factors, such as competition, market share, demographics, legislation, economy, and technology.

Strategic information systems planning begins with a statement of business issues or business objectives, most of which may have been given formally to commence the project. Of course, the statements received may be too vague or general, and it is necessary to sit down with business management and describe the business requirements in some detail, with the processes and functions that must be handled. Any current business systems, including those that are less than ideal, should also be described and assessed.

The following are some guidelines with respect to business issues and objectives:

a.  It is not necessary that a formal business planning process be in place before the IS strategic planning process is begun. If such does not exist, any statement of business issues and objectives will do as a starting point.

b.  Most business objectives as stated in company business plans are overly conceptual. They are not precise enough to be used verbatim in IS strategic planning. In some respects, they lack either measurability, achievability, or issues-resolvability. Therefore, the business objectives statements must undergo a strategic analysis to be refined enough for achievable implementation programs to be developed.

c.   Statements of business issues and business objectives, no matter where they originate (top management, users, corporate offices), should be accepted as "givens" by IS planners. Business issues and objectives should not be challenged or critiqued, even though they may appear to be only conceptual or otherwise invalid according to our criteria. To challenge them is to invite dissension with the business units, and to foreclose further productive discussions. At a later time, once the appropriate strategic analyses have been accomplished, there will be ample opportunity to discuss differences or disagreements that may exist.

An alternative to business objectives for strategic planning is to develop a **statement of business issues.** This is necessary where coherent business objectives statements often do not exist. In other cases, while they may exist for the perusal of top management and certain users, objectives statements are not made available to the IS organization. Also, the company's objectives statements, where they exist, are often overly conceptual and read more like policy or mission declarations than objectives statements. For example, an expression like "To improve our customer service image" is typical of objectives statements found in company business plans, but is hardly sufficient as a declaration of purpose to launch an IS planning effort.

**Figure 4-3, Business Objectives/Strategy Summary,** is a sample of one approach to describing the information obtained in a brief form. Another approach in a situation analysis is to take an inventory of current business requirements and processes, and develop **process matrices.** Accounting is an example of a business process. The matrix would show the availability of automated systems supplying controlled information on one axis, and the business processes on the other axis. It would illustrate how readily the desired system information could be assembled. More of the information in process matrices should be readily available to the IS study.

When the statements about business issues and objectives are either non-existent, vague, or too general, the IS planners should develop a set of the business issues surrounding the particular phase of the business that is being considered. This should be done in conjunction with the interested company line and staff units in preference to working alone. Working alone is better, however, than not developing business issues at all.

**Figure 4-3**

### BUSINESS OBJECTIVES/STRATEGY SUMMARY

| Business Objective | Business Strategy | Impact on Functional Area | Business Plan Cross-Reference | Other Factors |
|---|---|---|---|---|
| | | | | |
| | | | | |
| | | | | |
| | | | | |

**B.**      Identify Information Services Issues and Objectives:

The survey group should describe and assess all current IS capabilities which may have an impact on the strategic plans being considered. The information should be readily available to the group, but it may not be immediately obvious or it would have been considered previously. Approaches to identifying IS issues are:

● The routine contacts between operational management and IS

● Business Plans Analysis (BPA)

● Business Systems Planning (BSP) approach

Part of such an analysis is the assessment of both current and possible future technology. Frequently, strategic planning becomes a high priority because new technological innovations in terminals, communications, customer-used equipment, or required services have suddenly become of great importance to the business. In other cases, the planning is started because a senior manager has thought of a concept which requires new equipment and new approaches. In such cases, all parts of IS management should be drawn into the discussion, possibly through brainstorming sessions or requests for written ideas, to try to find the best reply to management. Key IS issues may then become critical in reaching a feasible project plan.

The result of this review of the IS capabilities and the desired approaches to reaching the business objectives will be the surfacing of **Information Services issues.**

After raising all relevant issues through the analysis of the plan documents and the resulting discussions, next, select a few of the most important, or primary, issues for strategic analysis. Some guidelines on selecting primary issues are:

- For each particular business issue or objective, no more than a few primary IS issues should be selected for strategic analysis.

- Do not treat IS issues as a shopping list of all possible choices. To do so would needlessly fragment the planning effort. With so many topics to be addressed, the analysis could be carried out only superficially, if at all.

At this point in the Situation Analysis, there are three assessments which could be done, depending upon the size of the projects being considered and the complexity of the process involved. These possible assessments are:

1. Do a **business systems assessment** by comparing business systems with business process **(systems-to-process matrix)**, and determine the extent of systems support to each of the business processes.

2. Do a **technology assessment** by comparing present business systems against several state-of-the-art technologies **(business system/technology matrices)**, and by grading each of the business systems on a scale of "1" to "5" against certain predetermined technology criteria.

3. Do an **IS organizational assessment** by identifying and grading current IS organizations on business processes, business systems, and state-of-the-art technology. The purpose is to answer the question: "To what extent does the present IS organizational structure support the business processes and systems, and facilitate advanced technology applications?"

These assessments would then be direct input into the Strategic Systems Objectives Report to complete the Situation Analysis.

## C.     Develop Strategic Systems Objectives:

Before the initial Situation Analysis is completed, the findings and conclusions to this point should be summarized and the next steps planned. **Figure 4-4, Information Services Opportunities, Problems, and Strategy,** is a sample form for the type of summary analysis that would be helpful for discussion, review, and further analysis. The possible IS strategies summarized on this form will probably not correspond to the strategies that will finally evolve after further analysis, but they will give direction to further study.

This step will summarize the work that has been done so far, and will give direction to the subsequent effort.

**Figure 4-4**

### INFORMATION SERVICES OPPORTUNITIES, PROBLEMS, AND STRATEGY

| Business Objectives | Opportunities | IS Problems and Constraints | Possible IS Strategy |
|---|---|---|---|
|  |  |  |  |

## 4.1.4.2   PHASE II - BUSINESS PLANNING

### A.     Analyze Business Plans:

Having identified the business issues and objectives, reviewed and assessed the current business systems, and identified the Information Services issues and objectives, the next step is to review the business planning process and describe the particular business function being analyzed strategically. In this way, there is less likelihood of a misunderstanding among IS, the users, and top management over which business functions will be analyzed, and which company organizations will be affected by the proposed business systems. The most popular method for analyzing business functions has become Business Systems Planning (BSP), which is used in many IBM installations and is well documented by IBM. The outputs of a BSP analysis usually consist of a display of the company's business process set against the various business systems supporting the process. These outputs can be a great help in resolving business and IS issues.

There are three possible steps that can increase the effectiveness of this analysis of business plans, and the correlation of the IS plans with them. These steps are:

- Participate in the corporation's operational planning process and identify major **operational business objectives** to be addressed in the IS planning process.

- Work with the long-range business planners to **develop a methodology** for determining the **impact of business plans support** on the IS organization at both the divisional and corporate levels.

- Identify opportunities to establish **linkage between the IS and business plans** in each step of the planning process.


**B.      Describe Objectives for the System:**

The business planning process may not necessarily produce a written set of objectives that can be directly used in the system analysis process or in the subsequent development. The objectives may be clear to business management, but not specific enough to plan systems in detail. Such qualitative objectives may be quite adequate in the original situation analysis, but in the analysis of the business plans to link them to the IS plans, a description of objectives is needed as is usually developed in the Feasibility Analysis stage of the System Development Life Cycle.

Next, develop concrete IS accomplishment objectives from the list of business objectives now at hand. Doing this will require:

- Identifying the operational business objectives in data processing terms.

- Stating the management goals for the system in such terms as functions, capabilities, response time, etc.

- Making business forecasts of the activity and volume to be expected with the final system.

Clearly, these will be preliminary analyses and forecasts only, to be refined later. They allow for an estimate of the time and expense that will be involved in the planning, development, and subsequent use of the system. They are the base on which the strategic analyses will be accomplished.


**C.      Prepare Strategic Analyses:**

The particular strategic analyses that will be conducted at this stage of planning will depend upon the size of the projects being considered. Strategic planning first involves the generation of feasible alternative courses of action to meet business objectives. It then follows with an analysis to determine what impacts the alternatives may produce. Finally, the analysis is refined into final objectives. The IS strategic planning process is designed to answer the following questions:

- What is the nature of my business, and what do I really want it to become?

- Who are my customers (users, top management, etc.)? What are their wants and needs, now and in the future?

- Who are my competitors (e.g., users, equipment, vendors, competing projects)?

- What is my organization's capability (strengths and weaknesses)?

- What are my objectives?

- What strategies do I want to pursue?

- What are my expected risks, costs, and rewards of following each strategy?

- What can I reasonably achieve?

Thus, the first step in preparing strategic analyses is to identify appropriate **strategic inputs and assumptions.** Strategic inputs are the products of various strategic analyses that have been conducted throughout the organization and the management decisions pertaining to them. By analyzing these strategic documents, we can often find ways to approach IS issues that are more consistent with company environment and management style than those which use internally generated IS data alone.

In the past, companies have customarily conducted strategic planning activities in the early part of the plan year, so that the study products could provide inputs to the long-range and annual plans. Recently, however, more and more companies are making strategic planning into a continuous process which is conducted throughout the entire year as required, particularly when important business issues surface. This change in direction is fostered by the awareness that strategic considerations are always timely. Strategic studies should be conducted whenever legitimate business or IS issues are known to exist and qualified people are available to do it.

Four different types of strategic inputs may be considered:

1. Technology Forecast

2. Business Plans Analysis

3. Strategic Analyses (developed previously by user/IS groups)

4. Strategic Assumptions (developed by various staff groups)

This group of four strategic inputs is then put through an analysis consisting of three parts:

1. Summarize Strategic Inputs

2. Correlate Inputs with Issues

3. Summarize Findings

## Part One:  Summarize Strategic Inputs and Assumptions

Examine business plan documents and other **strategic inputs,** and identify opportunities for IS to contribute more effectively to the company's bottom line.

Each of the strategic activities conducted during various phases of the planning process is summarized.  Strategic activities usually yield documents which the IS people can review.  Those documents need not be strictly IS in their subject matter.  Other sources of strategic information that may be informative are:

- Business units plans

- Corporate staff offices memoranda

- Management committee conclusions

- Outside consultants and auditors' reports

## Part Two:  Correlate Inputs with Issues

- Conduct **strategic analyses** dealing with key business and IS issues in response to long-range corporate plans.

- Analyze senior **management goals** enabling IS to set objectives for future business systems.

- Participate in the corporation's strategic planning process and identify major **strategic business objectives** to be addressed in this IS planning process.

The various strategic inputs which were developed by people inside and outside the company earlier in the plan year, or in previous years, ought to be correlated with the IS issues.  In this way, strategic information can be helpful in resolving the issues.  **Figure 4-5, Correlation of IS Issues with Strategic Inputs,** is a sample form that can be used to display the results of such a correlation analysis.

Decide on the appropriate strategic inputs to include in the analysis. Strategic business and IS analyses are usually broad in scope, as are the strategic inputs derived from them.  For example, the technology forecast, as an example of a strategic input, is usually an overview of the present and expected future technology environment, broadly stated.  Accordingly, it would be expected that such a forecast would include a number of technology topics in addition to those of immediate interest.  Consequently, all of the strategic inputs should be examined, and only the ones should be selected which are relevant in some way to the subject under discussion.

Figure 4-5

## CORRELATION OF IS ISSUES WITH STRATEGIC INPUTS

| IS Issue | STRATEGIC INPUTS | | |
|---|---|---|---|
| | #1<br><br>Technology Forecast | #2 & #3<br>Business Plans Analysis &<br>Strategic Analyses | #4<br><br>Strategic Assumptions |
| 1. Which of the company's business functions must be supported, and how? | | | |
| 2. What is the company's future business direction? | | | |
| 3. How can IS resources be best deployed? | | | |
| 4. What is the current status and future direction of the technology being considered? | | | |

- **Studying the correlation analysis:**  If the analysis is done correctly, and sufficient inputs are gathered to allow viewing the issues from several different perspectives, we should then be capable of summarizing the findings coherently.  However unrefined they may be at this preliminary stage of the planning process, nonetheless, the strategic summaries should be sufficient to instill confidence that a feasible set of IS objectives is being developed.  Developing the strategic summary, then, is a critical step in the IS planning process.

## Part Three: Summarize the Findings on Strategic Issues

- Summarize the principal strategic issues that have been agreed upon.

- Agree on the Critical Success Factors that will determine the outcome of the projects being considered.

From the correlation of issues and inputs in **Figure 4-5** and from the strategic analyses that have been made, this phase of the planning effort should be documented by a summary of the findings on strategic issues.  This should then be the definitive report for following the inputs and assumptions in the subsequent Information Service analyses of the technical considerations.

- **Critical Success Factors (CSF):** During the systems analysis of an IS project, it is normal for the analysts to produce a set of test data to apply to the finished system at a later date to verify whether it is, or is not, satisfying the requirements that were agreed upon. In the same manner, while the conversations with operational management are still in progress, it is important to mutually agree upon criteria for project success. These criteria are called Critical Success Factors. There is ample literature concerning their development and use.

At this point, therefore, before the more technical data processing studies, it is important to determine a set of Critical Success Factors. These should be established as a joint effort of IS management, systems personnel, and operations personnel, in addition to the affected users. Since they will be one of the measures of success of the projects involved, they deserve extensive thought and consensus among participants. They must be accomplished for Information Services and the users to be successful in their missions.

## 4.1.4.3   PHASE III - INFORMATION SERVICES PLANNING

### A.   Develop IS Issues and Requirements:

This next phase of strategic information systems planning is usually the more detailed and technical Information Services planning. It must be done in sufficient detail so that management will have a clear picture of both the opportunities and the difficulties involved. The various alternative solutions must be presented in a way that will allow decisions to be made, and will prevent unexpected problems from arising as even more detailed systems analysis is done. In order that appropriate IS support might be provided to business plans and objectives:

- Develop a set of **IS requirements, objectives, and opportunity areas.**
- Support with a set of **IS issues.**

IS will have a large stake in the outcome of the projects being considered, whether they succeed or fail. Therefore, this phase should include an analysis of the current IS long-range and short-range plans, and whether the requirements, objectives, and strategies can conform to the existing IS organization and operation. There may be a number of IS issues that need to be surfaced and discussed immediately, so that appropriate decisions can be made on agreement, funding, and handling of them.

For each IS objective that has been agreed upon to this point in the planning, the following questions should be asked:

1.   Is the objective measurable?

2.   Is the objective achievable?

3.   If the objective is achieved, will it resolve the issues, both the business issues and the IS issues?

This is not the time to stop and apply extra analytical effort to refine the objectives in ways that better fit the IS capabilities. This is simply the time to make an educated management estimate as to whether the objectives can be accomplished with either the existing staff and capabilities, or with purchased staff and operational support. The bottom-line IS issue is: If the other issues are resolved, can Information Services accomplish these projects in some way? Is there any way we can meet the requirements?

**B.      Propose IS Options and Alternatives:**

For any projects that are worthy of the management attention involved in strategic planning, IS planners should not presume to make key decisions on possible options, even if they appear to be technically obvious. There may be valid business reasons to choose other options. The types of options and alternatives that are developed and checked by IS personnel, then presented to management for selection, are:

- Develop a series of **alternative system solutions** with the assistance of the user divisions. These take the form of strategic options; for example, enhancement of current systems versus development of new systems, and identification of candidate business processes.

- Address **IS organizational alternatives** as a part of the year's planning cycle. Address important issues, such as centralization versus decentralization, distribution of IS organizations; appropriate assignment of IS activities to the various IS groups or user departments, and the proper role of the user in systems and data processing activities.

- Address the issue of **future equipment and software alternative configurations.** Analyze centralized, decentralized, and distributed equipment options. Also, analyze the issue of single versus mixed vendor environments, and so on.

- Identify significant voice/data/facsimile **communications alternatives** if a corporation-wide communications network is a prerequisite.

In all cases, describe the **strengths and weaknesses** of the various options from both the IS and the user's points of view. These options should not be presented in a highly technical manner, but should be stated simply and clearly for operational management to make decisions based upon the best estimates and experience that IS personnel can provide. It is quite valid for an analyst to express feelings and opinions from experience, if they bear directly on the subject at hand.

**C.      Create Impact Statements:**

At this point, considerable business planning and Information Services planning will have been accomplished. The proposed options and alternatives are being presented to management for decisions, yet there may still be some critical assumptions that should be emphasized, and there may be some opportunities or threats that should not be forgotten.   Business impacts created by the proposed systems, or impacts on particular functional areas, including IS, should be summarized on simple forms to attach to the options and alternatives information.  An example of a form that can be used is given in **Figure 4-6, Key Assumptions and Business Impacts.** This form could be useful in producing summarized impact statements that clearly point up opportunities or threats.

**Figure 4-6**

### KEY ASSUMPTIONS AND BUSINESS IMPACTS

| Factor | Key Assumptions | Business Impact Opportunities/Threats |
|---|---|---|
| Operational | | |
| Economic | | |
| Political | | |
| Regulatory | | |
| Labor Relations | | |
| Social | | |

## 4.1.4.4   PHASE IV - SETTING STRATEGIC PRIORITIES

**A.**      Establish Evaluation Criteria:

- Prepare a list of **evaluation criteria** to aid senior management in approving funding requests for new and enhanced business systems projects.

As the size, number, and complexity of IS project requests grow, they may well exceed the available financial resources and IS developmental personnel.  It is, therefore, necessary to establish evaluation criteria so that projects of most value to the organization can be accomplished first, and meaningful strategic priorities can be set.  Such criteria should be set mutually by user and IS management, as they must reflect both need and capability.  Some types of evaluation criteria could be:

- Projects with clear, quantifiable expense reductions and a payback of an agreed number of months.

- Projects that meet the needs of organizational change, or a recognized organizational necessity.

- Projects that support new and expanded products and services with attractive revenue forecasts.

- Projects that provide for critical decision-making capabilities.

**B.**      <u>Perform Investment and Cost-Benefit Analysis:</u>

- Follow the procedures for analyzing the projected **return on investment,** rate of return, or payback period for the proposed business system projects.

ROI estimates for the proposed projects should be developed in formats that are similar to the ROI calculations made for all other operational projects in the organization. It is quite feasible for Information Services to fit their estimates and calculations into any form that is generally accepted by the user management for other types of projects. Methods can be developed for assessing the worthiness of, and applying objective figures to, "soft" as well as "hard" projects with documented expense reductions. If there is a business necessity for the project, it is likely that operational management can estimate its value.

**C.**      <u>Establish a Priority Ranking of Options:</u>

- **Rank** the various business processes and automated systems in accordance with predetermined selection criteria. Other factors which enter into the **priority-setting** process are apparent degree of technical feasibility, extent of business plan support, and satisfaction of critical success factors.

Systems options usually have varied costs and time for accomplishment. The review of the options is meaningless unless some effort has been made to:

- Rate the options for fit with the requirements.

- Estimate the allocation of resources required for each option.

- Recommend a priority ranking of the options.

The **strategic options** that are still being considered at this point should all have reasonably good fit with the original business and IS objectives, but it is possible that newer ideas have been introduced by operational management, newer technological methods have become feasible, or substantial cost/features trade-offs have been discussed as the analysis has proceeded. It is important, therefore, before recommending a priority ranking of the options proposed, to summarize a rating of the options for fit with the original and modified requirements. It must be clearly understood by all participants where business or technological issues have forced a different direction in the thinking of the analysts, which may artificially change their proposed priority ranking scheme.

An estimate of the **allocation of resources** should be made for each option being considered, as the costs and efforts involved may well affect the ranking that is being considered. In practice, estimates of the allocation of resources are made rather conservatively to give a good track record for IS on their planned resource usage compared to the actual after project completion. This also allows a certain amount of latitude on the part of IS management in handling special projects as the planning period proceeds. At this stage of planning, the estimates developed will merely be approximations anyway. It is helpful, however, to have comparable estimates available when choosing between various options. The recommended procedure, therefore, is to spend more effort on comparable estimates; that is, assume a base estimate for all the options. These will be the most valuable numbers in ranking the options.

There are a number of ways that priority ranking for project options can be accomplished if the options all have reasonably good fit with the original objectives, and the allocation of resources shows them to be acceptable to management. Guidelines for the ranking should be devised to fit the situations and should be presented to management for approval. The guidelines may be any of the following types:

**a.   Priority by organization need:**

Priority 1:   Mandatory projects with high-level support

Priority 2:   Necessary projects with high-level support:

- Organization Strategy
- Customer Service
- Product Improvement
- Expense Reduction (Should be close to $1 million minimum in large corporations to warrant consideration.)

Priority 3:   Desirable operational projects to improve efficiency or effectiveness.

Priority 4:   Operational projects to improve satisfaction of current requirements and requests.

**b.   Priority by return on investment:**

Priority 1:   Strategic projects which can be assigned priorities based on a five-year return-on-investment projection.

Priority 2:   Operational projects which can be assigned priorities based on a two year return-on-investment projection.

Priority 3:   Operational projects which were selected to satisfy current business requirements based on a two-year return-on-investment projection.

**c.   Priority relating to P&L impact:**

Priority 1:   Impact on revenues

Priority 2:   Impact on direct expenses

Priority 3:   Impact on overhead or indirect expenses

Whichever priority scheme is selected, the results of the estimation should be exhibited in tabular form with such headings as:

- Priority Ranking
- Business System
- Annualized Benefits ($000's)
- IS Estimated Development Costs ($000's)
- IS Estimated Annualized Expenses ($000's)
- Payback Period (Years)

The establishment of a priority ranking is, of course, a selection statement by IS management or the study team. It is valid and most helpful, however, if sufficient information is given to support the rankings, and the reasons for the calculations are available for consideration.

**D.**      **Make Funding Recommendations:**

- Make baseline funding recommendations for the selected, higher-priority IS projects that will be further considered in strategic planning.

These funding recommendations may be according to:

- Organizational unit
- Re-allocation of budget dollars
- A breakdown of the effort by systems
- The need of a particular strategic project

The funding recommendations should normally be in budget format, stating the organization involved, the dollars required, and the people to be assigned. If there are a number of projects, or the project is subdivided, percentages of the total should be given by type of strategic project (customer services, product line improvement, expense reduction, etc.), type of system (new development, enhancement, mandatory maintenance, etc.), or expense allocation of baseline budget dollars (business group, IS budget, DP operations, etc.).

The funding recommendations should clearly state whether they will be considered as part of the operating budget presently in force or being considered, or part of a special funding request which is being proposed.

**4.1.4.5   PHASE V - REPORTING THE STRATEGIC PLAN**

At this point in the strategic planning process, the various opportunities and options will have been explored and analyzed, and it will be time to refine the alternative proposals and to define the future business functions and Information Services requirements in a structured manner for further discussion. This will lead to the necessary management decisions and commitments to proceed with the selected projects and options.

**A.      Describe Proposed Architecture:**

Those who have been involved in exploring the strategic business and system alternatives should agree on preferred architectures to propose. The steps are:

- Develop a **strategic business architecture.** This will be a structured definition of the desired future business functions in terms of information flows, policies, procedures, management decision-making capabilities, and appropriate financial and operating controls.

- Evolve a **system architecture** which supports the business functions architecture developed in the previous step. System architecture includes office automation, distributed data processing, distributed database, communications, corporate data processing, and the corporate database.

**B.      Describe Proposed Strategies:**

At this point, it will be necessary to fine-tune the business objectives. It was pointed out in Phase II that the objectives as stated by business management should be accepted and used for subsequent analyses without appreciable discussion or criticism, if only to gain the full cooperation of all parties involved. By this time, however, the business and IS study team will have reviewed and discussed many other possible business objectives and will have found that some of the original objectives should be modified if management agreement can be obtained. Some changes in objectives may allow more attractive strategies to be employed. The steps are then:

- Describe the **strategic system alternatives** which will meet all requirements, but which have a degree of flexibility to meet continually changing business requirements.

- Describe the **options that exist** with regards to organizational strategies, meaning both IS structure and responsibilities, and the part user personnel will play in operating the system.

- Describe **equipment and software strategies** that can cope with the organization's many changing business requirements.

- Describe data, voice, and facsimile **communications strategies** to assure the organization of appropriate communications facilities as the systems are installed and future demands increase.

**C.      Compare Systems to Available Resources:**

The proposed system or systems will have been studied in Phase IV as to their resource requirements, and some measure of fit will have been agreed upon with either the present available or future proposed resources. This review of resource availability within budget constraints is a key section of the plan and should be stated clearly in summary form.

**D.        Develop Strategic Plan Document:**

The study group should get preliminary agreement with management before producing the final document, and then include all the descriptions and comparisons above which may be appropriate.

**E.        Obtain Necessary Management Commitments:**

If the document is circulated to responsible management and receives approval, the work of the strategic planning group is completed for the particular projects or time period involved.   Since strategic planning generally has no fixed annual calendar, however, modifications to a particular strategic plan, or the adoption of a plan to fit a particular budget, may proceed immediately.

### 4.1.4.6   PHASE VI - OPERATIONAL PLANNING

After a strategic plan has been developed and approved, it will be necessary to introduce its features, commitments, and costs into the next cycle or modification of the Information Services Annual Operational Plan and Budget Plan.  If special financial commitments have been received from top management to proceed immediately with the implementation of the strategic plan, or sections of it, the budget plan would have been thereby modified, and IS will be operating under a new base plan.   Management may decide, on the other hand, to wait for the annual planning cycle before implementing a particular strategy, and then the strategic plan will be folded into the rest of the operating plan as another set of projects.

When it is organization policy, there will be a long-range operating plan and forecast produced each year in addition to the budget plan.  For IS departments, the long-range operating plan and forecast will encompass estimates of all anticipated future development projects, including those being studied as strategic plans.

However it is handled, after a strategic plan is approved, it will be introduced to the regular IS planning process to comply with any company policies and to meet the Controller's office requirements for expense and capital forecasting.

**A.        Enter Systems Analysis Phase of System Development Life Cycle:**

Once the projects that have been handled in a strategic plan have received all approvals, the necessary funding, and the required personnel, the planning process will move into the Systems Analysis phase of the System Development Life Cycle.

**B.        Proceed with System Development:**

The particular projects that have been selected in the strategic planning exercise will then be passed to the Systems Development group for detailed operational planning and for systems development.

## 4.2     NOLAN'S SIX STAGES,[10]

The familiar "stages theory" of data processing development is shown in **Figure 4-7, The Stages Theory.**

**Figure 4-7**

### THE STAGES THEORY

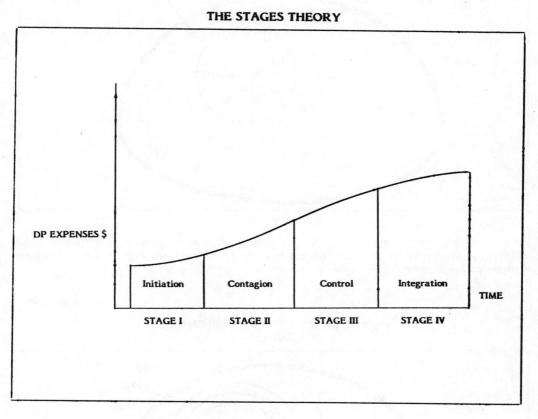

---

[10]     Richard L. Nolan, Nolan, Norton & Company

This held true in the 1960's when data processing, compared to the organization's operations, was as illustrated in **Figure 4-8, Company Computer Environment 1960.**

**Figure 4-8**

COMPANY COMPUTER ENVIRONMENT 1960

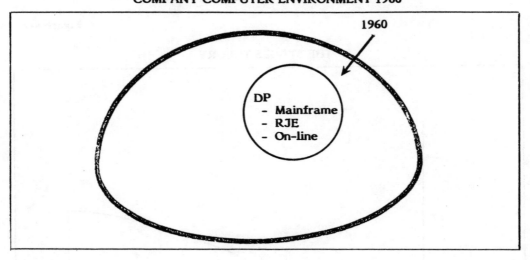

It also held generally true to the 1980's, when data processing continued to be relatively separate from other operations as illustrated in **Figure 4-9, Company Computer Environment 1960-1980.**

**Figure 4-9**

COMPANY COMPUTER ENVIRONMENT
1960-1980

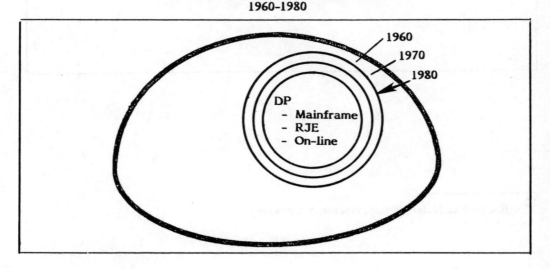

In the 1980's however, there has been a marked change in the relationship, and data processing is now integral to the general operations. This is shown in **Figure 4-10, Company Computer Environment, 1980-1990.**

Figure 4-10

## COMPANY COMPUTER ENVIRONMENT
### 1980-1990

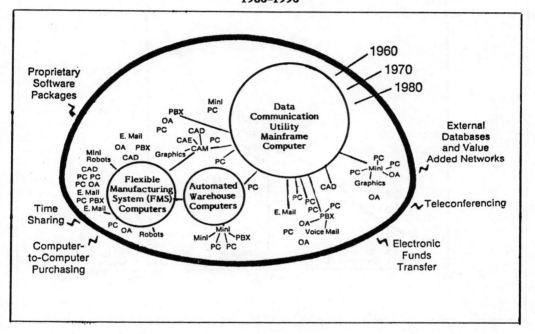

The advent of the installation of strategic information systems, communications, databases, end-user computing, engineering and factory automation, and voice systems has caused a seven fold projected increase in computer expenditures from 1980 to 1990.

The result has been a technological discontinuity that has called for an extension of the stages theory. **Figure 4-11, Restated Stages Theory,** illustrates the effect of the micro era.

**Figure 4-11**

## RESTATED STAGES THEORY

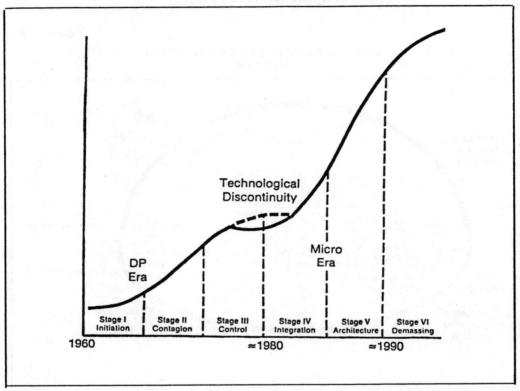

This has been described in the literature. Stages I to III, from 1960 to 1980, had a relatively stable technology. The effort was data processing, and the computers handled tasks rather than functions. There was a highly structured control environment with clear lines of administration. The efforts were highly documented.

End-user computing has been dominant in Stages IV, V, and VI. There have been three classes of technology driving the growth:

1.  **Functional Niche Applications,** including such things as work-stations, computer aided design (CAD), and process control.

2.  **End-User Productivity Applications,** including office automation, personal computing, and ad hoc computing.

3.  **Utility Applications,** where the old-line data processing is being re-engineered to form the base of administrative systems.

The microcomputer era has brought about the technological discontinuity. There are many ways we use micros, such as in office automation, personal computing,

computer aided design, robotics, and so on. The fact is, while traditional data processing is flattening out, the new data processing uses of micros are moving up rapidly.
The discontinuity in management has been dramatic. On-line computing and database
development were structured, centralized experiences. Micros, on the other hand, are
decentralized, although they still require central leadership.

   **Figure 4-12, DP Is Evolving To The Advanced Stages,** points out that the
problems of the mid-1980's are those of managing the diversified technologies. By
1990, the expenditures will be considerable, and it will be necessary to exert strong
central leadership to build the necessary computer architecture.

**Figure 4-12**

## DP IS EVOLVING TO THE ADVANCED STAGES

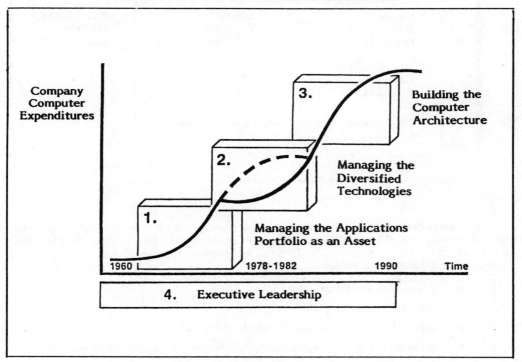

   **Figure 4-13, Computer Architecture Product Spectrum, Post-1975,** shows the
broad band of products that make up Information Services. The growth products of the
1980's include the office automation, personal computer, and distributed computer
products. While the telephones and the main DP computers are relatively stable, the
growth products are quite volatile, with frequent shakeouts. For example, VisiCalc had
70% of the market, yet Lotus 1-2-3 overtook it in one year. Osborne was first, but was
replaced in usage by Compaq.

**Figure 4-13**

### COMPUTER ARCHITECTURE PRODUCT SPECTRUM
### POST - 1975

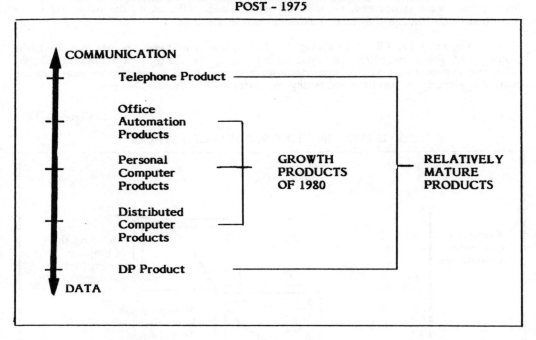

Companies that obtain a strategic advantage with the computer generally redefine the factors of competition rather than applying the computer to the traditional factors of industry competition. Typical examples of strategically managing the diversified technologies have been:

- Deere and Company using FMS
- Merrill Lynch using CMA
- Citibank using Automatic Teller Machines (ATM)
- American Hospital Supply using microcomputer customer order entry

Managing the diversified technologies requires development of effective techniques and new approaches. There must be a redefinition of the management discipline necessary for end-user computing and communications. The impact of these changes has caused the need for the following:

- Necessary visions in strategy and direction setting.

- Consideration of overall costs, benefits, and their ongoing measurement, rather than Return on Investment calculations.

  Success criteria must be established, looking at three levels: senior, middle, and lower management. New possibilities must be looked upon as ventures, with prototypes and pilots developed.

- Data Resource and Information Centers should be established, with both accountability and authority for results.

- Communications and End-User Computer Architecture must have central standards and guidelines established.

- User accountability and authority must be clearly understood for operational changes.

- There must be central leadership supplied for this period of discontinuity which entails a great deal of cultural change in the organization.

- Someone must follow and predict the future applications and technical resources to be expected. Technology scanning must be an ongoing task of senior information management.

These needs are clear and must be effectively handled. A good approach is to consider the position of a Computer Functional Executive (CFE). This is shown in **Figure 4-14, Structuring Executive Leadership for Computer Technology.** The position must be in place to take advantage of strategic opportunities.

**Figure 4-14**

**STRUCTURING EXECUTIVE LEADERSHIP FOR COMPUTER TECHNOLOGY**

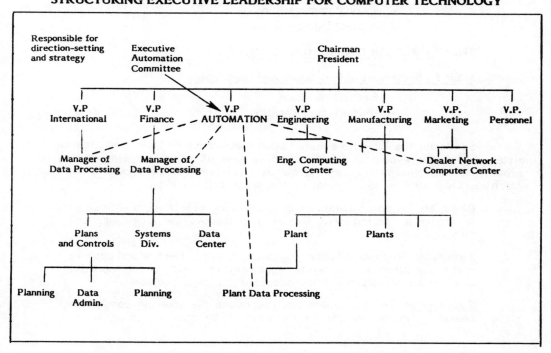

A VP Automation, or CFE or CIO, would have all types of data processing and computing reporting in a dotted-line relationship. the position would be responsible for automation leadership, planning, and implementation. The position could report to an Executive Automation Committee that would be responsible for direction setting and strategy. As pointed out by Barnard, the essential functions of the Computer Functional Executive would be:

a.   To provide the system of communications

b.   To promote the securing of essential strategic efforts

c.   To formulate and define purpose

Such a leader would take a different approach to management than the EDP manager of 1973, or the "New Breed" Information Systems manager of the late 1970's. The approach is summarized in **Figure 4-15, Leadership Attributes.**

The steps to be taken by the person filling this position are listed below:

### STEP 1 - Firm Understanding of Perceived and Real Problems:

1.   Common management framework

2.   Strategic systems alignment

3.   Baseline
     - Against a healthy organization structure
     - Against competition
     - Against industry leader

### STEP 2 - Workable Organization Structure

### STEP 3 - Statement of Key Issues and Objectives:

     - Recharting issues
     - Cultural considerations

Similarly, the Executive Automation Committee or Executive Steering Committee should also evolve in function and responsibility. A steering committee is normally for direction setting, and it spends a relatively small amount of time on its activities. Over a three- to five-year period, its functions can be:

**Direction Setting:** Establish company-wide objectives and policies for computer technology. Review and approve the long-range and strategic plans.

**Rationing:** Review and approve annual budgets. Review and approve major computer-related capital appropriations, such as for facilities and hardware. Screen and approve major strategic projects.

**Structuring:** Develop, maintain, and revise the steering committee charter. Review and approve organization structure and changes.

Figure 4-15

## LEADERSHIP ATTRIBUTES

| | EDP MANAGER 1973 | NEW BREED INFORMATION SYSTEMS MANAGER (late 1970's) | COMPUTING FUNCTIONAL EXECUTIVE 1980's |
|---|---|---|---|
| Views Himself As | Technologist | An Operating Manager | A Functional Executive |
| Approach | "Hands-On" | Closely Involved | "Hands Off" |
| Role Model | "We" | "Us" | Others |
| Personally | Strong-Willed | Direct | Flexible, Diplomatic |
| Short Term | Tomorrow | 3-6 Months | This Year |
| Long Term | One Year | 12-24 Months | 5-10 Years |
| Develops Expertise | Centrally | Concentrated | Distributed in Units |
| Deliverable | Report | System | Organizational Change |
| Rallying Point | Expertise | Force Of Personality | Common Vision |
| Demands | Personal Loyalty | Departmental Loyalty | Loyalty to Common Vision |
| How To Do It | One Way | Several Ways | Many Alternatives |
| Technology Perspective | One Legitimate, Others Dangerous | Limited | Many Deserve Consideration Consideration with Control |
| Thinking | "Right" | Pragmatic | Abstract |
| Political Base | Functional | Narrow, Built By Service | Broad, Built Through Relationships |
| Facilitate Change By | Installing Technology | Policy Is Law | Guidelines |
| Constituent Base | Professionals | Narrow | Widening |
| Decisions Reached | Independently | Rapidly-Without Consensus | By Negotiation, Conflict Resolution |
| Attention Focused | Project | Targeted, Some Alienation | Broadly, Open Doors |
| Senior Management | Limited Interaction | Executes Initial Concerns | Leads, Counsels |
| Assistance To Units | Control | Audit, Review | Common Exposures, Opportunities |

**Staffing:** Selection of key managers for the computer activity.

**Advising and Auditing:** Monitor and review major projects. Advise and audit key managers' performances.

Most companies feel that the relative effectiveness of a steering committee is greatest in the direction setting and rationing functions.

The impact of the type of thinking that would create a CFE (Computing Functional Executive) and a steering committee could be considerable. Such changes could lead to:

a.  **Gaining a Competitive Edge:** For example, terminals in customers' offices and product differentiation can dramatically affect competition.

b.  **Repositioning the Business:** Information technology can aid in market innovation that may or may not be computer oriented.

c.  **Running the Business Better:** The new technologies can aid considerably in the management of key resources.

There are two inverse problems that must be faced in planning and managing modern computing. These are:

● Bottom-up focus without top-down vision

● Top-down vision without bottom-up capability

The issues are clear for this time of discontinuity and change. They are:

1.  There must be policy direction from the top. Authority and accountability must be assigned, and clear investment criteria must be established.

2.  Resources must be supplied to support this major change. There must be management commitment and organizational change to meet the problems.

## 4.3     ROCKART'S CRITICAL SUCCESS FACTORS

John F. Rochart's concept of Critical Success Factors (CSF) has proven to be as useful for planning strategic information systems as it has long been for discussing traditional systems with management.  A useful planning methodology for strategic information systems, using CSFs, is described in the report entitled, "A Planning Methodology for Integrating Management Support Systems[11].

This report traces the extensive impact of information technology on organizations, and describes the concepts of Decision Support Systems (DSS) and Executive Support Systems (ESS), with their links to the traditional system infrastructure.  The development of the CSF approach to understand the information requirements of the CEO is described, with Rockart's original definition of CSFs as "those few critical areas where things must go right for the business to flourish."  CSFs are limited by the skills and objectivity of the analysts using them, and are time dependent, but these are both common limitations to all strategic planning efforts.

The CSF process does provide a design focus.  It can help direct the investment in technological infrastructure to achieve strategic goals.  The critical information set indicated by CSFs clarifies the support of strategic goals.  The process of generating CSFs and eliciting the critical information set involves personal interviews with key management.  This is described in **Section 1.4, Engaging Top Management in Strategic Planning.**

**Figure 4-16, A Strategic Planning Methodology,** illustrates the steps necessary to build strategic systems.  Such an analysis builds on the critical information set to define high-payoff MIS opportunities, and to begin the development of a strategic data model.

This function may be carried out in several ways, but generally follows the top-down planning orientation of methodologies such as BSP.  The strategic data model attempts to identify the major sources of data classes that are required, and how these sources interrelate.  It provides a tangible link between the strategic directions being followed and the design and implementation of the systems.

There is a growing experience with strategic information systems planning approaches that use the CSF method as a strategic requirement definition.  For example, Arthur Young (Arthur Young & Co., 1983) has used the CSF approach to provide the **strategic** direction for the information systems plan in over fifty planning engagements.  They combine the CSF approach with a modified version of the BSP methodology to provide the basis for building a strategic data model.  This links the competitive strategic direction that is being followed with the comprehensive data resource of the firm.

---

[11] **"A Planning Methodology for Integrating Management Support Systems,"** John C. Henderson, John F, Rockart, and John G.  Sifonis, Sept. 1984, CISR WP #116, Center for Information Systems Research, Sloan School of Management, MIT.

Figure 4-16

## A STRATEGIC PLANNING METHODOLOGY

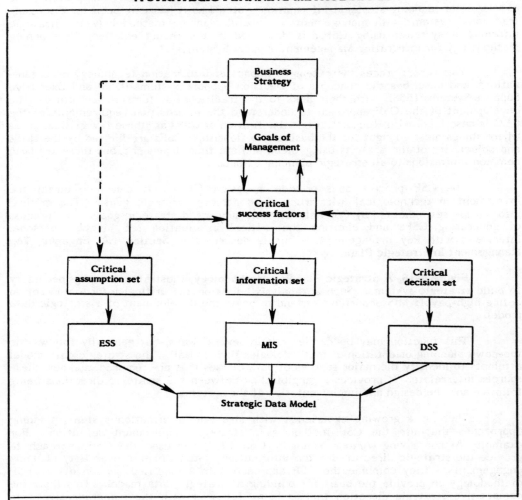

In **Figure 4-16,** the critical information set, the critical decision set, and the critical assumption set, all serve the same function. They are differentiated depending upon whether the system being developed is an MIS, a DSS, or an ESS. This provides a means to integrate major activities in DSS and ESS with the MIS action plan.

In summary, the planning methodology starts with a top-level strategic business analysis to identify high payoff opportunities and to predict information requirements. Information needs of all types are integrated through a strategic data model. As shown in **Figure 4-17, An Integrated Framework for DSS, ESS, and MIS Planning** this strategic data model also depends upon the results of a more detailed information and technical analysis. There must be a connection between the strategic thrust of the organization and the technical level. This provides the opportunity to reflect the operational requirements of lower-level management and staff, and to identify existing data resources.

The upper half of **Figure 4-17** provides a strategic perspective for establishing priorities and implementation plans. The lower half is a planning process that yields specific hardware/software, major application systems, and data architecture recommendations. The strategic data model is a lens through which senior management can focus on the technical requirements of strategic information systems development. It also provides a mechanism for the systems professionals to determine investments in the technological infrastructure that meet the critical strategic needs of the firm.

**Figure 4-17**

**AN INTEGRATED FRAMEWORK FOR DSS, ESS, AND MIS PLANNING**

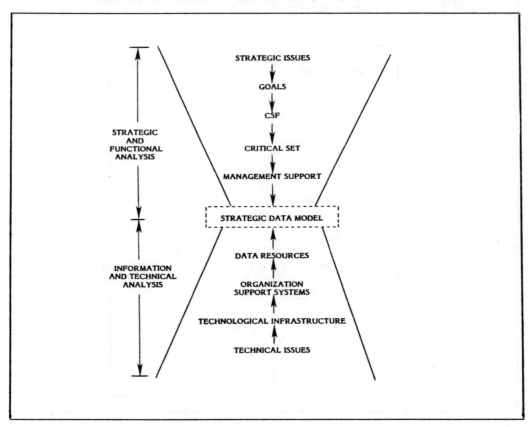

The application of this method in practice is described in more detail in **Section 1.4, Engaging Top Management in Strategic Planning.** One approach is outlined in **Figure 4-18, The Planning Process.** This technique provides a basis for debate, and a method of identifying primary and secondary opportunities for strategic systems. The critical assumption set for ESS systems, and the critical decision set for DSS systems can be voted on, and a decision made on the course to take.

**Figure 4-18**

## THE PLANNING PROCESS

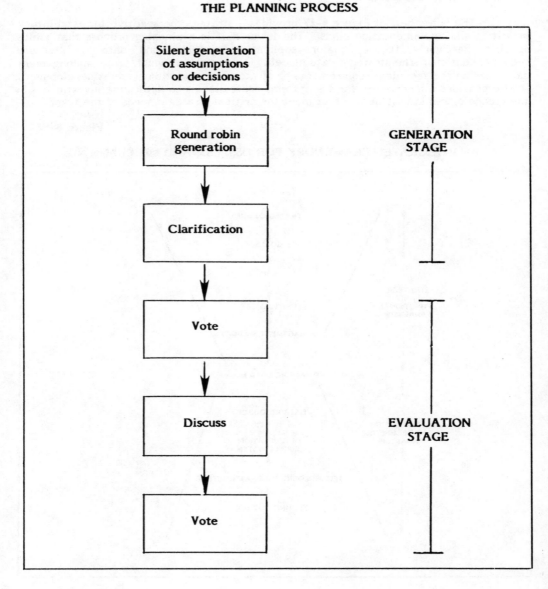

The process of surfacing critical assumptions, information, and decisions, and translating these issues into requirements for strategic management support systems provides important input into the development of a strategic data model for a firm. The model is presented as a modified entity/relation model that defines data classes and their relationships. Combinations of these data classes can portray subject area databases. Each CSF will project on this model differently. The model provides a means to examine and communicate strategic data requirements.

Such discussions enlighten operational management about information systems problems, and illustrate how the strategic information system plan could be better integrated with the strategic business plan. The management of the assumption set is in the domain of executive management, and the responsibility for ensuring the validity of the assumptions rests clearly with executive management.

It has been found that the methodology does provide a means to integrate strategic systems and other MIS systems. The strategic data model serves as a linking device between the strategic data needs of top management and the operational and technical needs of the IS organization.

The group techniques complement the traditional CSF approach by increasing communication between individuals. CSFs and goals are challenged, and there is an implicit link from the assumption set back to the organizational goals and the overall business strategy.

The role of information technology in the competitive advantage of the firm is rapidly increasing. However, the opportunity for competitive advantages cannot be fully exploited until management can coordinate its investments in professional and management support systems to ensure that they will impact the strategic issues of the firm. This approach is a way of coordinating those investments in an efficient and effective manner.

**4.4          McLEAN'S STRATEGIC PLANNING FRAMEWORK**

Professor Ephraim R. McLean co-authored a book with John V. Soden after a conference on strategic planning participated in by major private and public sector organizations.[12] This material was obviously developed under the original paradigm of strategic systems before "competitive advantage" became the key words to include. It is centered on the strategic information systems **planning process,** however, and it still offers a completely valid and tested approach for moving from the objectives and strategies that have been agreed upon to implementation plans for strategic MIS systems. In addition, it is one distillation of the strategic planning experience of such firms as IBM, Standard Oil, Mobil, Procter & Gamble, Xerox, Trans World Airlines, TRW, and a number of government, health care, and education enterprises.

This approach is, indeed a **framework** for strategic planning. It centers on, "How is the Information Services organization contributing to the overall success of the enterprise?" It delineates a process for deciding on the **objectives** of the MIS organization; on changes to these objectives, on the resources used to attain these objectives; and on the policies that are required to govern the acquisition, use, and disposition of these resources. Strategic MIS planning, as outlined here, typically occurs at infrequent intervals, and is triggered by the need for an enterprise to resolve a particularly substantive strategic issue, or issues, that involves the MIS entity. This process is, therefore, still completely valid.

**4.4.1     STRATEGIC PLANNING TASKS**

The first task in strategic planning, as shown in **Figure 4-19, MIS Strategic Planning Framework,** is to set the MIS mission; that is, to define the charter of the Information Services organization. This broad definition of organizational role must naturally be done within the mission and purpose of the overall organization of which MIS is a part. Sometimes the MIS organization receives this mission as a given; other times it is arrived at through mutual discussion with top management.

Once this mission is set, the next task is to **assess the MIS environment** -- to consider the opportunities and risks which are present now and might be present in the future. This would include consideration of such things as:

- The objectives, strategies, policies and plans of the host organization.

- The competitive position of the overall organization.

- The user groups within the organization -- their needs, their current use of MIS resources, and their perceptions of the capability of the MIS organization.

- The present and emerging technology for information processing, such as the rapid growth of microcomputers.

- The ability of the MIS organization to effect change.

---

[12] **Strategic Planning for MIS,** Professor Ephraim R. McLean, the University of California, Los Angeles, and John V. Soden, McKinsey & Co., Inc., Wiley-Interscience, New York, 1977.

Figure 4-19

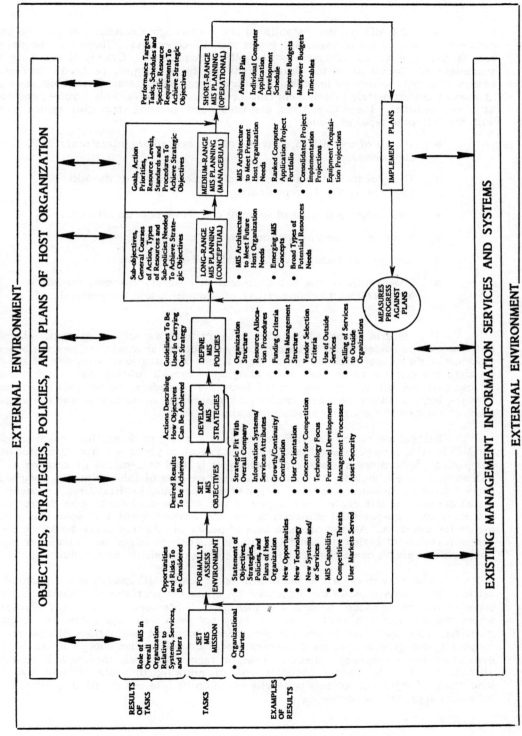

MIS STRATEGIC PLANNING FRAMEWORK

195

With the MIS mission established and a thorough appraisal made of the environment, it next becomes necessary to **set the MIS objectives.** These are the desired results that are to be achieved by the MIS organization. Closely linked with the statement of objectives is the development of the strategies, or broad courses of action, that will be needed in order to achieve these objectives. Thus, objectives and strategies are intimately interwoven; consideration of one invariably involves consideration of the other. These objectives, and their accompanying strategies, typically deal with the following types of items:

- The fit of the MIS objectives with the overall organizational objectives.

- The growth, continuity, and level of contribution of the MIS function within the organization.

- The classes and types of systems and services to be offered.

- The role of users in systems development efforts.

- The type of management and staff to be developed.

- The posture of the MIS organization vis-a-vis the user, the host organization, the competitive environment, and the professional milieu.

The determination of policies is a critical aspect of strategic planning. Policies are the guidelines to be used in carrying out the strategies. They are specific statements that cover such things as the internal organizational structure of the MIS division; the criteria to be used in deciding upon overall funding levels and resource allocations; the use of steering committees; the procedures to be used in selecting vendors, buying outside services, and/or selling services to outside users; the employment of a database management scheme; and so forth.

**Setting the policy** for how the company is going to decide how much to spend for MIS is seldom directly addressed, and it is an area of particular frustration for many companies. Sometimes a mixture of techniques is used as a means of arriving at the MIS budget. These include, for example, a fixed percent of sales or assets; comparable expenditures of similar companies, adjusted for size and profitability; whatever the major company profit centers will agree to pay for; base amounts, plus discretionary increases for high-potential projects; and/or the amount spent last year plus adjustments for inflation. All too often, a lack of policy in this area leads the MIS group to concentrate its attention on justifying the acquisition of major new computer equipment without giving much concern to the underlying reasons for such equipment.

Policies with regard to the allocation of scarce MIS resources are particularly critical, since they provide the guidelines by which the portfolio of current and future projects will be selected, funded, and managed. Unfortunately, in many companies where these resource allocation policies have not been well established, MIS management has little incentive to perform disciplined economic evaluations of new project proposals, and general corporate policies are often not precise enough to be useful in evaluating these proposed projects. Thus, in many instances, the implicit resource-allocation policy frequently becomes one of allowing the MIS division the self-indulgence of selecting projects primarily based on its interest in utilizing the latest in information processing technology.

Although such policy-setting activity is admittedly difficult, it is essential that it be done, in order that subsequent, more detailed planning efforts may have a better chance of success.

### 4.4.2    PLANNING TO IMPLEMENT MIS STRATEGIES

As shown in **Figure 4-20, Implementing MIS Strategies,** the plans which are needed to implement MIS strategies can be of several types, each of which has the goal of translating the MIS objectives and strategies into increasingly more detailed and specific plans.

**Figure 4-20**

## IMPLEMENTING MIS STRATEGIES

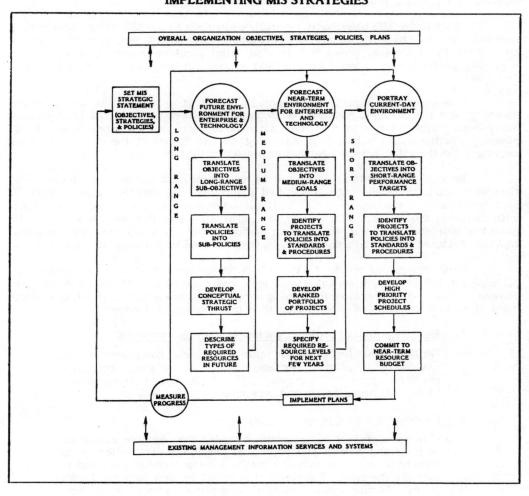

**Long-range MIS planning** deals with meeting the **future** MIS needs of the host organization. It is largely conceptual in character and can have a horizon of from five to seven years or longer. It does not deal with specific projects or even groups of projects, but with emerging types of user needs, and with approaches that might be useful in addressing these needs. It must also plan for the organizational philosophy to guide the MIS organization of the future and for the skills and capabilities that will be needed in developing and managing future systems. An example of this type of plan is the information systems design architectures that are being developed within a number of organizations.

**Medium-range MIS planning** is what many organizations call their long-range plan. It is the planning that is necessary to meet the host organization's **present** MIS needs, projected two to five years into the future. It is a portfolio of projects, ranked by importance, and coupled with projections for their implementation. It also involves the planning for hardware and software acquisitions and conversions, and for the staffing of multi-year projects and developmental activities.

**Short-range MIS planning** is generally equivalent to the MIS annual planning. It involves detailed budget preparation, manpower scheduling, and the creating of timetables for individual projects. It also often includes quantitative statements regarding performance targets for the MIS group. It is relatively operational in character.

The choice of a particular approach or set of approaches to MIS planning, assuming that the **strategic planning** has been properly done, is particularly important. Many organizations falter in that they attempt to carry out all three types of MIS planning simultaneously before first mastering the intricacies of the short-term plans necessary for the effective management of present activities.

Ideally, the MIS strategy should be translated into current-day decisions by first developing the long-range conceptual plan, then the medium-range managerial plan, and finally, the short-term MIS strategic objectives, such as to build credibility with users. It should focus first on simple, operational plans that include very specific goals and objectives for improving current performance. Then, once the MIS organization has mastered its short-term challenges, it can extend its planning horizon.

Most companies would find a major investment in long-range conceptual planning for MIS to be of little value until they have mastered medium- and short-range planning. Short-range operational planning is relatively straightforward. The development of medium-range plans generally involves the following activities:

1. **Identify potential projects, including strategic projects:**

   Gather ideas for projects relating to new computer system development efforts, enhancements to existing computer services, upgrading of ongoing MIS activities, and strengthening of the MIS organization and personnel.

2. **Evaluate and rank projects by priority:**

   Filter the project opportunities by using the resource allocation policies and overall MIS objectives previously established, so as both to select those projects that will be undertaken next and to identify the types of projects that might be undertaken in future years. At this point, strategic competitive advantage projects will come to the fore.

3. **Translate these projects into schedules of activities, resource requirements, and action steps:**

   That is, define the means, requirements, and plans of action for implementing the selected MIS projects.

## 4.4.3   IDENTIFYING POTENTIAL PROJECTS

The first step in the development of an information systems plan is to identify those information system projects that have a high potential for the organization. There is a wide variety of approaches that can be used to scan for these new opportunities for system development.  The following are some of the most common:

a. **The isolated approach** - where the MIS organization reacts to environmental factors by modifying existing systems to meet new legal or regulatory requirements; proposes retrofits to existing computer systems to enhance their cost or operating characteristics; or uses its own "intuition" regarding new strategic opportunities.

b. **The emulative approach** - where the MIS organization picks up ideas for new projects from the successful computer systems of other companies, similar in size or industry group.

c. **The bottom-up approach** - in which MIS systems analysts interview either selected user executives or, in certain company situations, all major user groups so as to identify the major decision areas, possible information gaps, and operating inefficiencies which could be improved through the use of better computer systems.

d. **The reactive approach** - in which the MIS organization simply responds to decisions made by either the chief executive officer or some high level corporate executive as to which are the most appropriate new computer system projects for the MIS division to undertake.

e. **The derived top-down approach** - used when the host organization has no overall strategy.  It involves a detailed analysis of the company, in order to hypothesize an overall corporate business strategy from which new computer system ideas can be selectively developed.   These ideas are then further refined through interviews and appropriate systems analysis.  In other words, if no overall business plan exists - you make one up, and then use this as a basis for your planning.  This can be dangerous unless you have a good sense of where your company is going.

f. **The top-down approach** - where the MIS organization develops new services and projects as an outgrowth of the company business plan that already exists, and the strategic opportunities that arise.

g.  **The interactive approach** - the MIS organization interacts with other parts of the business during the normal company planning cycle so that the identification of MIS project ideas, and assessment of their likely business impact, are integrated into the planning activities of management throughout the company on an on-going basis.

The important task then for the MIS executive is to select the particular approach or combination of approaches that best fits the company's unique situation - and that is feasible to implement.

## 4.4.4   PROJECT SELECTION

Invariable, there comes a point in this planning process when the collected ideas for new projects must be sorted out so that the highest priority applications or services can be undertaken in the near term. A problem of many planning efforts is the failure to perceive, in advance, for the need to establish a means for conducting such a screening. Since the MIS effort is a service function to the entire enterprise, this sorting out of priorities is difficult, even when well-chosen resource allocation policies have been established. A simple chart to aid in carrying out this ranking is shown in **Figure 4-21, Sample Project Portfolio Overview,** where the project ideas are listed, and the previously-selected resource allocation criteria are applied to each project to the maximum extent possible. The major challenge here is to obtain a summary evaluation of these projects without entering into a detailed project feasibility study, since the primary objective of this effort is not to decide which projects should be undertaken, but which should be investigated and analyzed further. At this point, attractive strategic opportunities should rise to the top of the list.

Figure 4-21

### SAMPLE PROJECT PORTFOLIO OVERVIEW

| APPLICA-TION/ SERVICE IDENTITY | BRIEF DESCRIP-TION | OPERATING EXPENSES ESTIMATE | OPERATING BENEFITS ESTIMATE | USER SPONSOR | RESOURCE ALLOCATION CRITERIA | | | | | | | |
|---|---|---|---|---|---|---|---|---|---|---|---|---|
| | | | | | DEVELOP-MENT COST ESTIMATE | DEVELOP-MENT TIME SPAN ESTIMATE | ROI ESTIMATE | RISK ASSESS-MENT | CORPOR-ATE STRATEGY FIT | MIS ARCHI-TECTURE FIT | OTHER CONSIDER-ATIONS |
| | | | | | (FUNDED, ALREADY UNDERTAKEN) | | | | | | |
| | | | | | (FUNDED, NOT YET UNDERTAKEN) | | | | | | |
| | | | | | (NOT FUNDED, UNDER CONSIDERATION) | | | | | | |

To make these difficult priority rankings, many corporations have established computer applications steering committees in which judgments regarding these alternative investments in new systems are made on an ongoing basis by selected members of top management.    In this way, a continuing consensus regarding the need for new system development activities is obtained.    In cases where trade-offs and compromises must be made, the affected individuals and user organizations have an active voice in the decisions.    Some of these committees have not been as successful in carrying out their prescribed role as they might have been.    The overriding problem in such cases is that they are unable to resolve the many competing demands for limited MIS resources. More often than not, this failure is due to the absence of a clearcut resource-allocation policy, one which provides unambiguous guidelines for choosing among projects - guidelines which are firmly routed in business considerations, not technical ones.

## 4.4.5    DEVELOP ACTION PLANS

If an appropriate approach to the scanning and ranking of projects is taken, then the third step in planning (the development of the associated resources and activity schedules) is somewhat more technical in nature, although vital in reaching such important decisions as computer equipment selection.    Generally, these project schedules are quite precise for the near term and somewhat more general for future years. And this is as it should be, since the primary purpose of the planning effort is to make near term decisions that are consistent with a longer term direction, not to decide on specific computer system projects that are to be undertaken three or four years in the future.

## 4.4.6    FEEDBACK

It is important to recognize that the planning process and resulting decisions are dynamic, not static.    As the bottom part of **Figures 4-16 and 4-17** indicate, there is an important feedback loop, one which measures progress against plans, and ultimately, against the objectives and strategies themselves.    Nothing should be felt to be fixed or "cast in concrete."    Many an MIS executive has wailed "but this isn't the way we planned things last year," forgetting that a plan is not a forecast **of** the future, but a way of being better prepared **for** the future.    Plans and strategies should be flexible and able to be modified and changed as circumstances dictate.    Following a plan too closely is almost as bad as ignoring it entirely.

## 4.5        KEEN'S CREATING THE BUSINESS VISION

Dr. Peter Keen, Chairman, Informational Technology Services, has done considerable consulting in strategic planning for telecommunications. Telecommunications is a complex and fast-changing function that significantly impacts both the business and the computing activities. Through the electronic delivery of business information and services, it is becoming a key to market innovation and gaining competitive edge.

A whole host of technical issues have arisen, especially in defining the long-term architecture, in determining the migration path, and in assessing which technologies and vendors to bet on, and when. In addition, complex financial issues are surfacing in funding telecommunications, including the business case for a large-scale electronic highway system, not knowing what kinds of volume and traffic will be involved.

Dr. Keen has spoken widely about the need for creating the business vision for telecommunications planning. He points out that a major difficulty for the IS function is that business managers have unclear pictures of how IS can make a significant difference. The situation is clouded by vague words like "productivity" and "competitive edge". Many business managers still see the technology as disruptive, mainly concerned with automation, and a source of increase in their budgets. One of the functions of IS is to help create "photographs" of the future to sharpen the sense of where the organization is moving, where the business wants to go, and what that means to the business manager in terms of what is needed from IS. IS needs to derive these photographs from business people so it can help set priorities  for development, and create the necessary long-term telecommunications architecture.

Dr. Keen suggests that a "formalized" vision is necessary, and should be consciously created, because there is no established tradition for talking about business in technical terms. We still explain the technology, then relate it to the business, rather than the other way around. A business vision helps put some authority together with responsibility, and should be presented in a formal paper. It sends the message, and gets to the thinkers who have access to the doers.

The dynamics of innovation move in a set sequence from vision to technique, as follows:

a.    The **vision** is a clear picture of the effective organization. It is a photograph of a feasible and desirable future. It determines the architecture.

b.    The **architecture** is a business, organizational, and technical blueprint. It determines the process or education, the organization, and so on.

c.    **Mobilizing** action follows. This is a process of educating, explaining, and organizing.

d.    Then **technique,** or traditional planning, is used for business justification, design, and delivery.

e.    Finally, there is **sustained action,** on a two to seven year horizon.

This is a new planning process which is really simple, and it makes the future concrete. The only near vision is "fog", where we don't know what is happening. The "office of the future" has gone the way of the "paperless society". But there must be **commitment.** Commitment by memo is worthless. There has to be sustained action for several years.

There are several reasons for the need for **vision:**

1.  There is no established tradition for thinking about technology in business terms.

2.  Telecommunications has a trans-organizational nature.

3.  Lack of pictures gives rise to ambiguity and uncertainty.

4.  The historical management process for DP has been a barrier to innovation.

5.  There is a problem of generating momentum for a radical change.

Technology has not been thought about in strategic business terms because the concentration from MIS has been technology-push, rather than the preferable demand-pull. MIS has had a limited awareness of business trends and the opportunities offered. The salient issue is that technology has had limited visibility and impact. Even when managers have been willing to participate, they have not known how to do so because of:

- concepts and vocabulary;

- a lack of self-confidence in the subject;

- the fact that the organizing focus of MIS and the level of detail has been elsewhere;

- computers being treated as a magic wand, with "analysis paralysis."

A good starting point is the **exemplars** approach. Get pictures of successful work from the industry. Make the examples business-centered.

Because of the trans-organizational nature of telecommunications, there has been a natural departmental/functional/professional focus on corporate issues. There is a need to respect the reality of decentralization, and establish the criticality of coordination. The historical focus has been, unfortunately, on applications rather than infrastructure. There has been no natural consensus on the opportunities, needs, or priorities. There has been no middle forum for the sharing of viewpoints, and building a synthesis.

Telecommunications, however, is an enabling technology where the payoffs are mainly from sharing. Such advantages as lateral communications, distributed coordination, common highways, and access to shared resources come from cooperation.

The ambiguity and uncertainty have arisen because technicians have invented the future. Most managers see major uncertainties and risks in technology, cultural change, deregulation, and the use of vendors. In addition, they find that experts frequently disagree. They want clear pictures of the future presented to them, rather than a lot of assertions and hopes.

The historical management process for data processing and telecommunications has always been a barrier to innovation. Instead of coordinated direction, there has been delegation. The MIS focus has been on cost and cost savings rather then on investment and opportunities. There has been quite an unclear mandate for telecommunications. There has been a separation of functions for voice and data that has been difficult to bridge. There has been a slow movement up the telecommunications management learning curve from the cable room era, to the telephone utility era, then sometimes to the position of a phone and data utility. What is needed is the final step of thinking of **telecommunications as a business resource.**

There is a need to gather the momentum for a radical change. There is more than one way to approach the problem. Some of the lessons that can be learned from the implementation literature on the **effective management of change** include:

- Capture the vision and follow an evolutionary approach.

- Come bottom-up with technical possibilities.

- Find the "felt need" and crystallize it, using the vision process for strategic "unfreezing".

- Use consultants to unfreeze organizational inertia.

- Work on the ambiguous "resistance" through training to acceptability.

- Have "entry" projects to build credibility and trust, and to bridge the culture gap.

- State clear operational goals that are feasible.

- Use political influence and control, beyond mere "involvement".

Telecommunications for business strategy is a relatively unknown approach and it implies radical change. Some of the problems are:

- It is a revolutionary approach to most people.

- It is top-down, because the coordination is required.

- There is no felt need for the telecommunications infrastructure; there is only a felt need for the resulting applications.

- It has a significant impact on the organization's culture, jobs, and work style.

- There is a resistance to the vision because of the fear of personal obsolescence.

- There is a culture chasm between the business and the technology.

- Users have a sense of helplessness.

The **goals for the vision** are numerous, but there are some that are key. First, there is a need to shift the focus and the terms of the debate from technology to business. Next, there is need to provide a forum for sharing. The two sides must be brought together, with all that are concerned. Third, always highlight policy issues rather than the operational telecommunications issues. Fourth, send the message across the whole organization. They will all be affected.

### Goal 1 - Shift the focus and terms of debate:

A new style of corporate planning and thinking is needed that is business-centered. It must be opportunity-based, rather than problem-based. A longer-term planning horizon is required to break out of the cost justification box. Mind sets must be opened up, with a new vocabulary established. The focus must be on the planning **process** rather than on specific plans.

### Goal 2 - Provide a forum for sharing:

Every manager in the corporation is needed to help synthesize the corporate view from the functional and departmental views. There must be mutual education between the technicians and the business people. Assumptions must be surfaced from all departments. Objectives need aligning, and agreements need to be flushed out.

### Goal 3 - Highlight the policy issues:

A meaningful commitment is required with mandates and directives from responsible managers. You have to get to the "doers" to get it done. The architects must create an architecture that represents corporate policy.

### Goal 4 - Send the message:

Create a **vision paper** that is brief, concrete, exciting, and realistic. Make it transportable: up, across, and down the firm. Make it a "Rohrschach" test for people thinking about telecommunications and business strategy. Set it up as the reference document for discussion. Signal your own role and behavior. Try to transform the interest from commitment, to policy, then to architecture.

There is a style of thinking that is needed in the vision process that can be described as adventurous realism. You focus on **competitive examples** that always get interest. Use pictures from industry, and documented exemplars. Show the self-justifying benefits. **Highlight the risks** and tradeoffs; don't try to hide them. Center on the competitive opportunity and the defensive necessity. Ask for "state-of-the-art" in technical, application, and organizational approaches. Emphasize leading versus following. Point out **divergence versus convergence.** Look at the extremes, and bring out the "perhaps ifs?" Make everyone a contributor, but avoid a cumbersome planning process.

The **vision paper** should be about 8 to 15 pages. Words well written can be powerful and the paper can have tremendous impact. Documents can unleash a surprising amount of innovation. The typical contents of a vision paper are:

1. <u>**Executive Summary:**</u> our vision for telecommunications.

2. <u>**What is happening in the marketplace:**</u>

   ● Trends in the industry - electronic delivery base for existing and new products.

   ● Customer trends in use of services, own technology base.

   ● Competitive pressures within industry, from non-bank competition.

   ● Strategic role of telecommunications in retail, corporate banking, domestic and international.

   Should contain brief (one to three sentence) exemplars throughout section:

   **KEY ONES:** Renters, Merrill Lynch, Citibank, Texaco, Exxon, insurance, shipping, Chase, American Express, ADP, Giant, Sears, Manufacturers Hanover, Dun and Bradstreet.

3. <u>**Where we stand in telecommunications:**</u>

   ● Strengths: domestic base, SNA experience, first rate operations.

   ● Current plans (mainly consolidation and extension of domestic capability).

   ● Areas where telecommunications is key in supporting Executive Committee's stated priorities.

   ● Priority opportunities and problem areas (especially in international area).

**4.6          AVON PRODUCTS' STRATEGIC PLANNING - PRESSURE POINT ANALYSIS**

John J. Walsh[13] emphasized the need for strategic planning for Office Automation. He said that the focuses of strategic planning are to:

a. Support the business environment and the organizational goals and directions.

b. Define the effort from a management, technical, and administrative perspective.

c. Identify key issues.

d. Establish a strategic directional foundation for the functions through the decade.

e. Provide a planning framework.

f. Develop a series of strategies to maximize the broad goals of increasing profits, increasing productivity, reducing information float, reducing/avoiding costs, and reducing risks.

g. Better anticipate and plan for uncertainty and change.

He pointed out that the first step in planning was to determine the **key issues** involved, in this case in the automated office. This included management issues about needs, demands, functions, services, costs, risks, and obstacles. This includes what strategy and implementation decisions need to be made before they "make themselves". Problems of security, privacy, standardization, and centralization are all factors that could be key issues. There are many; they are complex; and there are a variety of organizational implications. They are issues of concern to management. The problem is, how can they be presented in a way that makes sense and shows their relationships?

On the one hand there are **external pressures for change.** These may be regulatory or technical, or they may be general trends in energy, inflation, technology, disclosure, and experiences. On the other hand there are **internal pressures for change.** These may be corporate issues, employee concerns, and user issues, such as resistance to change, unionization, capital, regulatory, and software availability. The following questions related to the planning activities must be examined:

● Where are we? (current environment)

● Why **should** we change? (the issues)

● What **could** we do? (the strategic alternatives)

● What should we do? (recommended alternatives)

● How can we get there? (strategic and action programs)

These are five universal questions for strategic planning, so this type of analysis has broad uses. These are the five basic steps in a **Pressure Point Analysis.** They can be used for any approach to strategic planning. Pressure Point Analysis thus consists of the following five steps: (see **Figure 4-22, Pressure Point Analysis-Summary Diagram).**

---

13 John J. Walsh, Avon Products, Inc., in a presentation given at the International Conference of Wang Users in 1980

### STEP 1 - Where are we?

Develop a profile of the existing environment in terms of cost, strengths and weaknesses, pressures for change, and environmental uncertainties.

### STEP 2 - Why should we change?

Identify the key issues facing the corporate environment.

### STEP 3 - What could we do?

Examine the strategic alternatives in terms of costs, benefits, pros, cons, risks, and consequences, both if selected and if not selected. Examine the obstacles, contingencies, and potential bottom line opportunities.

### STEP 4 - What should we do?

Present the recommended alternatives to management along with the strategies, resource requirements, and possible action programs.

### STEP 5 - How do we get there?

Refine the action programs for the implementation of the plan.

The users must be involved in all elements of the planning and implementation, including goal setting, strategic planning, budgeting, and linking the plan and the budget.

In this view, strategic management covers a five-year period or longer, while tactical management covers a one to two year period. Operational management, then, is on a daily, weekly, or monthly basis.

**Strategic management** is concerned with adjusting the business over time according to the ever-changing conditions and requirements of the environment. The environment includes society, the market competition, and advances in technology. It involves the setting of long-range objectives, the establishment of overall priorities, and the selection of strategies (the approaches and the methods) to be used to meet the objectives.

**Planning** involves setting the objectives and developing the plans necessary to achieve them. It states what is going to be done, by whom, with what resources, and within what period of time. It also involves obtaining and combining the human and physical resources needed for the work activities to be performed in order to meet the objectives.

In the office automation arena the prime opportunities and impact are, of course, in the areas of cost reduction and displacement and reduced information float. Walsh pointed out, however, that this can lead to competitive advantages and enhanced decision support.

Pressure Point Analysis offers a framework that is readily understood by management, and it provides a good "talking paper" on strategic issues.

Figure 4-22

# PRESSURE POINT ANALYSIS–SUMMARY DIAGRAM

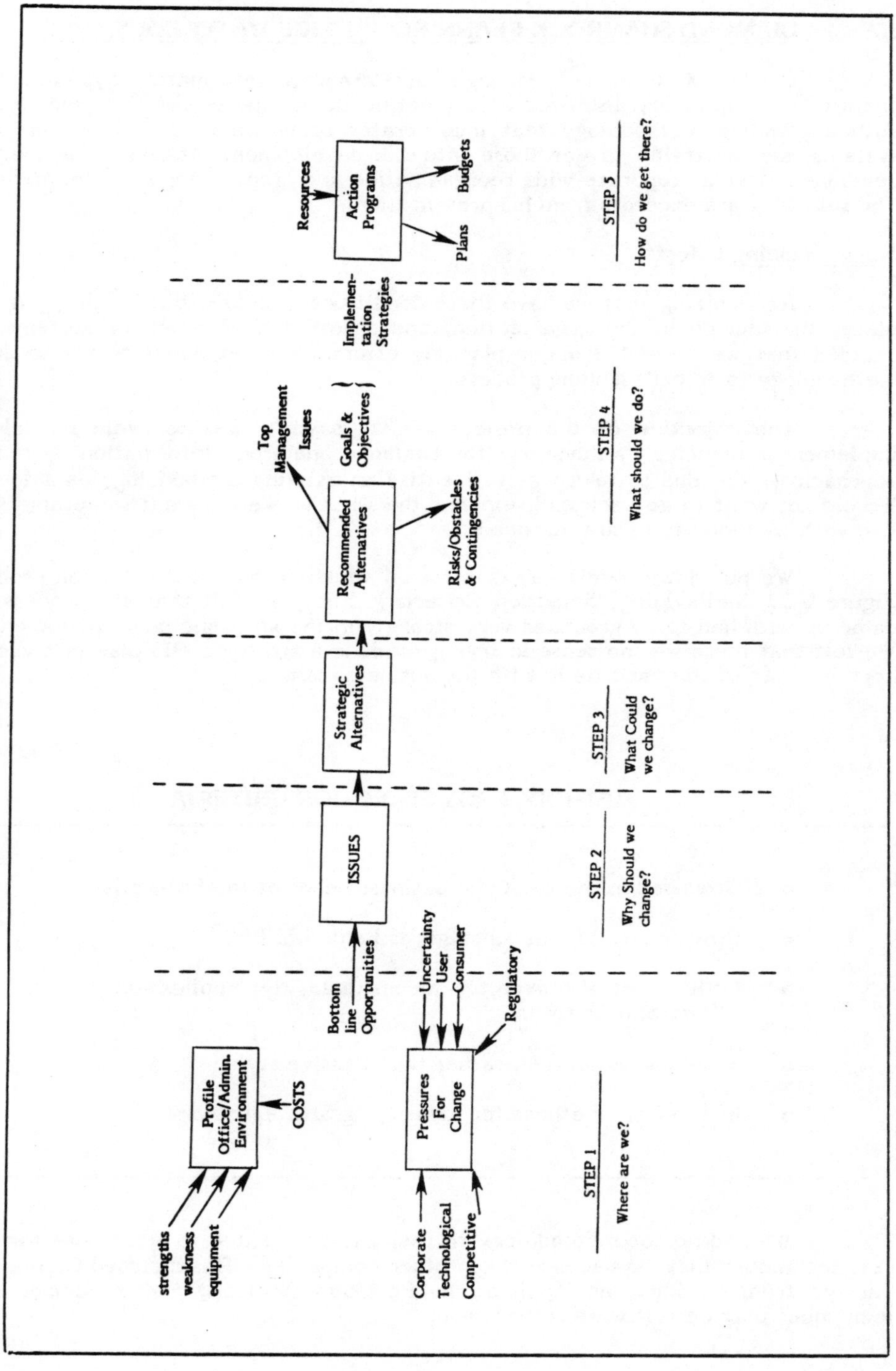

strengths
weakness
equipment

Profile
Office/Admin.
Environment

COSTS

Bottom
line
Opportunities

Uncertainty
User
Consumer

Regulatory

Pressures
For
Change

Corporate
Technological
Competitive

STEP 1

Where are we?

ISSUES

STEP 2

Why Should we
change?

Strategic
Alternatives

STEP 3

What Could
we change?

Recommended
Alternatives

Top
Management
Issues

Goals &
Objectives

Risks/Obstacles
& Contingencies

STEP 4

What should we do?

Implemen-
tation
Strategies

Resources

Action
Programs

Budgets

Plans

STEP 5

How do we get there?

**4.7       DIAMOND SHAMROCK PLANNING  -  PRICE WATERHOUSE SISP**

Gordon M. Campbell, Manager of Corporate Information Systems, Diamond Shamrock Corporation, discussed at a meeting their experiences in trying to come up with a planning methodology that incorporates some ways of looking for strategic systems, and of trying to get those into the development process. The method was developed after a corporate-wide reorganization and great changes in the marketplace. The following are excerpts from his presentation.

**Major Planning Effort:**

Recognizing that we have these conditions to deal with: the changing market-place, the change in the organization, and a lot of duplication of systems, it was decided that we needed a major planning effort. We set about to try to develop a methodology to do our planning process.

The **objective** of the project, as we saw it, was to **evaluate, select,** and **implement** a planning methodology for Diamond Shamrock Information Systems. The **approach** we decided to take was **to identify an existing methodology as a foundation.** We did not want to go back and reinvent the wheel. We did want something we could live with, and modify to suit our needs.

We put down a few key criteria on which to base our selection process **(See Figure 4-23, Methodology Selection Criteria.)** First, we felt that any process that we came up with had to be grounded very strongly in the strategic needs of the enterprise. We felt that there was no sense in trying to make a strategic MIS plan in a vacuum. It certainly had to start and tie in with the business plan.

Figure 4-23

### METHODOLOGY SELECTION CRITERIA

- Grounded in the strategic business needs of the Enterprise

- Provide a solid, but "change resilient" I.S. Plan

- Utilize best of proven techniques (e.g. CSF; Application Portfolio Analysis)

- Should be Proactive, rather than Passive style

- Incorporate methods for identifying Strategic Systems

We had no set methodology to use, and we wanted to try to use some of the best techniques that we had seen from other companies. This included Critical Success Factors from Rockart, an Applications Portfolio Analysis, and a number of other techniques that we felt were rather good.

We also recognized that the particular management style of the MIS director and his team of people is more proactive than passive, and we wanted a methodology that would fit with that kind of MIS style.   Certainly, we wanted a way of incorporating how to draw out strategic systems from the organization, get them identified, and get them into the process.

We assembled a list of methodologies to decide which ones to focus on **(See Figure 4-24, Alternative Methodologies Review.)** There is a fuzziness between what is a development methodology and what is a strategic planning methodology.  We had to sort through a much longer list to come down to a few that we consider the serious strategic approaches.  We, looked at the traditional IBM approach, BSP and BSIP.  We looked at Critical Success Factors, and felt it was a little too limiting, though a good technique.   We looked at a McAuto product, which they called Information Systems Transition Planning.  We thought that it was too traditional for what we were looking for.  Because we happen to have Price Waterhouse as a auditing firm, we brought them in, and they introduced us to Strategic Information Systems Planning, (SISP), which is their approach.

**Figure 4-24**

### ALTERNATIVE METHODOLOGIES REVIEW

- BSP/BSIP - Traditional IBM approach

- Critical Success Factors

- Information Systems Transition Planning - McAuto Product

- Strategic Information Systems Planning - Price Waterhouse

**Strategic Information Systems Planning:**

We told Price Waterhouse that we were interested in looking at their methodology to see if we could make it fit our needs. We looked at the methodology in more detail and did an assessment of its strengths and weaknesses **(See Figure 4-25, SISP Assessment.)**

Figure 4-25

### SISP ASSESSMENT

**STRENGTHS:**

● Structured/thorough analytical approach

● Good techniques for information gathering

● Starts with Business orientation and C.S.F.

● Addresses all the key elements to produce an I.S. Strategy

**WEAKNESSES:**

● Needed repackaging for Client use

● Project-oriented (needed more dynamic update methods)

● Passive I.S. role (adjust to Proactive style)

We felt that the approach was well structured and a thorough, analytical approach. It had some good techniques for information gathering. It included things we were looking for, like Critical Success Factors. It seemed to address all the key elements. All the pieces were there to produce an IS strategy.

We have modified the Price Waterhouse SISP for our use, and we have identified two of our business segments, one of which is a new venture. It is on a small enough scale that we think we can take the whole process from start to finish and still be able to manage a pilot of the methodology. The other project is focusing in on some of the technical services areas of the business.

**SISP Stages:**

**Figure 4-26** helps to capture the essence of the planning methodology. It might be termed an input/output diagram. It shows the basic inputs to the planning process to the planning methodology, as well as the outputs. It also represents the base case, before we made any modifications.

In the first two stages of this, you are doing a lot of interviewing and drawing information via the senior executives and line managers. With these non-MIS people, you can get a handle on what the business environment is. This is a somewhat indirect approach to try to find out what your competition is doing, what the suppliers are about, and what your customer needs are. Basically, you are looking for opportunities and threats. You are trying to understand the business before you get into the MIS planning itself.

The bottom box on the chart is the **strategic IS opportunities.** We have not come up with any great methodologies for finding that out. We are going to be experimenting with some different techniques.

In Stage II, you are trying to refine things a little further. You take some of the opportunities that you have identified, and combine them with an analysis of your applications portfolio. Typically, you find in an applications portfolio that you have some things that are relatively new and some things that are old. In the coal business, we had a system for tracking our heavy earth-moving equipment. The whole point of that system was to identify when a piece of equipment became more expensive to repair and rebuild than it was to scrap and replace. At some point, you may want to scrap your investment and replace it entirely. Those are the kinds of opportunities we are looking for in that area.

**Figure 4-26**

## SISP STAGES

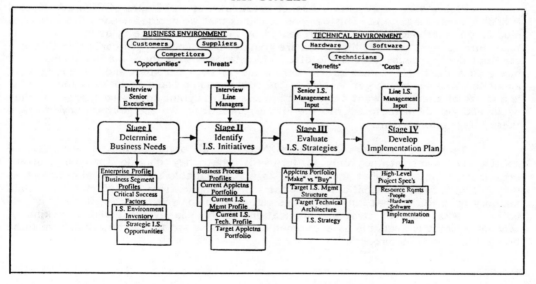

In this stage of the process, you are also looking at what the MIS environment looks like. Does it match the needs of your corporation, or should it be changed? This is one of the things that people consider to be sacred cows. I don't think it should be. It has to be looked at from time to time, and I think this is an appropriate place to look at it. Actually, it is much better if it comes from within MIS, than to have someone at the top come down and tell you to do it differently. We should be proactive in that area.

You certainly have to look at the technology, the changes that are going on there, and how that helps you in applying the strategies. In the latter two stages, you are starting to get more of the input from the MIS side. Then you get into the hardware and into the technology in more depth. You look at the software that you have, and you ultimately end up with some kind of strategy, which is made up of an applications portfolio, where you would like to be, and what your IS management team should look like if you were to change. It may not require changing, but you should at least look at it and decide. You should also look at what your technical architecture should be. That does not necessarily continue on the same path that you have been on. We have taken a look at some very major changes, and we will probably implement some of them in our technical architecture. We are prepared to look and see if there are some better alternatives than we have.

Finally, you take the results and develop some high-level project specifications. That is getting into the fuzzy border line, where you don't want to go too far in detail, but you want to be able to deliver enough to the development groups so they have a starting point and they can make some sense out of it. Certainly, you have to look at what it is going to take to implement the plan. That is what the resource requirements are, and that is the piece that is going to have to tie in with your annual budgeting cycle.

### SISP Phases:

Figure 4-27 represents a further breakdown of the Stages of Figure 4-26, and it adds another stage to it. This was one of things that we decided needed to be done to modify this methodology. It is represented by Phase K, or Stage V, at the bottom. It takes into account the fact that there are going to be changes. You cannot do this as a one-shot deal, because that is too often what happens with these metholologies. You hire a consultant. He comes in. He does a one- or two-year study and you end up with about ten volumes which get shelved in the corner and no one ever looks at them. That is a waste of time. We want a dynamic process that is going to absorb changes as they occur and get them factored into the MIS organization. We are going to have to take these things into account.

Technology changes are things that face all organizations. They must be continually looked at, not only in terms of what they can do for your current organization, but also what they can do to make available strategic applications that may not have been practical before. What are the implications of a 10 megabyte main memory on a PC? What kinds of things can that do for you now that it could not do before? What sort of strategic applications might you evolve given that kind of technology that is available as a common base? Those are the factors that have to be brought back into the process.

**Figure 4-27**

## SISP PHASES

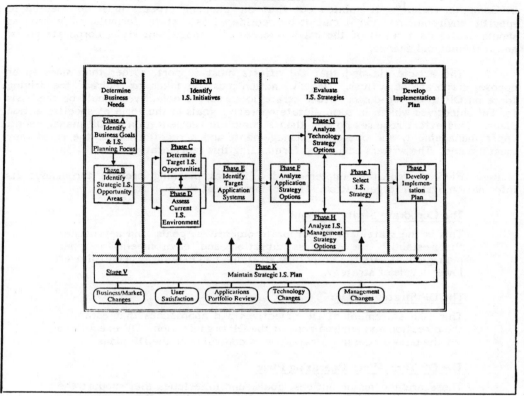

**4.8      FLUOR CORPORATION - STRATEGIC PLANNING**

An excellent article on **Adapting DP Strategy to Management Style,** appeared in Computerworld.[14]  It pointed out that the planning process must be adapted to specific environments, and it cannot be considered as a static formula.  The process should evolve as a result of the driving forces of management style, corporate goals, and technological change.

The article claimed that DP efforts must support, rather than sidestep or oppose, corporate objectives.  Decisive action must be taken to redirect the driving force on DP to be top-down.  Broad strategic corporate objectives should be the basis for DP objectives which, in turn, dictate operating goals in the form of specific action plans.  This effort requires no less than a complete reorientation of DP management, upper management, and operating management, and a redefinition of the roles they must assume.  The writers advocated formalizing this reorientation.

Fluor Corporation implemented a formal planning process throughout its Information Systems organization.  The components of the plan are:

**The Corporate Strategic Plan:**

This is the statement of corporate objectives, goals, and approaches that establish the business direction and environment.  Upper management sets the corporate strategy, and establishes control over lower levels of strategy.

**The DP Strategic Plan:**

This is a statement of DP objectives and approaches that establish the direction and environment of the DP organization.  DP executives set the data processing strategy with control over the DP plans.

**The DP Three-Year Operating Plan:**

These are the major actions, goals, and milestones that support the objectives in the DP and corporate strategic plans.  DP management and user management together develop specific long-range goals and activities.

**The DP Operating Budget:**

This is the precise presentation of the costs and benefits of the projects and functions included in the upcoming year's DP budget.  DP management, DP staff, and user staff work together to set one-year activities, goals, and milestones.

**Reporting and Control Mechanisms:**

Procedures, formats, and organizational structure that facilitate progress and financial reporting against the budget.  DP staff sets up data processing reporting and control systems.

---

[14]   Robert E. Lief, Robert D. Dodge, and Ralph L. Ogden, **Adapting DP Strategy to Management Style,** Computerworld, Dec. 5, 1983.

One of the problems, of course, was how DP was to secure the support of top management. First, they informed top management about the purpose and methodology of the planning process before it was initiated. This required the diplomatic expertise of the top DP executive to assure top management that DP was undertaking the effort on management's behalf, to provide better service. Second, the plan was expressed in business language as much as possible. Third, top management was clearly given the veto power over any part of the DP plan, since DP was looked on as a service organization.

The DP strategic plan contained:

- Structure of the DP organization
- Hardware capacity and configuration
- New application development
- Productivity and competence of the DP staff
- Injection of new technology
- Computer security
- Financial performance
- Administrative policies and procedures

They felt that this was a useful starting point for developing specific objectives and strategies. They preferred explicit strategies, such as "Decentralize DP", rather than vague statements such as "Enhance user productivity through increased use of the computer." They tried to make the strategies consistent with the original corporate strategy. They felt that the astute planner must be able to distill meaningful information from statements that are general and tainted with political overtones. He must be a visionary who can discern trends from scanty or unverifiable data, and extrapolate them to make predictions.

The strategic plan is realized through the operating plan. When formulated, the operating plan must be double-checked for consistency with the DP and corporate strategic plans. Once it is agreed upon and approved, it becomes a contract between DP and the rest of the organization.

**4.9**            **VETERANS ADMINISTRATION - STRATEGIC PLANNING**

The purpose of the Veterans Administration ADP and Telecommunications Strategic Plan is to set forth the agency's strategies for accomplishing automation objectives. It provides an overview of the evolution of ADP and telecommunications in the VA, and describes the organizational context on which that evolution is occurring, as well as the technical approaches being pursued.

**The Strategic Plan is arranged in three sections:**

1.    The **Executive Summary** presents a concise overview of the current environment in which the ADP and telecommunications planning takes place, and out of which the strategies and objectives are being developed.

2.    The **Introduction** focuses on the background of the VA's planning effort, the ADP technological directions and the technological environment, and an organizational needs analysis which assesses the requirements of the departments and the agency's approach to meeting those requirements.

3.    The **Strategic Plan** details the VA's current ADP planning strategies. It includes a description of strategy development in which the agency's programmatic objectives are presented.

The efficient management and delivery of VA benefits require accurate and timely information. To ensure that such information is available, the VA maintains an ongoing information resources management program. A major portion of this program is the ADP and telecommunications function.

The VA approach to ADP and telecommunications planning is derived from the **VA Integrated Management System (See Figure 4-28)** which is cyclic in nature. This system is initiated annually by goals, objectives and guidance issued by the Administrator. It is supported by policy analysis and revision, program planning, budget formulation, program and budget execution, program evaluation and post-policy analysis.

The long history of VA's use of ADP technology to support programmatic areas resulted in various large and independent application systems designed and developed for different users. Many of these application systems were designed and developed before state-of-the-art innovations such as database technology, on-line interactive capabilities, and telecommunications networking. Furthermore, little consideration was given to the standardization and interchange of organizational data between and among systems and users. Their current information technology strategies attempt to exploit fully current technologies and to plan for, design and develop application systems to comply with the principles and practices of information resource management.

The **VA ADP Planning Process** is predicated upon the fact that ADP is but one activity in information resources management. This philosophy has been the principal focus in the ADP planning process. **(See Figure 4-29).** Because of their commitment to become a state-of-the-art ADP user, the VA developed three basic technological strategies on which all operational ADP plans are based. The strategies are to integrate systems and data to the maximum extent possible, to provide end-user on-line computing capability through office automation and computer utilities, and to provide a VA-wide telecommunications network for efficient and timely movement of data between and among various organizations at field stations and Central Office. They intend to exploit these strategies for the development or redesign of all future application systems. **(See Figure 4-30).**

**Figure 4-28**

## VETERANS ADMINISTRATION INTEGRATED MANAGEMENT SYSTEM

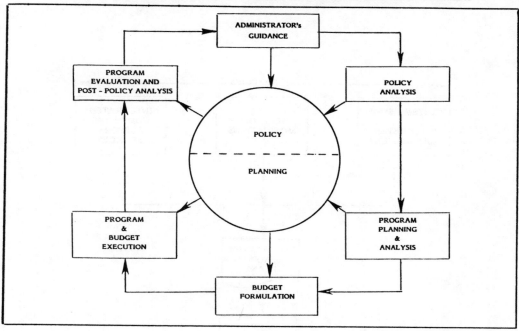

**Figure 4-29**

## ADP PLANNING INFORMATION

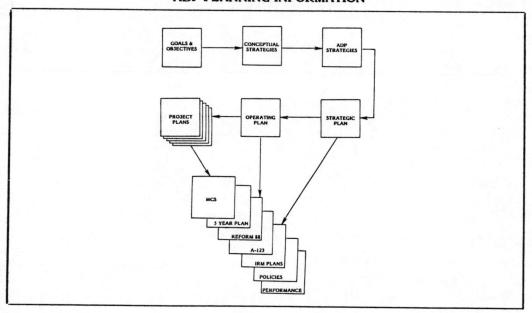

**Figure 4-30**

## STRATEGIES

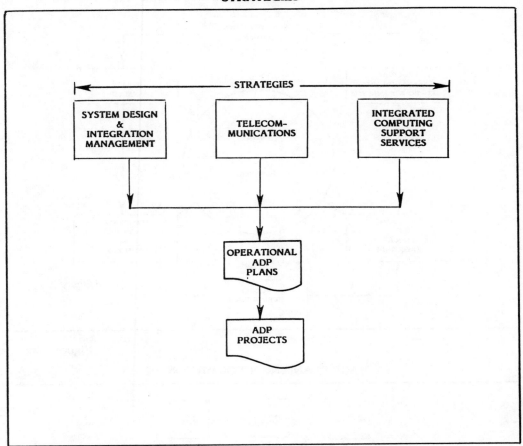

They intend to further refine the VA ADP planning process to ensure an integration with agency ADP policy development for a successful strategic and operational integration of plans and implementation efforts. Their objective is to provide an ongoing planning and policy development process by which planning and policy are constantly supportive of one another, and of the goals and objectives of the VA. (See Figure 4-31, ADP and Telecommunications Plan)

Figure 4-31

## ADP AND TELECOMMUNICATIONS PLAN

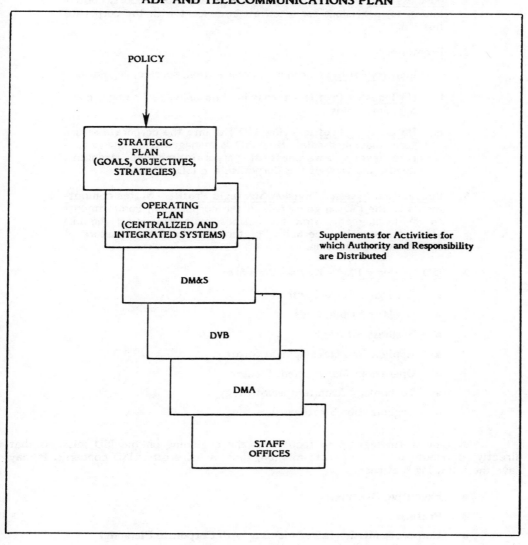

**4.10    MAJOR INSURANCE ORGANIZATION'S STRATEGIC PLAN**

The strategic planning of the Information Systems Division of a major insurance organization has proven to be successful, and accepted by management. It is divided into five major parts:

1.  **Corporate Mission** - A succinct statement of what the business is, and general perspectives. This may emphasize being a profit leader, increasing marketshare, or improving the service level.

2.  **Information Systems Division Mission (including each major business unit)** - A succinct statement of areas of support, contribution to, provisions for, etc., all in concert with the corporate mission.

3.  **Framework:**

    a.  **Industry Profile** - products, competition, service, regulation

    b.  **I/S Industry Profile** - trends in philosophy, technology, management, roles.

    c.  **I/S Division Profile** - How ISD fits into the corporate structure, plans and role. How ISD is managed from the corporate level. Awareness of corporate mission, strengths, needs, and view of the Corporate and ISD missions.

4.  **Information Systems Division Strategic Profile** - States commitments to the ISD on-going role in the corporation; commitments to meet, augment, etc., the business unit strategies; the ISD view of new roles, methods: pictures of the future posture of ISD in the organization.

5.  **ISD Strategic Plan** - Key sections are:
    - Critical Success Factors
    - Goals and Objectives
    - Business Strategy
    - Applications Development Strategy
    - Operations Management Strategy
    - Technology Architecture Strategy
    - Organization Strategy

A typical strategic plan focuses in the beginning on the ISD missions that directly contribute to the corporate mission, then includes other ISD concerns. It may have the following sections:

- **Executive Overview**
- **Preface**
- **Corporate Mission (after meeting with Corporate Planning)**

- **Information Systems Division Mission**
- **Situation Analysis (opportunities, issues, and constraints)**
- **Industry Profile (business diversification, organizational and marketing issues)**
- **Information Systems Industry Profile**

  **Examples are:**
  - Application development trends
  - The changing role of information systems planning
  - Trends towards integrated information systems
  - Scarcity of information systems resources
  - The rising demands for business information
  - Organizational implications

- **Information Systems Division Business Profile**

  **Examples are:**
  - ISD strengths and weaknesses
  - Corporate analysis relative to the ISD
  - Forecasted corporate demands

- **Information Systems Division Strategic Profile**

  **Examples are:**
  - ISD will manage information as a strategic resource.
  - ISD will meet the business information needs of management.
  - ISD will provide competitive and cost-effective products and services.
  - ISD will operate as a business unit.

- **Information Systems Division Strategic Plans**
  - ISD Critical Success Factors

    **Examples are:**
    - Competitiveness
    - Value-added service vs. cost
    - Productivity
    - Innovation and creativity
  - ISD Goals and Objectives

    **Examples are:**
    - Develop a business profit-center structure.
    - Be properly organized to accomplish/support ISD business.
    - Market products and services inside and outside the organization.
    - Administratively control corporate information resources.
    - Develop quality systems that are cost/benefit effective.

- Increase participative system development.
- Improve quality of personnel through enhancement of skills.
- Improve systems availability and responsiveness.
- Integrate Office Automation with Corporate Information Systems

- ISD Business Strategies
- ISD Application Development Strategies
- ISD Operations Management Strategies
- Technology Architectures
- ISD Organization Strategies

- Appendix A:  Current Applications

- Appendix B:  Future Products

An example of their **Executive Overview** is as follows:

The basic philosophy underlying our goals and strategies is the planned positioning of the Information Systems Division for the 1990's, so that we can take advantage of new technologies in order to produce competitive information systems.  These systems will assist the corporation in effectively competing within the industry, and the IS Division in effectively competing within the corporation and the IS market.

This positioning will require creative and innovative methodologies for designing and developing business information systems.  Systems and applications will be designed to address strategic issues and opportunities of the corporation based on a full understanding of the information needs of our business for effective decision-making at all levels of the enterprise.

Analysis of the trends and challenges of the IS have substantiated the rationale for our strategic profile, which in summary is:  to manage information as a strategic resource, to meet business needs of corporate management, and to provide competitive and cost effec- tive products and services while operating as a strategic business unit.

In order to reach this strategic position, the IS Division will adopt the business application portfolio approach.  This approach will be an enhancement of the current METHOD/1 methodology which includes strategic information planning, systems and application design and project development activities.

In order to develop competitive systems while maximizing corporate resources, applications will be designed and developed under the sponsorship and direction of user management.  This participative development approach will be a major factor in developing and implementing systems which more completely address the business needs in a profitable and timely fashion.

The Information Systems Division will adopt a business unit organizational structure that can be both competitive and flexible to meet the dynamic changes within the IS industry of the future.

This plan identifies and describes the strategies that will set a course and direction for the ISD business over the next five years.

The **Information Systems Strategic Management Cycle** is illustrated in **Figure 4-32.**

**Figure 4–32**

## INFORMATION SYSTEMS STRATEGIC MANAGEMENT CYCLE

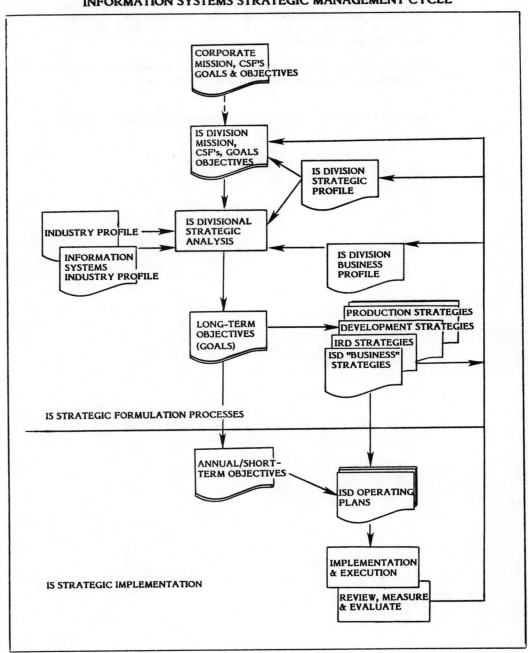

# SECTION 5

## TELECOMMUNICATIONS STRATEGIC PLANNING

### SECTION OVERVIEW

Telecommunications planning is complex. Effective planning calls for first creating a vision of the major business opportunities, then linking them to telecommunications. The telecommunications planner must focus upon the critical issues in a structured manner, and provide a strategic framework which will improve short-term operations while supporting the long-range business mission.

There are a number of problems in telecommunications planning, principal of which is getting the integration of IS, telecommunications, and business planning, while frequently there is fragmentation of the telecommunications responsibility within the organization.

Three approaches to telecommunications planning are briefly discussed. These are: a) the strategic business plan approach; b) the information architecture approach; and c) the incremental approach. In the first approach, telecommunications planning considers the overall strategic plan of the organization. The second approach is devoted to supporting the current structure of the organization, while rationalizing better communications techniques and considering the strategic value of information. The third approach is concerned with maintaining the existing structure, while performing the moves, changes, and additions that are required. Planning worksheets are provided for the first two approaches which touch on the strategic aspects of providing computer services and communications.

## 5.1    STRATEGIC AND OPERATIONAL PLANNING OF TELECOMMUNICATIONS

Managing telecommunications in almost any organization today is not a job for the fainthearted. Often telecommunications is looked upon by senior management as an expense that cannot be avoided. Often the investments in telecommunications have no obvious "payback" that the manager can use for justification. Often the various communications organizations are fragmented between divisions and/or by voice, data and video. Also, telecommunications projects often require three to five  years of sustained investment before significant payback can be shown, yet conditions are changing rapidly. Planning in this environment is very difficult and it is because of the complex nature of telecommunications that planning is important. The more complicated the environment, the more reason one has to plan.

Effective strategic planning for telecommunications involves **creating a vision** of the major business opportunities and linking them to telecommunications. Examples abound of businesses gaining competitive advantage through planning and sustained investment in telecommunications systems. Understanding business opportunities and merging them with telecommunications capabilities can provide the business with new and exciting products that can differentiate your business from the pack.

It cannot be done in a vacuum, however. The planning process must find ways to involve management in the effort. Without this participation, plans often become little more than a stack of technical schematics with funding requests attached. One thing to keep in mind is that planning is a process, not an event. The planning activity itself promotes understanding, improves communications, and helps generate awareness of the difficult issues relating to telecommunications among the various organizational units participating in the planning effort. The first time it is done it will not produce as a solid a result as the fifth time it is done. The organization learns the process as it repeats doing it by being exposed to terms, issues and the process itself. To be proficient one must study and practice. Similarly, organizations become proficient and learn by repeating the telecommunications planning effort. Don't become totally discouraged if management isn't banging down your door to help in the process, or if the result of your first effort is not quite as good as you had in mind originally. Make sure to set expectations that are appropriate for your organization's background and keep trying. The results will improve with practice.

Telecommunication is one of the remaining areas where computer technology will make a significant difference for firms who choose to plan strategically and invest properly. It will take vision and foresight to do it well. Planning for, and investing in telecommunications technology is difficult, and that is the reason it isn't done well by many organizations today. Building the telecommunications network often requires that the business make investments in computers, software, communications equipment, personnel and facilities with little "hard," short-term business benefit shown. The benefit comes when the application traffic on the network starts paying-off in terms of productivity gains, competitive gains, or shifts in marketshare. It is often extremely difficult to predict ahead of time the specific uses to which the network will be put and hence, to show clear payoffs.

An often used but good analogy is that of the highway system. Governments must invest in building roads and highways that open new access routes to new or remote geographic locations. This is often done without specific knowledge of the kinds of traffic that will use those highways, or to what purpose. Major investments in highways and roads are made with few specifics, and usually place significant financial (tax) burdens on the citizens in the given area. What usually happens once the roads are built is that new industries are created and new markets are opened. Basically the highway system enables these to occur.

Telecommunications networks are similar in nature to that highway system. They do not in and of themselves produce major revenue and profits for the business. This, of course, is not true of all projects. There are those who are selling telecommunication services to other businesses. For the most part, these are companies who have been investing heavily for many years and now have developed a telecommunications capability that has value in the marketplace. However, our emphasis is on those whose need is to develop, maintain, and operate an effective network that meets the needs of the business. The telecommunications network enables the business to enter new markets, offer new products, deliver old products in new ways, manage itself more efficiently, and provide a host of other uses. Building the network often takes years, and once built it has certain operational characteristics that, if not planned well, can limit the business capability. The lack of effective planning can leave the business in a reactive position, constantly patching the network together, trying to meet market need or to match competitive thrusts. Done well, the network can provide the information and data highways that provide the business with competitive advantages, productivity gains and effective operational support. In effect, the telecommunications network can become the enabler for new technology uses and new business opportunities. The lack of a telecommunications network can become a constraint to those opportunities.

Effective planning enables the network builders to design, or architect, the network in a way that enables it to best serve the strategic business needs of the present and future. Integration of the computers, systems, and networks in a cost-effective manner is a major consideration of the designer. Computer and communications technology is evolving at an extremely rapid pace. Suppliers are constantly competing in this lucrative market and hence, the capabilities of the systems are growing rapidly. The network architect or designer must contend with this constant change and insure that the equipment and systems can connect in an effect manner. This issue of connectivity is a major one that planning helps minimize. Effective planning helps insure that the network that is built will connect in an efficient manner with the devices that will use it and provide the traffic on the network.

It is very difficult to integrate technologies that are designed and built by different vendors or that use different types of internal processors with different ages of the equipment. Often they are not designed for the specific purpose to which they are being put. In some cases the technology is designed specifically not to connect easily with other vendors' equipment. If not planned and executed well, the cost of operating and maintaining the network can become staggering. Operating and maintenance costs normally become greater than the development cost in just a few years. Planning allows the designer and builders to develop a network that will run efficiently. A lack of planning that is both organizational-wide and department-specific can lead to the building of a network that the business cannot afford to operate because of the difficulties of connectivity and integration.

Viewing telecommunications as the highway system that will enable the business to run new applications that open new markets, or increase productivity, enables management to look upon the money being spent as an investment rather than an expense. Building effective telecommunications networks and accomplishing the planning necessary to insure that the most appropriate networks are built is, in effect, an investment in the company's future.  This, perhaps for many organizations, is the most significant outcome of a successful telecommunications planning effort.   The change of mindset from expense to investment is one that can have profound effects on the direction of many businesses.

Another major hurdle the telecommunications planner needs to overcome is that of organization.   In many companies the responsibility for voice and data communications are split.   Additionally, in many organizations data communications and systems planning are done by different organizations.   Systems will eventually create the data "traffic" that travels on the telecommunications "highway" system. Planning of this kind requires an integration of direction.  The planner must be prepared to interface and communicate with a large number of organizational units, and to do the best job possible synthesizing the information gathered from these various units. Obviously, the more centralized the responsibility for voice, data and systems the easier the planning effort will become.   The lack of organizational centralization, however, is not a valid reason to abandon the planning effort.

Voice and data communications may have very different requirements, but sharing of facilities and the infrastructure can often provide the business with network cost savings.  Each line of business or SBU in the organization usually has different requirements, and decisions on functional requirements versus cost tradeoffs are unavoidable.   The impact of these can often be minimized by an effective inter-organizational telecommunications planning effort.   The planning process can bring consensus and common understanding, find innovative solutions, provide a consistent approach for all units, and become the basis for networks that meet more of the businesses needs for a given level of expenditure.

This organizational diversity often leaves the telecommunications planning function fragmented and without direction.  When this is the case, the telecommunications planners have an obligation to the business to find forums in which they can participate in common planning.  Providing a planning process that is consistent and fairly applied can go a long way toward improving the overall and SBU specific telecommunications environment.

## 5.2    PROBLEMS OF TELECOMMUNICATIONS PLANNING

The telecommunications planner is faced with change in every direction. In the regulatory environment, the breakup of the Bell System in the U. S. has provided more options than ever before to the planner. It has also made evaluation of competing alternatives more complex. In the area of technology, advances in local area networks, fiber optics, microprocessors, new workstations, and cabling media have proliferated at a very rapid rate. Where there was once dozens of products, there are now hundreds. Within the organization, the telecommunications planner is faced with constant demands from users, particularly as MIS expands its way into every corner of the organization through on-line transaction processing and office automation. In the international area, some privatization of overseas telephone monopolies has yielded a few more options than before. In many countries, control over telecommunications is used as an indirect way to regulate the activities of multinational corporations.

In light of these changes, what are the special planning considerations? What is the order in which things should be decided? How is this information to be communicated to end users, to MIS, and to top management? Among the many problems faced by today's communications manager are:

- Inexact knowledge of the organization's inventory of equipment and facilities.

- Too much emphasis in telecommunications planning on equipment and facilities.

- Lack of integration in the organization's IS, telecommunications, and business planning.

- The fragmentation of telecommunications responsibility within the organization.

- The introduction of many more equipment manufacturers and service vendors.

- The inability to get, motivate, and keep good personnel.

With the upheaval in industry and the booming costs, the effective management of telecommunications is recognized as an essential business activity. Senior management realizes that, no matter how well-developed the data processing environment, it can be a helpless giant without an efficient communications system.

One of the keys to successful telecommunications planning and management is the avoidance of the pitfall of becoming immersed in seductive technology and failure to:

- Focus upon critical issues in a structured manner

- Provide for a **strategic framework** which will improve short-term operations while supporting the long-range business mission.

- Identify new opportunities

- Minimize risks

- Abandon marginal efforts and lower cost projects

- ● Address multiple audiences effectively

- ● Anticipate and plan for change

No matter what the future developments of telecommunications technology are, or the range of user requirements, in order to avoid chaos and severe business risk the telecommunications plan is an essential document. This manual is designed to guide the information manager in the development and preparation of the organization's telecommunications strategic plan. It is also intended to demonstrate the importance of telecommunications to the achievement of the organization's overall goals.

**Figure 5-1, One View of the Telecommunications Planning Process,** illustrates the bottom-to-top planning activities that operate in concert with the top-to-bottom management decisions.

**Figure 5-2, Telecommunications Functional Environment,** exhibits the relationship of telecommunications to the rest of the organization.

**Figure 5-1**

## ONE VIEW OF THE TELECOMMUNICATIONS PLANNING PROCESS

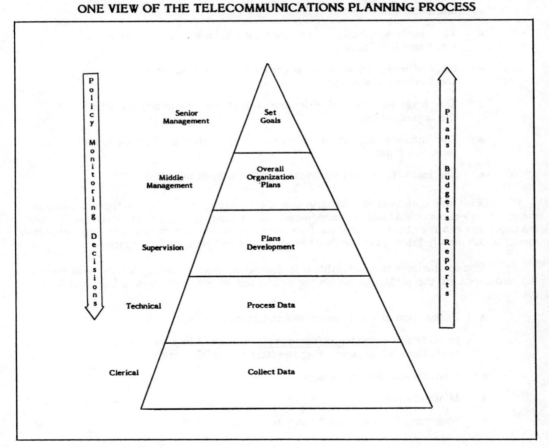

Figure 5-2

## TELECOMMUNICATIONS FUNCTIONAL ENVIRONMENT

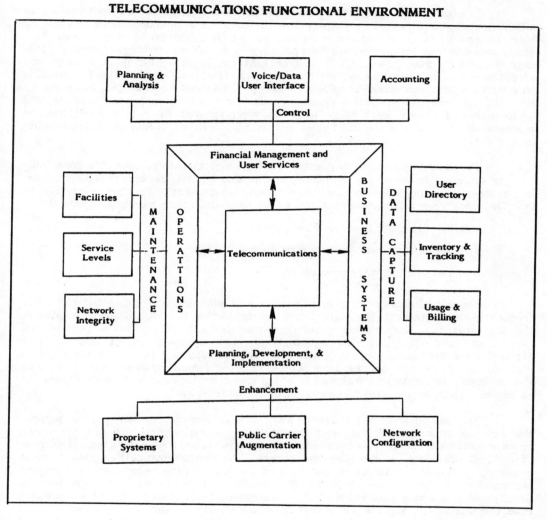

## 5.3     THREE APPROACHES TO TELECOMMUNICATIONS PLANNING

Telecommunications are complex and expensive, and have a direct impact on all the operational aspects of a corporation. Effective telecommunications can only be built if there is a business demand to be met and a business thrust to be followed. This would indicate that telecommunications planning is, by nature, strategic planning. This is only partially true, however. It is true that the implementation of a large and effective telecommunication system can be most effectively accomplished if there is an overriding strategic business necessity for it. This must be balanced, however, by the fact that telecommunication systems reach into every corner of the business, and often include the very large voice network, meaning that there is a great deal of mundane operational planning that must also be accomplished to reap the total benefits of a telecommunications system.

The telecommunications planner must always, therefore, take into consideration the different levels of the data being communicated, and the operational priorities in a system, depending upon how inclusive the telecommunications system is intended to be. There are three different approaches to telecommunications planning. These are:

- The Strategic Business Plan Approach

- The Information Architecture Approach

- The Incremental Approach

These approaches to telecommunications planning are quite different, but frequently must interact. The highest level is considering the overall **strategic plan** of the organization. The telecommunications plan is centered on the support of the overall strategic thrust of the organization. This approach is, of course, most attractive for the planner, as the justification for the system is readily obtained. Such planning usually centers on specific strategic communications systems, and establishes the necessary technological framework which can later be examined to determine its ability to support less strategic communications functions also.

The second level is the development of a telecommunications plan to support the current structure of the organization, and to rationalize the use of better communications techniques in the regular operations. It has by far the greatest amount of technological detail in the planning process. The telecommunications planner must examine, in detail, the structure and flow of the information being used in managing and conducting the business, both for the present and the future. The key here is usually not in the **strategic value** of the information, but, rather, in the **efficiency** and **effectiveness** of handling the greatest flow of information through the network.

In the third, and lowest, level of telecommunications planning, the planner is concerned simply with maintaining the existing network architecture and the plan of equipment. The work is concerned with the routine moves, additions, and changes that are required without altering the network architecture. The planning is at the level of the efficiency of providing an adequate ongoing service.

These approaches will all be briefly outlined in this section because they are seldom independent. It is difficult to think of a new strategic telecommunications system that does not impact the existing operational system, and does not have many moves, additions, and changes (MACs) to be performed. The telecommunications planner is thus required to think of each of these levels together, rather than separately. Simultaneous planning is required to insure that the actions taken on each level are consistent with the other levels. It is necessary to be prepared to be able to justify the smallest action in terms of the largest objective. In the usual case of strategic planning, therefore, a hybrid approach which combines the other approaches is needed.


## 5.3.1    THE STRATEGIC BUSINESS PLAN APPROACH

The strategic business plan approach views telecommunications planning as an extension of the overall mission of the business. Telecommunications is a tool, often the key tool, that must be developed as an extension of the overall strategic mission of the business. The telecommunications planner is required to translate the overall strategic objectives of the organization into the "nuts and bolts" of the telecommunications infrastructure.

It is most helpful for justification and prioritization if the nature of the business is such that the development of certain telecommunications systems can be a strategic weapon in the competitive arena. One example might be the development of a new, aggressive telemarketing system. In such cases, telecommunications ceases to be simply a back-office support mechanism, but becomes a bold, strategic weapon being used by the firm. In these cases, the prominence of the telecommunications manager is greatly enhanced, but the risks of failure are much greater, because any problem is much more visible.

In most organizations, even when communications is a strategic weapon, the relationship of the telecommunications plan to the overall strategic plan of the organization is one of **support**. It is rare when telecommunications by itself moves out of the support role, and constitutes a strategic objective or a tactical move of the organization by itself. Therefore, it is usual that the various constituent aspects of the strategic plan must be analyzed to determine their telecommunications implications, whatever those may be.

Telecommunications frequently provides **input** into the strategic plan, however. There is frequently a relationship between the telecommunications function and the strategic plan of the organization in which the input from the telecommunications function is one of the keys to success. This can be of great interest when the telecommunications staff has been monitoring the activities of competitor organizations, and has found certain strategic advantages that have accrued from aggressive use of telecommunications and information technologies.

If the telecommunications function is able to combine its efforts with the Information Services function in giving top management a comprehensive, integrated plan, then the political impact of the proposal is greater, and the chances of approval are correspondingly better. In some organizations the Chief Information Officer (CIO) is capable of coordinating the planning of both the telecommunications function and the IS function. In those cases, however, the direct input from the telecommunications group to senior management is correspondingly limited.

In those cases where the telecommunications function is not able to have direct input into the strategic plan of the organization, the planners must derive their priorities from their interpretation of the overall strategic direction that the organization is taking.

The technological implications can readily be derived on a preliminary basis when the overall strategic plan mentions specific organizational changes or new services being offered. In those cases, when new competitive applications of information technology are called for, Information Services will usually plan the lead role in determining the telecommunications priorities. In some organizations, IS has been combined with, or put over, all aspects of telecommunications, both data and voice. This facilitates determining the telecommunications priorities, but does not simplify the technical considerations.

Thus the overall concept of the telecommunications plan should be derived from the strategic plan of the organization as a whole, whenever that is feasible. The actual realization of this can be quite difficult, however, since it involves translating what may be very general goals or strategies into quite specific ideas for the telecommunications infrastructure. This process of translation can be aided by breaking down the overall data flow into several steps. **Figure 5-3, Strategic Plan Considerations,** is a simplified worksheet that can be helpful in crystallizing the key points. This worksheet simply notes the points without defining them in detail, but it can be a good starting point in thinking through the strategic implications of the plan.

Figure 5-3
(Page 1 of 2)

### STRATEGIC PLAN CONSIDERATIONS

| Strategic Goals of the Organization | Informational Correlary | Role of Technology | Role of Telecommunications |
|---|---|---|---|
| Note (a) | Note (b) | Note (c) | Note (d) |
| | | | |
| | | | |
| | | | |
| | | | |
| | | | |

Figure 5-3
(Page 2 of 2)

### STRATEGIC PLAN CONSIDERATIONS

#### NOTES

(a) The strategic goals of the organization must be put down in terms which may or may not relate to technology. It is important to realize that many goals of the organization do not have a specific solution which is answerable with a technological fix. It may be the case that technology may not help at all. Thinking through this process, however, should help in answering this question.

(b) Many of the strategic goals of the organization will have an informational aspect, since each function in business has an informational aspect. For each of the strategic goals of the organization, it is important to try and make a note of the informational correlary. Taking and filling orders, responding to customer requirements, communicating with regulatory authorities so as to avoid penalties -- each of these types of information-oriented actions has its basic genesis in a strategic goal of the organization. Also, there may be several informational correlaries to each of the strategic goals set forth for the organization. In that case, these are listed underneath each other in the worksheet.

(c) The role of technology must be considered next as a function of each of the informational correlaries which have been specified from the overall strategic goals of the organization. Each of the informational correlaries must be broken down to determine the specific technological infrastructure, if any, through which it is currently supported. Obviously, those information flows and structures which are not heavily supported by technology, but which are directly derived from the strategic goals of the organization, deserve a great deal of careful consideration.

(d) After the specific technological infrastructure for each of the major informational correlaries derived from the strategic goals of the organization has been identified, the telecommunications aspects of that infrastructure must be specified. This would include the following types of information:

- Voice or Data Component
- Current Main System
- Rate of Growth
- Presence or Absence in Current Plans.

## 5.3.2    THE INFORMATION ARCHITECTURE APPROACH

The information architecture approach to telecommunication planning is intended to assess the need for telecommunications based on the underlying flow of information throughout the business organization. It corresponds to techniques such as Business Systems Planning in the Information Services arena.

The information architecture approach is particularly useful at the inter-departmental level, where decisions must be made regarding the linking together of systems. While the sum of the actions taken will support the overall strategic plan of the organization, the information architecture approach provides a detailed analysis at the micro level.

### STEP ONE:  Mapping of Information Flows

The first step in the information architecture approach involves drawing up maps of the overall information flow throughout the organization. The planner starts at the most general level, with statements such as, "marketing provides information to sales, which informs production and accounting." It then proceeds to break down the general information flows into successively greater detail.

Basic questionniare survey techniques and review of computer operations can be used to determine the relative amounts of data flow along each of the major paths. At the top level of analysis, it is also important to determine the basic priorities and importance of the various data flows.

Three worksheets are designed to allow consideration of three levels of information architecture, starting at the most general, and progressing to more detailed levels of analysis. The three levels of information flow are:

- Organizational

- Departmental

- Individual

The number of maps and information sheets needed to create the detailed mapping of the information architecture can become quite great. For example, an organization with ten major divisions, each having ten departments, each with ten major tasks and five channels of communication could create a total of 10x10x10x5 = 5000 individual feeder sheets for the mapping exercise. Fortunately, the number is usually less, and some can be combined.

**Figure 5-4, Mapping of Information Flows - Level One,** can be used as a worksheet for the overall organization. In drawing out the various maps, use of color coding for information flows is advisable. The worksheet information is simply a set of statements from the maps.

**Figure 5-5, Mapping of Information Flows - Level Two,** can be used within each major division of the organization.

**Figure 5-6, Mapping of Information Flows - Level Three,** can be used within each major departmental section.

Figure 5-4
(Page 1 of 2)

## MAPPING OF INFORMATION FLOWS – LEVEL ONE

| Major Organizational Divisions Of The Firm | Allocation Of Administrative Resources | Major Changes Of Communication |
|---|---|---|
| Note (a) | Note (b) | Note (c) |
| | | |
| | | |
| | | |
| | | |
| | | |
| | | |

Figure 5-4
(Page 2 of 2)

## MAPPING OF INFORMATION FLOWS - LEVEL ONE

### NOTES

(a)    The first level of analysis starts with the overall divisions of the firm. How is your firm organized, and what are the major organizational sections. The specific examples vary according to the firm. For example, "Eastern vs. Western Region" or "Manufacturing vs. Financial Services" parts of an organization.

(b)    After the major organizational divisions have been identified, the allocation of administrative resources is specified for each one. What is the current consumption of administrative resources for each of the major organizations identified? Note: It is possible to put in place of administrative resources the total amount of resources dedicated only to information and telecommunications technologies in the organization, if this is known. To be able to do this will be of great advantage as successively greater details of the information architecture are specified.

(c)    The major channels of communication between the various major organizational divisions is specified. The specification must include some generalized measurement of the volume and cost, if possible, of each of the major communication flows.

Figure 5-5
(Page 1 of 2)

## MAPPING OF INFORMATION FLOWS – LEVEL TWO
### (Within Each Major Organizational Division of the Firm)

| Identity And Function Of Major Departmental Sections Of The Division | Allocation Of Administrative Resources | Major Channels Of Communication |
|---|---|---|
| Note (a) | Note (b) | Note (c) |
|  |  |  |
|  |  |  |
|  |  |  |
|  |  |  |
|  |  |  |
|  |  |  |

Figure 5-5
(Page 2 of 2)

## MAPPING OF INFORMATION FLOWS - LEVEL TWO
### (Within Each Major Organizational Division of the Firm)

### NOTES

(a) After having identified each of the major divisions of the organization, the individual departments which make up the divisions is specified. Within each division, each major department is listed, along with its principal function. It is crucial to make note of the function, since it is the relationship between the overall function of the department and its function as contrasted to the corporate mission which helps later in setting priorities for change. Generally, each planner knows of the relative importance of each division and departmental section but, occasionally, a careful re-analysis of these relationships will yield a few surprises and priorities can be adjusted accordingly.

(b) Again, at this most detailed level of analysis, the share of allocated administrative or information and telecommunications resources are specified. Obviously, the total of the resource for each section must add up to the given entry for the division at the first level of analysis.

(c) The major channels of communications are specified for each of the departmental sections, in particular which channels connect together different departmental sections. This is crucial information and may be the highest level of detail to which the telecommunications planner is able to go without very extensive research. If an organization is very large, with many departments, then the basic channels of communications between departmental sections will be constantly changing, making a periodic up-dating of the information necessary.

Figure 5-6
(Page 1 of 2)

## MAPPING OF INFORMATION FLOWS - LEVEL THREE
### (Within each Major Departmental Section of the Division)

| Identity And Function Of Each Major Task And Its Role In Supporting The Business | Allocation Of Administrative Resources | Major Channels Of Communication And Support Technologies |
|---|---|---|
| Note (a) | Note (b) | Note (c) |
|  |  |  |
|  |  |  |
|  |  |  |
|  |  |  |
|  |  |  |
|  |  |  |

**Figure 5-6**
**(Page 2 of 2)**

### MAPPING OF INFORMATION FLOWS – LEVEL THREE
**(Within each Major Departmental Section of the Division)**

---

#### NOTES

**(a)**  After the top two levels of analysis have been completed, it is necessary to go to the next level of detail. Here, the functions of each
major task within the identified departments are specified. The task
must be listed, along with a note regarding its importance, and relationship to the overall mission of the department.

**(b)**  Here, the allocation of resources (either general administrative, or
information and telecommunications expenditures) is related to each
individual task. In many cases, this will be a form of estimation. This
estimation is difficult because (1) records are rarely kept at this level,
(2) people sometimes do several related tasks simultaneously, (3)
equipment and information technology is many times allocated to
many different tasks, (in which case it is necessary to interpolate).
For example, how do you allocate the costs for the departmental word
processing pool, or for the departmental photocopier?

**(c)**  For each of the tasks identified, the major channels of communication,
within the department, are identified. The technologies which support
those flows of communication are also identified. Note is made of the
relative sophistication of the channels being used, and the degree to
which they are automated. The goal of this analysis is to identify
which specific technologies in the telecommunications arena are being
used in support of specific tasks related to the end-product of the
business.

In a truly large organization, there cannot be a single "map" which sets forth the basic information architecture of the organization. Some organizations are so large that, should such a map be created down to significant detail, it would constitute literally volumes of information and dozens if not hundreds of pages. It could never be drawn out on a single sheet, unless there was much reduction and very large CAD-type equipment was used for the final production work. However, regardless of the challenge, this type of exercise is necessary. The determination of necessary detail is subjective. Generally, in order to save time and resources, the level of detail and analysis is specified only as far as is necessary for a specific project.

### STEP TWO: Identification Of "Communications Intensive" Areas

After the basic information flows throughout the organization have been identified and specified down through several levels of detail, the "communications intensive" areas of the organization are identified. These areas of the organization are those major pathways through which the bulk of the vital information of the firm passes.

The communications intensive areas of the firm are the most important to pinpoint from the point of view of telecommunications planning. Allocation of tele-communications resources should be targeted primarily on the most communications intensive areas of the firm, as determined by the real flows of information.

Organizations using the information architecture approach are often surprised to find that some communications intensive areas have been completely overlooked, and relatively unimportant communications areas have been over-computerized. The information architecture approach helps to avoid these two problems.

The definition of **"communications intensity"** will vary from organization to organization. Also, there are many different ways in which communications intensity can be measured, or quantified. In the most extreme cases, the measurement approach would involve careful analysis of specific numbers of documents or pieces of information being transmitted. A high degree of accuracy would be yielded by this approach. It would be a beautiful **analytical** exercise. But the telecommunications planner must ask **"Is this necessary"**? In any analysis, there is always a balance which must be maintained between the accuracy needed and the costs and time required to make the analysis. In this case, the worksheet simply asks for a judgment as to whether the communications intensity is **"High, Medium, or Low."** Although this is a loose measurement, it may be accurate enough in most cases to accomplish the task of prioritization for investment, which, after all, is its only real purpose.

**Figure 5-7, Communications Intensity,** is a worksheet for ranking "communications intensive" areas.

Figure 5-7
(Page 1 of 2)

## COMMUNICATIONS INTENSITY

| Administrative Function | Ranking Of Strategic Importance (High, Medium, Low) | Ranking of Present Intensity (High, Medium, Low) |
|---|---|---|
| Note (a) | Note (b) | Note (c) |
| | | |
| | | |
| | | |
| | | |
| | | |
| | | |

**Figure 5-7**
**(Page 2 of 2)**

## COMMUNICATIONS INTENSITY

<u>NOTES</u>

**(a)**    The administrative function is identified from the previous worksheets in the information architecture series.

**(b)**    A subjective ranking is made regarding the relationship between the strategic mission of the organization and the specific function which is being analyzed. These functions should get particularly high marks when they involve interfaces with customers, for example, and particularly low marks when dealing with strictly internal matters.

**(c)**    A subjective ranking is made of the present level of communications intensity. Communications intensity is a measure of the dependence of the function on information and communications. High volumes of information, or requirements for quick response communications, or other factors, can all combine to produce a high rating for a function's communications intensity.

**(d)**    **GENERAL NOTE:** The purpose of this exercise has been to establish that there is a careful and balanced relationship between the business value of various administrative functions, their information intensity, and the resources allocated to their information and telecommunications technology infrastructure. In other words, those administrative functions which have been given a high rating for value to the organization as a whole, should enjoy a similarly high rating for their present communications intensity. If they do not, then investments should be brought into focus to rectify the balance. In those cases where areas of low strategic importance have been invested heavily, the best strategy is to neglect, and wait until investments in more important areas regain their appropriate level.

### STEP THREE:  Development Of The Automation Plan

After the basic and most important flows of information have been identified, measurements are taken to determine the relative degree of automation which has been applied.  In general, the goal is to add investment of telecommunications resources towards those information flows in the organization which are both vital and have heretofore been under-invested and ill-supplied with appropriate technology.

In order to do this, a listing of all the areas where priority telecommunications investment is to take place is drawn up.  This list of priorities forms the backbone of the telecommunications planning effort, at least in the initial stages.

Although the identification of priorities for automation has been accomplished, this is only one of the first major steps in creating the plan.  After priorities have been established, consideration must be given to costs, technologies, and implementation.  The development of priorities for telecommunications is only one step in a very long and complex process.

### STEP FOUR:  Derivation Of Telecommunications Priorities

From the automation plan, the priorities for telecommunications are derived.  Automation of information flows throughout an organization involves much more than the telecommunications function.  Automation of information flows which have previously been paper-based is of particular concern to the MIS department.  When office automation is introduced into various areas of the firm, telecommunications follows.

Telecommunications priorities may be derived from the office automation efforts coordinated through the MIS department.


## 5.3.3    THE INCREMENTAL APPROACH

In any organization, there is a constant shifting of people, departments, and priorities.  Each of these changes present implications for the telecommunications function.  Regardless of the overall grand strategic objectives of the organization, or the theoretical approach which might be taken in forecasting new telecommunications traffic between departments, any telecommunications manager must face the current backlog of moves, changes and additions that are of on-going concern.

One approach to this problem is **"incrementalism"** -- the technique of accomplishing large goals through gradual changes in the installed base of equipment. Assuming no drastic changes in the objectives of the organization, or in the underlying managerial or operational structure, incrementalism is a viable approach, particularly as it emphasizes that equipment be fully depreciated before being replaced.

The incremental approach is usually involved with the moves, additions, and changes (MACs).

Any telecommunications plan must take into consideration the on-going projects which burden all development efforts. The hard-pressed telecommunications manager frequently expresses difficulty in keeping up with the basic moves, additions and changes to the present system, apart from beginning any new initiatives. MACs are responsible for a great portion of current expenditures in many organizations.

The backlog of on-going projects is another area of irritation to many telecommunications managers. "Fire fighting" is the process of simply maintaining the present system to keep it from significantly deteriorating.

### 5.3.4    WHICH IS THE "BEST" APPROACH TO PLANNING?

Choosing the approach which is best depends on many factors. The chief factor is the rate of expected change in the telecommunications function in your organization. If telecommunications is vitally important to your business, then the **strategic approach** must be constantly kept in mind. If the organization is constantly re-structuring, then the **information architecture** approach is best. If things are relatively stable, and you are concerned primarily with cost-cutting and minimization of exposure, then the telecommunications planning function should take a low profile approach.

In many cases, however, the astute telecommunications manager should be aware of all levels of the telecommunications process and be able to respond to questions regarding each level. Ideally, actions pursued at each level should be consistent with objectives at all other levels.

# APPENDIX

## CASE EXAMPLES OF STRATEGIC PLANNING

### SECTION OVERVIEW

Strategic planning is approached in different ways by different organizations. Despite the accepted definition of "strategic planning" that is used in this manual, and the many articles that have been written at the universities, the process is viewed in various ways in actual practice. The one common thread is that, in strategic planning, the business plans are preeminent, and the Information Services plans are developed for the optimal support of the business thrust that management has decided upon.

This appendix contains several examples of actual organizational strategic plans for Information Services groups. The examples include:

- The use of a planning database by a large bank, which describes the approach taken in a strategic situation where planning is continuous to match the operational reality of the frequent changes that must be faced and planned for.

- The Pfizer Pharmaceuticals approach, from the Chief Information Officer viewpoint, which describes the continuing interpersonal communications that are necessary, and the use of breakaway planning sessions.

- The American Medical International experience, which outlines a strategic planning process with examples of the choices to be made, the opportunities, the pitfalls, and ways to set up strategic information systems.

### A.1     CASE EXAMPLE - THE USE OF A PLANNING DATABASE BY A LARGE BANK

It is difficult to get close to operational reality with a fixed "annual" planning system. Frequently, the annual planning process has no real data, because it is divorced from the actual strategic planning and changes that are in process continually. In doing annual planning, usually a small team of people sit down and read what is happening in the bank, and then write down what they think will happen. That is then the plan. It is far separated from real operations, however, and never really gets down to the operations area. When there is strategic motion in an organization, the best planning is a virtually paperless process that extracts only a few pages from each business unit.

The planning process needs day-to-day operational feeds. This section describes an approach that uses a database concept, which has been called a "racetrack" concept. It uses databases, and performs a systems roll-up as a result of the objectives that are set. It has been found that the systems architecture actually dictates the planning.

The banking business has set a very fast pace, and there has had to be a change from paper-based to action-based planning. For example, the money markets own their existence entirely to automation. Treasury takes positions each time they make a major deal. They take a reposition twenty to thirty times a day. Money is shifted hourly. A large bank transfers billions a day in payments. So the planning system itself also has to be automated. The process favors continuous planning, not annual planning.

There should be no hang-up between strategic, long-term, and operational planning. **Strategic** means anything new, or anything with a substantial change to it. **Operational** planning addresses maintenance. In **long-term planning** we go through the capital investment process. But at the bank, we don't see things as being strategic, operational or long-term planning, at least not in the big volumes of paper that you read about. The following is an example of strategy for banking. We are in a branch banking state and have many branches. What is a branch? As you walk down the street, it's on the most prestigious, expensive corner of the block. The bank branch is a very expensive way to deliver services to people. There are basically three functions in the branch. First, there is the **transaction** function; going to a teller, cashing a check, making a deposit. Second, is the **marketing** function; the bank explains new products and services to the customers. Third, is **exception processing;** perhaps the customer missed a check out of his/her statement, something went wrong. It's called exception processing, and is usually performed by the clearance teller.

The **strategy** now is that the transactions will be dispersed out to ATM's, point-of-sale equipment, in all kinds of places which already exist for other purposes, for example, supermarkets and home improvement centers. Therefore, the branch function doesn't incur the cost of all this brick and mortar. The marketing function will be expanded through devices like Videotex, by which the customer can see not only the product, but how it will perform.

The strategy for the exception items is that it will be pulled away from the branches, and put on a central computer where the inquiry facility can be performed. Now branches have to peak their staff during the peak work hours, which is a very inefficient workload. That's how a **strategy** would be submitted. Very simply, in three to four pages.

## A.1.1    WHY INTEGRATED PLANNING DOES NOT WORK

Integrated planning does not work.    In our first exercise we set great objectives.  Our planning for information services would reduce duplications, redundancies and overlap.  It would make sure that nothing was inconsistent or ambiguous.  It would take advantage of commonalities.  For example, CD's tend to be processed in several places; in the front and back offices and in accounting.  We would bring all these things together and get cost reduction.  We would solve all of our issues and problems, and set a future direction which would not change a bit for the next ten years.  This was the Integrated Planning Methodology.  We collected the plans from around the bank and indexed them with columns.  There would be a column for the activity, the objectives, the beginning and ending dates, and for some of the business issues involved.  We collected data on all of our systems, some four to five hundred, and built a portfolio to describe them.  We then grouped them by applications; wholesale, retail, capital markets, treasury applications.  We classified their activities as front office, back office, customer oriented and that kind of thing.  We even did the architecture; which applications were IMS, CICS, DL/1, distributed, Digital Equipment, Office System, and so on.  Then we did a major analysis of them.  We built a lot of tables and we could see where we were covering the business with database and where we weren't, and so forth.  We took different cuts of the database and prepared an Executive Summary Report.

What happened?  We found that planning integration does not work.  In the first place, there is a **definitional problem.**  What is a system?  For planning to work, we have to define something called a system, because that is what takes several years to develop and has a useful life expectancy of ten years.  There are seven different kinds of systems at the bank.  For example, the shop floor defines a system as something that runs on System Management Facility on the shop floor.  The business people define the system as a trade.  The development people define it as input, processing, and output.  We had all these definitions and could not reconcile them.

Further, we have a **language barrier** between the business and IS.  For a trader to talk about short-terms and long-terms in annuities is just a foreign language to all of us.  Furthermore, integration implies **monolithic,** that there one, single answer for all of business's problems.  We are finding that business tends to be just the opposite.  It is competitive, focussed, broken out into customer groups.  Integration conveys **uniformity,** so there is no flexibility to respond to the customer.  We found that the main reason people do planning is to get the funding.  There is no further inducement to plan because they have what they need.

We then decided something which seems obvious, but which we hadn't noticed before, that there are lots of activities going on in the bank.  People are doing day-to-day planning, budgeting, and buying things.  They are over- and under-running.  They have problems on the shop floor.  They have problems with their testing.  Why not capture all of these operational feeds in some kind of database or sets of files?  We found that so-called "planning systems" really fall apart in the real world.  There is no congruence between the one-year plan, the five-year plan, and the capital expenditure plan, and what the business is actually doing from day to day.  However, an operating system is used constantly; for **project status, budget status, actuals** and so forth.  So we developed a planning system which **uses operational feeds.**  Certain things we have already automated, for example, the **project profile.**  This is a description of each project and system, who the project manager is, what the business objectives are, what the milestones are, what type of automation is being used, budgets and actuals, and cost allocations. We run an allocation system. Every dollar of IS expenses is allocated back to the users and to their products. We have also automated system profiles, terminal inventory, and the goals system. About to be automated, are the funding major project proposals, work requests (consultant control forms), the equipment and software inventories, business plans, and automation plans.

### A.1.2    RACETRACK CONCEPT

One of the project managers went home one night and drew a characterization of this architecture. A horse lover in the group called it a racetrack, because the track as you can see **(Figure A-1, Racetrack Diagram),** looks like a communications circle. On the racetrack are the operational files and databases. As we defined it, **racetrack** is a group of operational data files that roll up into a relational database for planning and MIS purposes. We must have relational databases because there is no single schema to define all of these files, therefore, we have to relate them. We have operational files feeding into a relational database. Actually there is a database on TSO/SAS, and we're putting them into a APR's Datacom database and Intellect. Since in the real world operational systems are distributed across all the operating groups, the racetrack files are distributed similarly. The racetrack environment has four major parts. The files can be flat or any type of file as long as they can be related either by key or by limits. We have Inventories, Financials, Profiles and Plans. Those are the racetrack databases feeding into a relational database.

**Figure A-1**

RACETRACK DIAGRAM

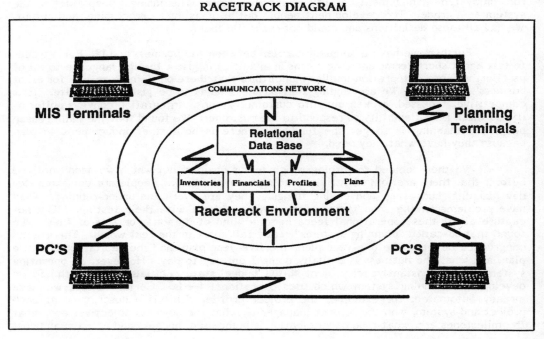

For MIS, this means that the cost center managers can see the status of their financials or their problems **(Figure A-1).** There are mail and messaging facilities. The planners can do what we will later define as system roll-up and do a three-to-five year estimate of development and ongoing operation costs. At the bottom, we are getting heavily into PC's. We have 7,000 MIS and planning terminals throughout the bank. We are uploading, downloading, and crossloading PC's because a lot of people actually want to take gulps of this information and play with it, for example, different budget estimates and that type of thing.

These are **distributed,** not monolithic, databases. On the left side of **Figure A-2, Distributed Databases on Racetrack,** are some of the databases. There is budgeting. PAC 2 is actual reporting, and cost allocation. The system depends very much upon master system lists. There is a master project list, a master system list, and a master cost center list. Coverage is shown on the horizontal axis, and you can see the following environments: IMS, MVS, TSO/SAS, Relational, and P/C. There is a wide technology coverage of these files. **Figure A-3, Racetrack Database/Inquiry Facilities,** shows some of the inquiry facilities: batch, RJE, Download or Interactive, for the databases shown on the left. These keep increasing, of course, with graphic ability.

**Figure A-2**

### DISTRIBUTED DATABASES ON RACETRACK

|  | ENVIRONMENT | | | | |
|---|---|---|---|---|---|
| **Databases** | **IMS** | **MVS** | **TSO/SAS** | **Relational** | **PC** |
| **Budgeting** | C | C | C | | |
| **PAC 2** | | C | C | | |
| **Cost Allocation** | | C | | | |
| **SDD Profiles** | | | C | C | C |
| **Business Profiles** | | | | F | |
| **Hardware** | | | C | C | |
| **Software** | | | C | C | |
| **Communications** | | | C | C | |
| **"Master" System List** | | | | C | |
| **Summary Info** | | | | C | |

### RACETRACK DATABASE/INQUIRY FACILITIES

| | FACILITIES | | | |
|---|---|---|---|---|
| Databases | Batch | RJE | Download | Interactive |
| Budgeting | X | | | X |
| PAC 2 | X | | | X |
| Cost Allocation | X | | | X |
| SDD Profiles | X | X | X | X |
| Business Profiles | X | X | X | X |
| Hardware | X | X | X | |
| Software | X | X | X | |
| Communications | X | X | X | |
| Summary Info | | | X | X |
| Ad Hoc | | | | X |

What is the principle of racetrack? Since we have an IBM shop we use SMF (System Management Facility). We attach the monitors to the machines, and it tells how the jobs are running and exactly what they are doing. We capture SMF data, and feed it to two different systems, one for user chargeback and the other for capacity planning. That is how a single thing expands into multiple uses. One of the principles behind Racetrack is that **data is entered only once.** The relational technique provides multiple views to physical databases. We have a limited number of physical databases, but by connecting by a relational "join," we can look at those as though they were just hundreds of files. We found that **only the physical databases need maintenance.** That means racetrack files are maintained, but relational files do not have to be maintained very often. The relational generates views automatically with no maintenance required.

Let's run a case study. Recently, the bank set an objective that all of the products would be fully costed. This means loans, deposits, trades or security transactions would have to be fully costed. This means we have to also cost out the data processing portion of the cost of a product. We have a problem, because most of our shops operate not on systems, but on projects. A project is a limited activity with a beginning and an end, a project manager, and an objective. Systems are just aggregates. We generally know about them, but we don't manage them. So to cost them, to do this system roll-up, we needed to define a project (**Figure A-4, Business Products/Functions**). We had to define all the data processing products. We had to define sub-systems before we defined systems. Gradually, you can roll up these projects. You can carry the budget in actual dollars up through the products. If this works out, it means you can look at a business product, like a loan, and determine any of its attributes (**Figure A-5, System Components/Attributes**). You can see how the

**BUSINESS PRODUCTS/FUNCTIONS**

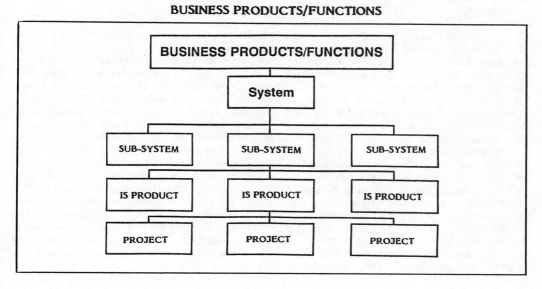

Figure A-5

**SYSTEM COMPONENTS/ATTRIBUTES**

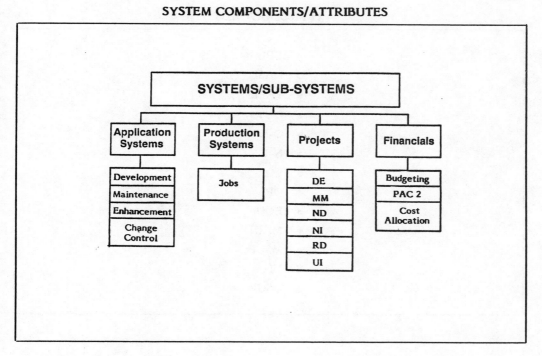

CPU cost is the development and ongoing cost, because anything that's carried through in the relational system has the attributes also carried with it. The attribute is just a descriptive.

Every project and system has a profile which describes what it is all about. We collect these and aggregate them and begin to roll them up. **Figure A-6,** is the **IS Product List:** CPU, DASD, output, on line, and so forth. These are all technical products which have an associated cost. Next, we get to **sub-systems. Figure A-7, Master System Roll-up List,** is a payment system, transferring about $50 billion a day. Only about half of the payment sub-systems are shown. Finally, we have to look at system components, **(Figure A-8, System Profile).** This is what we want to know about each of the systems. We want to know what the products are; the IS and bank products. We want to know the organizations involved, sponsors and cost centers. We want to know what functions are performed; for example, payment is basically the transfer of money that performs other functions. It determines whether your credit is good and whether you can pull money out of a deposit in order to make the payments. We also want to know the operations functions; the customer, the front-office, back-office functions, in order to control the system. And we need to know the whole technical environment; the applications systems in various stages, development, maintenance, and enhancement. There are hundreds of production jobs running on the floor, sometimes in several machines across two or three centers. We have the financials, the budgets, the actuals, and cost allocations. For this roll-up to work, all of these things have to be carried out all the way from hardware to system.

**Figure A-6**

**IS PRODUCT LIST**

- CPU
- DASD
- TAPE
- OUT
- O-L
- N-I
- VOI
- OPS
- EQU
- MAIN
- MSUP
- UI
- USUP

## MASTER SYSTEM ROLL-UP LIST
### Payment System

- Advices
- Automated Money Transfer System
- Bankwire
- Bank External Analysis
- Money Transfer System
- Special Instructions
- Clearing House Interface

- Communications Interface
- Compensation Inquiry System
- Customer Info File
- Fedwire Interface
- Fedwire System
- Manual Payment Entry System

## SYSTEM PROFILE

Project ID: _____        Revision Date: _____

SECTION A: GENERAL

System Name: _____

Bank Group: _____

Strategic Business Unit (SBU): _____

Principal User: _____

Location: _____        Telephone: _____

IS Group: _____        No: _____

Project Manager: _____

Location: _____        Telephone: _____

Software maintenance expenses for last (3) years:

        1st: _____

        2nd: _____

        3rd: _____

Annual Production Costs:

        1st: _____

        2nd: _____

        3rd: _____

System function Overview _____

The user is welcomed to the system, which is called "Integrated Planning." It is a development prototype, and a menu-driven system, including a help screen. The first menu is the main menu. The database directory is used to view all the master lists. For example, if there is a new cost center and you want to know whether that cost center is on, you go to the master directory. There are the planning profiles, and the matrix menu list. The matrix lets us know, for example, where the CPU's are located or what projects or systems CPU's are associated with. These are all done on the relational database generated out of our racetrack files.

## A.1.3    SECURITY AND CONTROL

A system like this scares a lot of DP people, because IMS does give the feeling that things are centrally controlled. When things are distributed, many DP'ers become very concerned about security. We do it in three ways. In the first place, we have ACF 2, which is IBM's security mechanism for mainframe files. If you have a PC and you are dialing the mainframe, between you and the mainframe would be a Series/I. A Series/I doesn't let anything go on until it dials you back to make sure you are the one that called. Finally, we have the concept of **shadow files.** In front of every master file is a shadow file. If you are a user, you may think you are inputting to the master, but you are really inputting to the shadow file. This protects the master file which is under central control.

The planning profile menu shows all of the application profiles; project and system profiles and plan indices. The first page defines the project, identifies the manager and gives other indicative information. It also shows the status by conversion, by migration, installation, and so forth, of this project.

There is **system classification.** You can define a system as anything, whether it performs switching or decision support, or MIS or transaction backup, front office, or customers. Another screen shows project milestones by quarter and year and are revised every month.

In the relational files, there is a "matrix" in which you can relate any of your attributes to find what's going on, for example, software classification. The matrix shows the letter credit project. It shows it is a delivery system, a switch, a relational system, a reporting system, it has communications and it also runs transactions. Why is this information valuable? We recently did a study of our switches to determine whether we should have one or more central communications. This matrix was useful because it showed all of the project systems which do switching.

We also have a graphics facility and a mail message facility. There are privileged fields in both the project and the system information that only people in particular circumstances can get at. Quality assurance also has a status field because quality assurance makes sure you follow the life cycle, do the testing, and so forth.

## A.1.4    RELATIONSHIP TO BUSINESS PLANNING

How does this relate to business planning? We envision that we are going to have business-related files and IS-related files, **(Figure A-9, Relationship To Business Planning).** If you look at a business profile the same way you look at an IS-related profile, you can describe it as technology; the switches, the functions it performs, the customer base. These will be profiled and put into the system. You could do the same thing with business automation plans; the funding proposals, and the coverage analysis. Relationally we can compare the business situation, to the IS situation, essentially do a coverage analysis.

**Figure A-9**

### RELATIONSHIP TO BUSINESS PLANNING

| Business-Related Files | IS-Related Files |
|---|---|
| • Business Profiles | • Budgeting |
| • Business Automation Plans | • PAC 2 |
| • Funding Proposals | • Cost Allocation |
| • Coverage Analysis | • System Development Profiles |
| | • Hardware |
| | • Software |
| | • Communications |
| | • "Master" Lists |

The two main purposes of racetrack are to give managers any information they want about any project or system, and to give them the planning facility through systems roll-up. The manager can go three, or perhaps five, years out on the big systems on estimates of development and ongoing costs. One of the things we do is called the "drop down ratio" which is, when we develop a system like payments, how fast is that development cost written off and what are the ongoing operations costs.

## A.2     CASE EXAMPLE - THE PFIZER PHARMACEUTICALS APPROACH[1]

Corporations such as Pfizer are continually evolving. In the past ten years there has been an evolution to a new systems organization that concentrates on building large, integrated databases, and interfaces to them. This includes the fundamental transaction processing. Complementing this are the information processing thrusts in the various businesses and staff divisions, where they take data as they wish, purchase it, and further process it for business-specific uses. Then there are the Information Centers, Office Automation groups, and so on. Pfizer has had a Systems Group, with a mission of the application of information technology to the management and operations of the business.

At one time, the mainframe CPU was the focus of all activity. Everything else was regarded as a peripheral to it, and not real computing. This has changed markedly, and is beginning to invert. The center of focus for the managers is becoming the PC workstation. The systems analyst has a new role of consultant and teacher to the manager. The systems organization has been evolving to concentrate on:

- Building large, integrated databases on mainframes;

- Building interfaces between mainframes, microcomputers, etc.;

- Installing commercial software for accessing the databases; and

- Developing methods of analyzing and using the data.

Many of the past systems and methods have become obsolescent, and new equipment and approaches are being proposed and installed. There are requirements for new systems goals (**Figure A-10, New Systems Goals**). There must be integrated databases, and there must be a plan with a business vision to move in this direction, and to consider the many hardware and software architectural problems that will arise. Specific plans are needed for:

- A Systems Architecture

- Office Automation

- Telecommunications

- Data Organization

In Pfizer, the long-range planning process considering these changes was developed by a few key people, in conjunction with a consultant, who developed an **actionable** plan. The **traps** of other plans that we intended to avoid were:

- The traditional computer capacity plan

- The formula business planning methodology

- The platitudes, such as "timely," "accurate information," etc.

- The one-time exercise, never to be revisited

- The unactionable statements

---

[1]     Dr. G.M.K. Hughes, VP Systems, Medical Education and Communications, Pfizer Pharmaceuticals Group, Pfizer Corp.

### NEW SYSTEMS GOAL

**Users will directly access data themselves and define output at convenient terminals/Personal Computers**

<u>**Why This Goal**</u>

**a.**   Users want data when they need it.

**b.**   Users want to be able to analyze data without having to call on others.

**c.**   Perusal of data stimulates questions and analyses.

**d.**   The changes in technology in the form of cheaper hardware and evolving software makes it possible.

**e.**   Without this goal, the backlog of requests will become unacceptable and/or users will go elsewhere.

The planning process was to take flip charts and begin to write every issue that could be thought of. These varied from highly technical to political turf building. A list of 75 issues for that year was rapidly generated. A number of questions then arose. These included:

- What is the purpose of the plan?
- Who is the audience?
  - Who will read it?
  - What will they do with it?
- What is to be the scope of the plan?
- What issues are to be tackled?
- What is to be the format?
- What is the time scale?

For example, in addressing who would be interested in the plan, we had to define clearly who the audience was for the plan. It was generally agreed that the audience consisted of:

- The Corporate Information Processing Committee
- The users
- Our direct management

- The systems staff

- Ourselves

Planning is needed to have a backdrop against which to make day-to-day decisions **(Figure A-11, Why Plan?).** We needed a vehicle for communicating our vision. We needed a vehicle for demonstrating that we had a viewpoint, listing the questions that we had addressed and the answers that we had at that time.

**Figure A-11**

### WHY PLAN?

- A framework for making day-to-day decisions

- A vehicle for securing the commitment of others

- A way of communicating the "vision"

- A statement of what the system intends to do

- A means of eliciting the views of others

It soon became clear how we were going to organize the document. We took those 75 issues that we had drawn up, and aggregated them according to perceived solutions. Some things were hardware issues, some were software issues, some were office technology, and so forth. There was nothing magical about the aggregations. They were simply done for readability of the document. It a truly integrated plan, they will obviously all run together. The first time through, then, the aggregated issues were the domains.

We used this strategy repeatedly until each domain became content-free: the hardware, software, database, personal computing, office technology, electronic mail, systems staff, and systems research. The details are not important, and what we decided for a hardware solution is not generally relevant, but we all have similar problems. It is interesting, however, that there are no universal solutions.

### A.2.1    THE PLANNING DOCUMENT

The purpose is to have some reasonably rational way to create a document. The intent is to create a draft document with some solutions, circulate it, then let it evolve over a period of, say, three months. The document includes the following:

- Scope
- Objective

- Background - issues, problems, opportunities
- Strategy (or tactics) recommended for each domain
- Projects
- Appendices

For example, we made a clear decision about software, an emphatic state-ment. There would be no more Third Generation languages used, such as COBOL, FORTRAN, or BASIC. That decision came out of this process, and we decided to make a statement about it.

## A.2.2    GARNERING SUPPORT

This was all very well for us to make these decisions, but we had to also convince other people. We needed to garner support among:

a.    Corporate Staff Groups

b.    The Users

c.    Divisional Management

d.    Divisional Systems Staff

We found the best way to garner support. Corporate staff groups are the first and the easiest. They correctly have a veto power, so it is important to clear such things as hardware selection with them first. If they insist on a certain type of equipment, the decision is quickly made, and you can proceed.

There is a variety of make-up of human beings among the users. In every division and every department there are a couple of people who read "Byte". They know a lot of jargon, and can be annoying, but usually their management trusts them more than you. So you must figure out who they are, talk to them, and get them to sign off by incorporating their phrases.

Divisional management can be easy, if you have established a track record. They are usually willing to grant the systems people the right to run the technology business. This is especially true if there have been precedents in other technical parts of the business. Technical people prevail on technical decisions. If, over time, you do not like some of their decisions, the technical people may be changed, but not overridden on simple decisions.

The divisional systems staff are usually the toughest. They may not be satisfied, and they may not believe you. There is nothing like a systems person to recognize that other systems people may be blowing "hot smoke." It may take one or two years to really get all the systems people on board, as opposed to paying lip service. It took us a year, and that was more than we had expected.

## A.2.3    THE CONTINUING PROCESS

This approach is a process. It is a process of writing down issues, debating them, writing down solutions, and going at it around and around. We have met every month, working from that planning document. Each time, we decide on which chapter to work on, and review it in detail. As time goes on in this continuing process, new problem areas crop up. If the items are currently inappropriate, or too far in the future for the first time around, we introduce them later on. We rework the old strategies. The PC models change, and everyone wants the new systems, so what is your response? What are you going to do with the old systems? The question of networking grows more complex every year. What is our policy on software upgrades? Do we upgrade everyone all at once? The document starts up-to-date, but continually needs editing. The documents must be controlled. Thus, the continuing process includes:

- Monthly review
- Identification of new strategies
- Rework of old strategies
- Recording the progress in the background.

We have a continuing process for recording our progress. As time went by, the focus shifted:

**From:**

- Headquarters Concerns
- Hardware and Software

**To:**

- Intra-company Communications
- Extra-company Communications
- Data Reorganization
- Communications

The second year, we had a repeat session in a hotel with the same planning group, again in Florida. This time, when we set up the flip charts, we found that there were only 64 of the original 75 issues left. We went through the process the same way. We found two new areas of focus: telecommunications and our regional field offices. They had not been considered the first time around.

We are satisfied with our planning process. We have a process for:

- Debating and Recording our Concensus
- Identifying New Issues
- Communicating to the Organization
- Managing Ourselves.

There are still a large number of issues to be resolved, and we will approach them in this way, systematically.

## A.3      <u>CASE EXAMPLE - THE AMERICAN MEDICAL INTERNATIONAL EXPERIENCE</u>[2]

This is a personal view of a strategic information systems project. The process is briefly outlined with the choices that have to be made, the opportunities, and the pitfalls of setting up strategic information systems.

American Medical International, Inc. (AMI) started with a standard set of business systems. One of the problems was that the systems did not fit the organizational structure of the company. New approaches to systems were developed by the planning group. The planning group became the system specifiers, and the Data Processing department executed the plans.

### A.3.1      <u>DEFINITION</u>

For a definition of strategic information systems, Charles Wiseman's definition, is appropriate: **"Information systems used to support or shape the competitive strategy of the organization."** There are two types of systems that actually do that. There is the set of systems that we are relatively familiar with; the systems we use internally in organization. There is **internal access to the system only.** There is a vast array of systems of this type. A new approach to accounts payable would fall into that category. The other type of system that can be strategic is one that has **both internal and external access to the system.**

We designed and developed an information system for AMI that ties together the purchasing function and the payables function into one integrated system. In a company with hundreds of locations in the U. S., purchasing became a monstrosity in the sense that we had about 120 purchasing agents, who were all doing more or less their own thing. They had corporate direction, but since that was paper-based, they would never know exactly where things were. If we have some 300 to 400 national contracts that all have a running time of one or two years, it would mean that about every day or so, one contract expires and a new one starts. Try and get that across to the people in the field. If we know that the company purchases about 25,000 generic items, and we multiply that by the number of vendors, we can end up with 120,000 to 150,000 items. It becomes a horrendous task to try and do that on paper. People just lose track. It was estimated the company was losing an enormous opportunity to save money simply by the fact that people could not adhere to the contracts. The paper just did not work.

Another reason that people could not adhere to the contracts was the accounts payable system, which was paper-based. The checks were automatically printed, but that was where the story ended. The paper flow, to get it to finally print a check, quite often made a situation occur where we would lose the opportunity to take discounts.

Corporate materials management had little clue as to what we were buying. They knew we were buying $1 million from Johnson and Johnson. But what was in that? Negotiations with the suppliers was always an impossible task because the supplier knew better than we did what we were buying.

---

2    **Wouter van Biene, Consultant, Information Systems Rancho Palos Verdes, CA**

We, therefore, developed a system that could deal with all of those functions, take away a lot of clerical tasks, and, essentially, streamline the whole functionality for purchasing and payments. That is an example of an **internal access to system** type of strategic system. It is definitely strategic. It crosses boundaries that were barriers before, and it allows the company to take better advantage of its purchasing clout. Therefore, it generates a strategic advantage in dealing with the suppliers.

The systems that tend to attract more of the attention because they are newer and are being looked upon as an innovative approach to information systems are those systems that have both **internal and external access.** Of course, the famous examples of American Airlines and American Hospital Supply are well known. There are definitely a number of elements in these systems that can be of great importance especially when we move into the service industry.

## A.3.2    THE IDENTIFICATION PROCESS

How do you identify, develop, and implement a strategic system? We never really developed a formal approach for these things. As head of IS, I was part of the inter-departmental committee for strategic planning. Strategic planning was a shared function between a group of executives. This made the coordination between the business plan and the IS plan straightforward. It is a very important step, because there is so much change in the information systems field and in its technology that can have a dramatic impact on the company. If IS were not in the strategic planning loop, it would simply be an erroneous approach.

Once you have decided to develop strategic systems, you will have to find the **creative element.** To a large extent, you can try to formalize the search approach. The ultimate thing is to create a spark where, all of a sudden, you realize that, if you do it this way, you will see these results. You find, "Ah ha! That is it!" And you have found a strategic system.

In the hospital management industry, since 1983, there has been one singular objective from the Boards: How do we increase utilization of our facilities? There is a lot of competition. Some of the competition is created by the hospital industry itself by creating out-patient services. It is also very much technology-driven. Hospitalization these days is not required for quite a few surgeries for the very simple reason that anesthesiology has moved ahead with such dramatic speed that the after-effects of anesthesia have become less and less serious. Therefore, you don't need to be in a hospital to recuperate from minor surgery.

If we want to increase utilization of hospitals, it can be done in a number of ways. The main point is to try to **identify your client.** For most industries, finding out who your client is is relatively straightforward. For a hospital management corporation, there is no simple answer to that question. There is not one group of people who can be identified as being "the" client. There are actually three or four clients who all play a role: the patient, who has a certain influence; the physician, the traditional client of the hospital; and more and more, in the last two or three years, the employers have become the clients. Employers, as you know, carry 80% or more of all the health care insurance in the United States. They have become more and more vocal about their costs. Cost, of course, can be reduced in a number of ways; one way is proper utilization of health care, and to avoid over-utilization. Somewhere in this employer area is also the insurance group as clients. To a certain extent, they are delegates of the employers in the sense that most large employers are self-insured. There is a relatively small group of people who are privately insured, so the insurance companies have a stake in these things.

AMI tried to develop programs to satisfy all three groups of users, because if you can't find your single client, the next best thing is to go after all three, and try to balance your efforts and give a general push to capture all three of them.

## A.3.3 WHAT INFLUENCES THE DECISION?

The question that you will have to answer is, what influences the decision to make use of a particular hospital? First of all, it is **convenience of location.** You go to a facility that is nearby. Once we put the bricks and mortar up, either through leases or through building, we are stuck there. The placement of hospitals throughout the United States has, for a long time, been a very big concern to all hospital corporations in their purchasing of facilities.

The second important issue is the **services performed for physicians.** It is interesting to note that the services provided by hospitals for physicians in the United States go further than anywhere else in the world. The reason for that is very simple, in order to capture your physician, you provide additional services.

Traditionally, the way hospital companies tried to deal with the two issues of location and service was to build medical office buildings next to their hospital. If you have the physician next to you, he would rather walk across the street than get into the car and drive a long distance.

Another issue is the **perceived quality of the facility and the staff.** There are two particular perceptions: the physician's and the patient's. Also, these days, there are the perceptions of the insurance companies and the employers.

The fourth influence is **cost.** Ask yourself if you would travel 200 miles to save 15% on the hospitalization bill. It just doesn't make sense. You can price yourself out of the market, however, if you are next to another glamorous facility, and you are twice as expensive.

## A.3.4 CASE STUDY

This case study is of a physician support system that was developed. The question we had to answer was, "What can we do to try and tie the client to our product, the hospital, in a way that is perceived by both parties as beneficial to their interests?"

In a typical hospital, you will find a number of information systems. Every hospital, of course, has a billing and an accounting system. Most hospitals do have a specific reporting system in their laboratories, or a laboratory information system. Since we are doing the transcription for all of these physicians, we would have some transcription systems, too.

The point was that, in order to enhance the service to physicians, we want to try to give the physician access, at his home or office, to these three, and potentially more, systems that are in a hospital. Why? It makes it easier for him. He doesn't have to run over to a hospital to get information. That became even more important where we started to implement in our hospitals what is known in the industry as a **hospital information system.** This essentially would gather information from all of these, integrate them into patient files, and add clinical information including the treatment of a patient on a day-to-day basis. All services provided for a patient would run into a hospital information system, which would have financial and statistical spin-offs to the accounting systems, which would send orders to the lab and receive information, which would receive the transcriptions, and which would be available throughout the hospital, wherever the physician or another medical worker would want to look at it. Hospital information systems include complete support systems for pharmacies, plus order-entry and results reporting. Everything you would want to know about a patient would be in there.

The obvious approach would be to put a terminal in the physician's office; create a port that would allow us to make the system connection. We do have that capacity, but that is not what we did. There was a very specific reason for it. First, was the fact that if you had a hospital that had not installed a hospital information system yet, it would mean that some hospitals would not be able to have this link. It would mean that we would have to have two solutions for a physician's support system.

Our next alternative would be to have these systems send messages to something that sits at the physician's office. Metpath used that approach, where lab results were sent back to the physician. That would mean that it would be either a one-way street, or it could mean multiple facilities would be needed, given the fact that the Transcription System, typically, would be a Lanier system. The Laboratory System would be either a micro-based or a DEC-based system. The Accounting System, typically, would be a DG-based system. We would run into all kinds of technical issues there.

We, therefore, decided, for reasons of data security, convenience and universality, to build a box between the systems; the Physician Support System. It essentially was going to be the recipient of information from these other three systems, and it would perform an electronic mail function for the physician. The physician could now dial-in to the system and review his mail. Everything that had something to do with the physician would show up in the Physician Support System.

Another reason we didn't use the Hospital Information System as a link was that it interfered with another objective that we had, which was in the laboratories and some other ancillary services. Why just use the laboratory for patients who are in the hospital? You may want to use it for outside services. If we have a physician who sends his patient's materials, blood samples, etc., to the lab, that patient would not feature in our Hospital Information System, not being a patient of the Hospital Information System. Therefore, this link would become unworkable in that approach.

We came up with the **electronic mail approach.** Electronic mail would allow us to shield the hospital at the intermediate box from any interference from the physician's office. If there was something going on, the furthest they would be able to get is the Physician Support System. They would not be able to interfere with any of the operations of these systems in the hospital. There was an added benefit of this approach: Physicians tend to refer patients from one to another. When a physician refers a patient from A to B, he likes to send an outline of what he knows about the patient to his colleague. If we have a whole set of physicians connected to this electronic mail, what is easier than to take the physical and the history that the hospital provided, and send it to the Physician Support System? We have created an added benefit by giving physicians a communication format between each other that can save them a considerable amount of time on a day-to-day basis. That is where the joint benefits are coming into the picture. You can admit patients to the hospitals, and put them up for surgery, and so on, through the accounting system.

The final feature we added to the system is a **pass-through window** into the Hospital Information System to do information retrieval. The physician can actually follow the day-to-day treatment of the patient, and all of the nurses notes, in a pathway through this system to the Hospital Information System. We have limited this to look only at the information because we are somewhat hesitant about liability in case a physician from the outside makes an adjustment to the patient's treatment.

## A.3.5    THE APPROVAL PROCESS

To get approval for a project you always need allies in your organization. Once we had developed an outline of what this could do, I went around the company to find the organization that would probably have the most interest in getting something of this nature on the road. There was a Market Planning department that really was interested in carrying this project. They had been developing micro-strategic plans for individual facilities. They knew very well, of the hundred facilities out there, which ones had what kind of problems. They had a lot of data right at their fingertips, and they knew how to interpret it. We immediately had our cost-benefit arm set up. We didn't have to do a lot of work in that field, and we didn't have to prove our credibility. They had the credibility.

## A.3.6    SYSTEM UTILIZATION ISSUES

There are some opportunities and pitfalls that one must be aware of when you go into this, and we feel we have dealt with them in an adequate way. The first one is the **system utilization issues.** We have to distinguish between "nice" versus "need-to-use." Most of the plans, the ideas, in the information systems arena that tie in the physician, fall into the category "nice." They are nice to have. It's a friend of the physician. Does it really make the physician into a user of your facility? Probably not. We don't have any physical means of tying him in. So, we added another category to the system that went to our corporate mainframe. On the corporate mainframe, we had the software available to put in his **insurance claims.** Since we insure some of our patients ourselves, he could expect a 48-hour turnaround to get his funds. That was nice. Now, if he used this system and put the patient in, two things would happen. First, the patient information would be copied out of the accounting system so he didn't have to do too much work. Second, if he then put his charges in, he would get his money, right away. So that helped. We also put in some other things that gave him access to National Database's reference materials and so on. That is nice, but it doesn't necessarily make him a user.

We then have the issue of **"first" versus "me too."** We were not the first to put such a system in all 100 markets, but we probably will be first in 70 or 80. Therefore, we don't necessarily get into the clutter situation where a physician already has the tools and devices to have these advantages with other facilities. The ease-of-use and effectiveness should be great. It should be **bombproof.** That is why we selected this option because it is relatively easy to control and to maintain. We were always worried that with the lab system, which is a third-party system that we don't control, it could very easily be that they make a change on their end and things elsewhere will "bomb" out. We just did not want to touch that.

**Support** is a major issue. That is a key element for a strategic system of this nature. As a starting point, we came up with a ratio of one field consultant for each 20 to 25 users. Over the years, we will see if we have to keep it that way or change it, but that is what we have based our plan on.

There is also **data security and confidentiality.** We decided in order to make this gateway somewhat safe, to use the dial-back approach, whereby a physician can have both his home and his office linked in for those physicians who have PC's. Where there are physicians who only have a dumb terminal, that is not an issue.

## A.3.7    HARDWARE ISSUES

Hardware is a big issue. This approach allowed us to have dumb terminals and personal computers attached. The questions is, should we have a **singular approach**? Considering the 20 or 30 markets where we will not be the first one to come in, and considering the fact that most of the physician office software is offered on personal computers these days, specifically the IBM PC, we decided that we needed to have an approach that would allow flexibility to have either a dumb terminal, which we could label "cheap" to anybody, or a PC where the physician would have to make an investment. He probably would already have one, so it was just a question of connectivity. Our strategy was that we would go both ways to be able to capture as much of the market as possible.

The second issue was the **"ownership" versus "gift"** issue. Metpath gave the equipment away. We decided not to do that. In our test phase we will give them equipment for a couple of months, but then they will have to buy it. With some good corporate discounts, I think these PC's will be relatively cheap. For our purposes, the IBM PC is the lowest grade PC you can have. It can just have one floppy and a couple of K core, and that would be it. However, if a physician wants to expand and put in additional systems and services on it, it can be done. That helps in the approach, but we felt that having a stake in it would be important.

There is the **service level.** Fortunately, since IBM PC's and DG's were standard in our hospitals, and we had a distributed support network for hardware services, we could offer the physician that we would maintain his hardware and work on an exchange basis. If his PC broke down, we would swap him one of ours. Service was resolved in that way.

## A.3.8   START-UP ISSUES

Start-up issues are important to look at because when you put up a system like this, which ultimately is estimated to run at an investment of about $10 million, management will not just say, "Sure, go ahead and do it!" You want to set up an environment, a **first test,** where you can be reasonably **assured of success.** It is important to select a group of clients that is likely to demonstrate the effectiveness of this strategic system most dramatically.

The second issue is to **keep the first test manageable in size.** We started out with ten physicians. We then increased that group to 20. The system is designed to handle anywhere from 50 to 250 physicians. It would be foolish to go too fast, because there is a lot of handholding involved in the first phase. I would recommend to **overstaff the test** in order to be able to provide handholding when the expected snags are shaking their confidence. That will happen.

You will also have to deal with **breakdowns,** especially in the beginning phase when communication, for whatever reason, just does not work. You want to minimize the impact that something like that has on the practice of your client. From that perspective, on this project with ten clients, we have about a one-to-one ratio in support personnel. That will now go to a one-and-one-half ratio. Slowly, but surely, we will whittle it down to one-to-twenty or twenty-five ratio. That is the approach we have taken.

This is very much focused on a hospital and service industry, but there are some general issues involved.